A BOY AND HI

CW00518886

A BOY AND HIS MOUSE

More postcards from the Net

Jon Casimir

ALLEN & UNWIN

First published in 1997 by
Allen & Unwin Pty Ltd
9 Atchison Street, St Leonards, NSW 2065 Australia
Phone: (61 2) 9901 4088
Fax: (61 2) 9906 2218
E-mail: frontdesk@allen-unwin.com.au
URL: http://www.allen-unwin.com.au

National Library of Australia
Cataloguing-in-Publication entry:

Casimir, Jon, 1964– .

A boy and his mouse: more postcards
from the net.

ISBN 1 86448 521 3

1. Internet (Computer Network)—Directories.
2. Web sites—Directories. I. Title.
004.678

Set in 11/13.5 pt Cochin by DOCUPRO, Sydney
Printed in Australia by McPherson's Printing Group

10 9 8 7 6 5 4 3 2 1

CONTENTS

INTRODUCTION

Why write a book about the Internet?

If I had a buck for every time I've been asked that question, I'd have a whole deer farm by now . . . okay, I'd have a pretty short and unsuccessful farming career if I didn't also recruit a few does, but I think you get my point . . .

Netheads can be quite blinkered when it comes to traditional media (you remember traditional media: books, films, television, newspapers and magazines, all that stuff). They think that the sound of the Internet exploding is the bell tolling for everything else. Their superiority complex tells them that other media should go quietly to the graveyard of the Brave Old World, and not embarrass themselves by sticking around as the younger, fitter competition takes the field.

'A book,' they snuffle. 'How dreadfully old-fashioned of you! For God's sake, they still make those things *out of atoms*!' Why not just make a Web site, they ask? Why not get with the times? How can a book possibly compete with the exciting, constantly shifting nature of the Web?

The idea that a book is old-fashioned, a relic of a previous media age, relies on a simplistic, binary view of existance. We're not in an either/or situation here. Media, like water, finds its level. Books have a role, as surely as the Internet does—the existence of one does not deny the value of the other.

Actually, I reckon the infiltration of the Web into our lives will make books more, not less, attractive to us. I'm very fond of the Internet, but spending so much time there only makes me more aware of the characteristics that make radio, television, newspapers and books important to me as well. Books are as sexy as all get out. They're tactile, sensual experiences. They're self-contained, discrete worlds, each its own little virtual environment, designed (it seems) only for me. Some of my best friends are books.

And beyond that, there is the simple point that not everyone who wants to know about the Net is actually *on* the Net. And many who *are* connected want other people to do the surfing for them — I go to some of these places so that you won't have to.

That said, it *is* hard to pull together a book about something that is in permanent flux. When you write about the Internet, you are always aware that you're taking aim at a moving target. Online ideas, cultures and trends often seem to have the life spans of mosquitos. Fads can be out of date before the ink dries or the HTML tags are put in place. Just when you think you've worked something out, it's not there to be understood anymore (the Taoists would have loved cyberspace). Sometimes, the target you were aiming at wasn't even there — it just looked that way until you fired and watched your bullets go straight through the mirage.

Still, just because it's hard, it doesn't also follow that it's not worth trying. Indeed, the problem of the complexity of the Net is the reason why a book is actually one of the very best kinds of ways to capture and catalogue it. Like real life, the Net is populated with innumerable species, places and events. Everything is somehow connected and yet, everything seems random. As an observer, the best way to deal with both situations is to roll up your sleeves and write about the minutiae. Take the fractal attitude that in the smallest of patterns the largest are revealed (and vise versa). The truth is in the detail.

A book like this gives me the chance to tell a lot of little stories about life on the Web. And, in the collection of those stories, I'm hoping that another tale is told, a larger, more organic tale. I'm hoping that the pieces will fit together into some sort of jigsaw, slowly creating a bigger picture.

I'm not sure what the picture will actually be. I suspect you may have to add a few pieces of your own to finish it. And I also have the feeling that it might be a different picture for different readers. But whatever that result, the thing that a book can achieve is the chance to throw so many elements together that the whole can be greater than the sum of the parts.

The only real drawbacks with writing a book about the Internet is that slow publishing deadlines mean that some things you write about may not be there by the time people get to read your words. But the Net is making that less of a problem all the time. It's slowing down too, not growing at anywhere near the speed it was in 1995 and 1996. In the course of pulling this book together, far fewer sites went walkabout than they did during the writing of the first one. So there's a very good chance that almost all of the thousand or so addresses listed in this book are still in their place.

And if they're not, then don't grieve for them. The Web can be a little like a garden. Some sites are perennial bloomers, and some burst into colourful life and disappear almost immediately. That's just the way it is.

I believe that it's enough to know that they were there, that in 1997, these were some of the things, people and places that combined to make up this Web. So this book is a slice of online life, a collection of Polaroids. It's a few crumbs off a very big table, my perpective on what the hell was happening. Anyway, let's get on with it . . .

casimir@smh.com.au
June 1997

OPENERS

How The Web Is Changing

IF YOU stare at the sun long enough, you can see anything. The same can be said of the Web—it plays tricks on the brain. And there are *waaay* too many people staring at their screens for *waaay* too long. The Web has thrown up crowds of sooth-sayers, pundits and futurists. They're all trying to work out what the latest trends are, what we're going through and what is around the corner.

They babble incessantly (me included) about the latest developments and what they mean. The logic of this babbling follows the same pattern as every other form of media: two people doing anything is a story, three is a trend, four is something you buy shares in. But really, they're all bluffing. The Web is too big a place, with too many people contributing to its growth, for it to be following simple paths. In truth, there are all sorts of ripples on the Web pond, all manner of move-ments. Like the Big Bang, it's not really heading in a direction—it's heading in every direction.

When people ask me what is happening on the Net (the second you put a book out, people think you're an expert—go figure), I blanch. Then I mumble a few things, a mixture of experience, anecdote and speculation, and stare at my feet. The following are some of those mumbles, some random thoughts about the forces which combine to bring us Web physics, some observations about what is making the Web tick.

Address Ubiquity

It was said they'd never catch on. It was said those dull, boring, maths-equation-type Web addresses would put everyone off the whole thing. Now they're sexy. Now everyone has them.

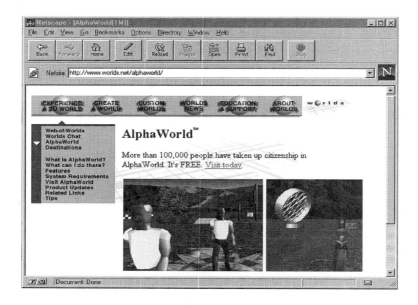

They have long since slipped the bonds of the broadcast and print media. They're everywhere you look, on flyers and handbills, billboards and bus stops. It's a rare ad break in commercial television that doesn't see one whizzing by. Papers have been adding them to front pages, television programs to credits. My favourite example of address ubiquity, and one that paints a thousand-word picture on its own, was a piece of graffiti seen on the wall of a toilet at Heathrow airport, which began with the words 'For a good time, try www . . . ' OK, it's not a big trend, but it's worth mentioning just to reflect on the speed with which it spread.

Bandwidth

It's increasing, but not at the rate the pundits promised. It seems that the increases in network quality are balanced by the extra traffic of newcomers. The demand for bandwidth jumps as fast as the supply can. So not much changes for most people. That said, the 56k modem is making inroads and we keep being assured that cable modems will bring joy and electronic liberty for all. For a hefty fee. There's been an enormous amount of hype around them, but little follow through.

Browser Wars

I get a headache just thinking about this one. By the end of 1996, Internet Explorer was claiming about 20 per cent of the market. How much more it will claim when the browser is built into Microsoft's next operating system is another question. Gates had his Net epiphany in December 1995, at a point in time when Netscape had a 75 per cent market share. So far, Netscape hasn't lost too heavily (it's been hovering around the 65–70 per cent mark), with Internet Explorer playing havoc with the smaller browsers. But the gap closes at a couple of per cent each month. Place your bets.

Cobwebsites

The older the Net gets, the more cyberspace junk there is; dead and dormant sites just drifting around, bumping into each other in the ether. Steve Baldwin runs **Ghost Sites of the Web**, a service which keeps track of those sites that are forgotten, but not gone, Web ventures which have succumbed to what he calls 'bit rot'. Baldwin doesn't just take a tilt at the little sites, he looks for the big and famous ones which haven't had a spring cleaning for some time, from **24 Hours in Cyberspace** to Pathfinder's own (now defunct) OJ Central. The beautiful irony is that the last version of the site I saw was dated 26 October 1996. There's an awful lot of tumbleweed rolling by . . .

Commercial Apathy

Commercial sites began to flood the Net in 1995. By mid-1996 it was becoming clear that many of them not only had failed to generate revenue, but had not even justified their costs. Business began to write the Net off, to take its eye off the ball. Many of these businesses should never have bothered with sites in the first place. Others had bad advice and bad site management. The Net's commercial credibility haemorrhaged. The smart Net early adopters began to rethink their strategies. But many didn't, and still haven't. It was very fashionable in the latter stages of 1996 to proclaim that the Web was dying. The facts, of course, disproved that.

Commercial Success

Revenue from advertising on the Web broke the US$25 million mark in 1996, according to the Electronic Advertising & Marketplace newsletter. The bulk of this, some $16 million, was shared between the top eighteen Web sites. The US research group Jupiter Communications estimated that the total revenue from shopping over the Internet was $1.2 billion in 1996 (that figure was expected to double in 1997). A great example of the success is **Amazon.com**, which went from nowhere to being the world's largest bookstore in less than two years. That, I think, is what they call growth.

Copyright

1996 and 1997 have really seen major companies developing an interest in the Net. In most cases, this led to two things: (1) they built crappy corporate Web sites; and (2) they shut down a lot of little fan sites for breach of copyright (see *The Copyright Wars Begin*).

Domain Consistency

The Web continues to grow like topsy. But in one way, we're living in the great settling period. It used to be that you bookmarked a site and it wasn't there the next week. It used to be that sites had appallingly long URLs, addresses you could never type in without making a mistake along the way. But somewhere back there everyone just went out and got their own domain name. They made it shorter and neater. And they stuck with it. The Net is not moving about anywhere near as much as it used to be. Every week, the number of broken bookmarks just seems to get lower, as sites get married and settle down in one place.

Event Obsession

The Internet, we have learned, loves an event. Or an excuse. In August 1996, the IBM Olympic site, dogged with its very public problems, was reporting up to 27 million hits a day. That's a lot of people, no matter how you do your calculations. Only three months later, in November, **CNN** claimed double that, nearing the 60 million mark on US election day. The **Heaven's Gate** cult suicide, in March 1997, set the Net buzzing. The official site of the cult was impossible to access, and others around the world mirrored it, watching their own hit rates skyrocket.

Fusion

It was pretty much inevitable. The Web has begun to assimilate other parts of the Net, to devour them by delivering the same services. More and more software is being developed to allow real-time and newsgroup-style chat on Web sites. All the things that you previously had to go to Usenet and IRC to do are now possible on the Web, and getting more widespread with each passing day. Will the other parts of the Net die back? What will avatar-based, three-dimensional chat do to this?

Geography

Here's an odd one. Whenever there has been philosophical discussion of the Net, the lack of borders has come up; the sensation of geographical collapse that a single, global network brings. This breaking down of physical barriers has long been seen as a virtue for the Net. And yet, geography (or a version of it) has been appearing on the Web. Major companies from **Yahoo** to **Microsoft** have decided that the public will find it conceptually easier to deal with the familiarity of geography in their Web browsing. Even smaller sites, such as the online conference **Electric Minds**, have seen value in replicating offline spatial concepts. Expect to see a lot more of it as sections of the Web head towards three dimensions.

Gravity

The more sites you have out there, the harder it is to get yours noticed. It's no longer enough just to get your site listed in the search indexes. Smarter site operators are considering the gravitational effects of the Web. The closer you can position yourself to the bigger sites, the hubs, the more you'll benefit from the passing traffic. The Net is not just about who you are, it's who you're linked to and who has linked to you. Many small, special interest sites, which can't do much about this problem, have found a way around it. The last year has seen the emergence of **WebRings**, collections of individual sites which share a common interest and band together to provide a topic-specific Web tour. You just click the button at the bottom of the home page and you're off to the next site in the chain.

Immediacy

The Web is speeding up. At the start of 1996, if your site had 'Updated Weekly' plastered across the top of the home page, people thought you were pretty cool, pretty respectable and diligent in your upkeep. A year later, the standard has moved much closer to the daily update. The Web wants, as much as a technology can harbour desires, to be a live medium. Or something very close to it. 'Updated Daily' is already starting to look pretty shabby. Will it be RIP time-based media?

Marketing Logjam

The **Batman and Robin** Web site was just one of many famous for months before its actual subject, the film, arrived. The Web has also emerged as a talk show circuit of its own, with film stars, TV stars and authors flogging their latest product. The marketers have grabbed the new technology with both hands, but it may yet explode in their grasp. For those of us not in America, sites like the **Independence Day** venture only made us aware of the poor service we were getting, the months we would have to wait to see the film. Will the Net make global industries *really* global? Will it force Hollywood into simultaneous releases in all major markets? If I have to wait three months to buy someone's new album in my own country, I'm much more likely to go to the Net and order it. The Net is making us better informed consumers, and more likely to complain. When an Australian television station dropped an episode of *Friends* in late 1996, its fan base went berserk, aware of what they'd missed because of all the episode guides on **Friends** Web sites.

Media Dominance

The big media players have begun to dominate. And despite all the forecasts that the Web would offer new and exciting niche publishing models which would see the offline media companies stewing in their own juices, many have quickly succeeded. Newspaper and news services have proliferated. The **Electronic Telegraph** has been the most hit content site (not a search engine) in England and Europe. **CNN** has set American records. In Australia, the **ABC** and **Sydney Morning Herald** (OK, I work on it and admit an interest in mentioning it) sites have been booming. The future is looking a lot like the past in many ways.

Paradigm Obsession

What is happening on the Web is rarely as interesting as the arguments about what is happening on the Web. Every few months or so, someone puts their hand up and shouts 'I have it! I've worked it out!' Every few months Web watchers come up with a new paradigm to discuss. 1997's buzzwords have been 'channels' and 'push'. It's not the Web, it's another form of television! If you don't agree, don't worry, there'll be a new one along soon.

Population Growth

The figures are so rubbery that they're basically meaningless. The **International Data Corporation** thinks there are around 40 million people online, and that seems as good a figure as any. I have heard estimates as low as 15 million and as high as 100 million. It just depends on who is talking and what day of the week you catch them on. What is important to note is that it is generally agreed that the figures are heading up (the predicted backlash has so far failed to materialise) and in most countries, the stereotype of the male, 25–40-year-old user is breaking down. One of the groups most interested in the Net these days is the retirees—it's no longer a young person's game.

Pranks

The Internet has a long folkloric history, of which pranks and hoaxes are a major part. My recent favourite was when Gena Lee Nolin, of *Baywatch* fame, announced she would Webcast the birth of her baby (Babywatch!), with a live feed from the hospital. It turned out to be an April Fool's joke. On a much crueller note, a fraud more than a prank, there was the case of the porn sites which asked users to download special picture viewing software before they could get their hands on the naughtiness. Trouble was, the software actually disconnected the modem from your ISP and reconnected you to a number in Moldavia, running up a massive phone bill, particularly for users who set their machine to dial silently.

Service Provider Shakeout

The bigger the Internet gets, the more money there is to be made, the less likely it is that the little guy will survive. That's the ugly truth of Internet *laissez-faire* capitalism for you. For one reason or another, every few months the ISPs claim that the major telecommunications companies (this happens in every country, it seems) are about to squeeze them out. Worrying about it is a perennial trend. But that doesn't mean it's not going to happen.

Three Dimensions

The Web, apparently, is greedy. Two dimensions aren't enough. There are all kinds of 3D experiments taking place on the Web, sites which construct environments that the user is able to move around in. You choose an avatar (a visual symbol) and move through the world, interacting by word (and by sound, in some places) with other visitors. In one way, they're like three-dimensional chat spaces, but they have the potential to be much more. The most popular is **AlphaWorld**.

Web Television

The first company to merge the Web and the television set was **WebTV Networks**, which created a system that could display Web pages on a TV screen using a little set top box and a remote control. The unit went on sale in the US in September 1996. This Web TV is not really the convergence that everyone is expecting though. It's only the beginning. Many believe real convergence will occur when, sooner or later, you don't think of the Net anymore than you think of the air TV and radio signals use for their delivery. This, of course, is hugely bandwidth dependent. When and if it reaches the point of possibility, anyone with a home video camera will be able to broadcast to the world. Given that half of commercial television now seems to be made up of video clip shows, will we notice the difference? The inherent danger, of course, is that the Web will move towards being a passive medium. And the big question no-one seems to be asking is: how do you design Web sites that work when viewed from 50 centimetres away on a computer screen, and three metres away on a TV screen? In the meantime, it's interesting to note that the TV industry is far more interested in digital television than Web mergers.

Workplace Restrictions

Being connected at work has been fun for the last couple of years. So few people in the average office had any idea of what the Net actually was that you could spend hours looking busy at your computer while actually slacking off and entertaining yourself. Now companies are beginning to restrict Net access. More and more stories of careful supervision of hours online are starting to emerge and it is becoming common for companies to restrict e-mail downloads to once or twice a day. It's a great way to get more out of your workers and less out of your technology. Once again, nobody wins.

Web addresses

Ghost Sites of the Web
http://cgi.pathfinder.com/netly/spoofcentral/ghostsites/

24 Hours in Cyberspace
http://www.cyber24.com

Amazon.com
http://www.amazon.com

CNN
http://www.cnn.com

Heaven's Gate Mirror
http://levelabovehuman.org/

Yahoo
http://www.yahoo.com

Microsoft
http://www.microsoft.com

Electric Minds
http://www.minds.com

WebRing
http://www.webring.org

Batman and Robin
http://www.batman-robin.com

Independence Day
http://www.id4movie.com/gateway.html

Friends Episode Guide
http://www.friends-tv.org/epguide.html

Electronic Telegraph
http://www.telegraph.co.uk

ABC
http://www.abc.net.au

Sydney Morning Herald
http://www.smh.com.au

International Data Corporation
http://www.idcresearch.com/f/idcf.htm

WebTV Networks
http://www.webtv.net

Push Media and the User Pays Syndrome

THE home page of **The Vatican** (yes, it has one—are you really surprised?) is a pretty stuffy affair. Though it has been through a major refurbishment, there's not a huge amount to see or do at the virtual Vatican. There are no online chapels and not much in the way of frescoes or statuary. There's not even a confessional booth—though to be fair, there are plenty of those **elsewhere** on the Web.

The most interesting part is probably the Vatican Information Service, which offers a daily news update in Castilian, English and French. Issued from Monday to Friday, the updates read a little like a newspaper's Vice Regal column. They tell you where the Pope is, what he's doing and who he's seeing (sparing you those expensive private investigator bills).

All in all, it's probably around 1,000 words a day of papal news. You can read these postings for free on the site—they are uploaded at the end of each day. But wait, there's more. You can also subscribe to the service and receive the updates by e-mail. You can join its automatic mailing list for US$400 ($515) a year. Yes, that's right: US$400pa just to add your name to an automatic electronic mailing list.

This seems rather steep to me. I could understand the altitude of the charge if the Vatican Press Office was express-mailing the updates in envelopes or faxing them at international rates. But they're not. They're sending them out as simple, efficient, mind-bogglingly cheap e-mails.

And what they're proving is that the Push Media believers (read: disciples) might just be right in their assertion that it will grow to dominate the Web. We're learning a lot about Push these days. It's being touted not only as the Web's future, but its salvation. Its arrival is being greeted with such relief that you'd think something was wrong with cyberspace, other than the fact that it doesn't generate fat rolls of cash for corporate rubber barons.

Everywhere you turn, software manufacturers, industry mags and pundits are getting all rosy-cheeked, flushed with the excitement of what they believe is the killer application they've all been waiting for. Finally, they seem to be saying, after years of putting up with the Net, it has a reason to exist. Even *Wired*, that increasingly ignorable former Bible (gosh, I've just had a flash of nostalgia for 1995!) of the online world, devoted a breathless, hysterical cover to it earlier this year.

Just in case you've been doing something more useful with your time, here's what the fuss is about. Push Media is a delivery system based on the logic that what the Web will do best is allow people to have their media diet tailored to them. Instead of just going to someone's site and pulling the information you want from it, the site and information will push its way to you, customised and ready for consumption. People, the theory goes, will pay for the ease of having things delivered to them, of having the surfing time and confusion cut out.

Simple versions of Push have already been in operation for a while. Using **Netscape**'s In-Box Direct technology, newspapers and Web zines, from **HotWired** to the **Herald**, are sending their home pages into the mailboxes of subscribers every morning. These home pages arrive on your desktop as HTML documents. The stories of the day can be clicked into without you having to go to the effort of accessing the site.

Pointcast is the most successful example of Push so far. The way it works is surprisingly straightforward. The Pointcast software regularly tells your computer to go to the company's site and download the latest news in your categories of interest (sports, business, arts and entertainment). It also picks up a few ads while it's there. Then, when your screen is idle, it

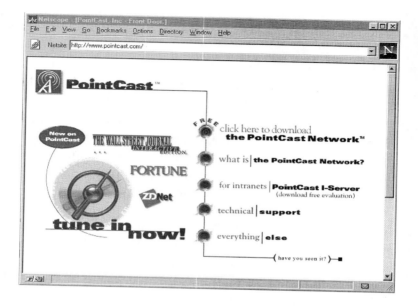

activates the screensaver function, popping up the news and ads for your perusal.

It finds news without you having to think to remind it. Or find it yourself. This has been an offer that a lot of people have found difficult to refuse. Pointcast says its site receives 40 million hits a day. But even if Pointcast has a few million users, that leaves tens of millions of Web inhabitants who don't use it. So exactly who is it that wants to be Pushed around?

Another company, Peak Media, takes a different, more subtle approach to the same kind of question. Its **Peak Net.Jet** software kicks into action when your modem is idle and sets out to download pages it thinks—based on your regular diet, the pages you go to most often—you might want to read.

These kinds of push technology are being built into Net browsers already. The new generation of products from Microsoft and Netscape are both huffing and puffing about

'Active desktops', additions which allow more integration of Pushed product.

Push Media is an obvious direction for the Internet to take, a fulfilment of one of its potentials but, make no mistake, there wouldn't be the buzz around it if that potential didn't also make it more attractive to advertisers. And that is because it makes the Web more like television — it makes us more like a captive target audience.

I'm not saying that Push Media is inherently bad, but the hype surrounding it so far has failed to take into account the complexity of the situation. Take the model of the personalised news service. Basically, it will work, and work blindingly well, for some people (those with highly specific business and personal interests), but not for all of us.

Human beings are just not that simple. We're complex, contrary and often contradictory creatures. And Push Media, like market research, is based on the theory that what we wanted yesterday is what we'll want today.

So that kind of Push will work wherever our relationship with the media is transactional, wherever we know precisely what we want and when we want it. But a lot of our media consumption is not transactional. Much of it involves grazing. It is based on browsing. How many stories did you look at in the paper today that you knew you were going to be interested in before you saw them? Were they the same interests you had last week?

Consuming media can be like buying clothes. You might know that you need a shirt, but you don't know which colour or fabric you want until you get to the shop. You need to try things on. Think about the way you buy a book or rent a video tape. You know you want something to read or watch, but you're often not sure what until you get to the store and have a chance to look around.

It's worth keeping in mind that the bottom line of Push media is revenue generation. After a couple of years of free experimentation, the Web now has its hand out. The goodwill and freedom of exchange on which it was built are (inevitably) starting to erode. There's a good, and fair, reason for much of this. The Web costs. And the revenue from advertising, in all but a handful of cases, has so far failed to match the drain of the sites. So, companies are understandably looking for other models to make the Web pay for their efforts. It used to be that it was only the porn sites which required you to register and fork over your credit card number. Now everybody's trying to get you to do it.

One of the most interesting players in this area has been the **New York Times**. When it launched a couple of years ago, it tried to make users pay for its service, a move that was doomed to failure. It was then left to watch as other sites, which contained information of a lower quality (but were crucially free) got all the traffic. The *Times* changed its mind, but not for the long. When you register now, it tells you that there's a charge of US$35 a month to access the site . . . but only if you're a foreigner. As if that makes any difference on the Net. As if you can't get a heck of a lot of the best bits of that paper via **Pointcast** for nothing anyway.

The *New York Times* may yet fail in its bid to charge at the front door. It wouldn't be alone. When Microsoft's **Slate** magazine debuted in early 1996, one of the many things it trumpeted was that it was going to start charging for access to the site by November of that year. Come the start of 1997, the notion had quietly disappeared.

The **Los Angeles Times**, on the other hand, keeps its daily news service free, but should you want to search the archive, well, you'd better crack open the purse. They charge US$1.50 for each story you call up from the menu, print or download.

For a little more (US$4 a story) they will find the stories you nominate and e-mail or fax them, saving you the browsing time. The research service goes back to 1985.

The **Washington Post**, which had been online since June of 1996, had taken most of its growing archive offline by the end of the year. Visitors can access stories going back only a fortnight. By the end of 1997, it was planning to have its entire news archive, back to 1986, online and accessible for a small fee. The **Wall Street Journal** charges both at the front door (US$49 a year) and for its searches.

After failing in its bid to launch a proprietary network, Microsoft has taken a second bite at the cherry with **MSN**, which has country-specific home pages for the United States and Canada, Australia, France, the United Kingdom and Germany. The service offers news, games and Web zines, but there's a monthly subscription fee.

At the moment, everybody is casting about, trying to find the revenue model that will work. Sooner or later, one will, and when it becomes the accepted wisdom—the Net is nothing if not sheep-like—we'll all have to pay more for the things we now mostly get for free. Though the reality will most likely be that we consume, as we do now, a broad media diet, with and without Push. Media is a giant buffet and Push will simply be another offering at the table. Some people will continue to get their news from TV. Others will go for radio or newspapers or the old-fashioned pull technology of the Web. More likely, people will fill up their plates with a little of everything.

Push Media will not become the be-all and end-all. It will be very successful and offer all kinds of new and useful points of access to information. The problem will arise when and if the people pumping the most money into the development of the Web get carried away with it. Because if, somehow, Push does achieve the level of dominance its advocates are tipping, we will have sacrificed something very special along the way. After all, what is the push behind Push Media about? It's about making money. And you know what? Making money is *their* problem. What did you come to the Net for? To spend?

In May 1997, *Hot Wired* columnist Mark Frauenfelder (as *Wired* declines, *HotWired* just gets better) quoted colleague Gareth Branwyn on the downside of the blind charge towards Push. Branwyn's words perfectly articulated what has been nagging me about the Push mania.

'I think at this time, when big media is trying to recast as a broadcast/couch-potato medium,' Branwyn said, 'it's good to remind people that the real beauty of the Net is the ability to exchange ideas, opinions, and your creativity with others; to build social networks. People are what interested me the most about the Net when I joined in '87, and people are still my main interest.'

If Push comes to shove, who will be the losers?

Web Addresses . . .

The Vatican
http://www.vatican.va/main-menu.html

Confess
http://www.fess-up.com/

Netscape
http://home.netscape.com/

HotWired
http://www.hotwired.com

Sydney Morning Herald
http://www.smh.com.au.

Pointcast
http://www.pointcast.com/

Peak Neck.Jet
http://www.peak-media.com/

Electronic Telegraph
http://www.telegraph.co.uk

New York Times
http://www.nytimes.com/

Pointcast
http://www.pointcast.com/

La Times
http://www.latimes.com

Washington Post
http://www.washingtonpost.com

Wall Street Journal
http://www.interactive.wsj.com/

MSN
http://www.msn.com

The Copyright Wars Begin

THE Net is a fan's medium. Anyone who has trawled around for more than a few hours knows that the official sites of films, actors, musicians and sports people are rarely as captivating as the fan-generated ones. It doesn't seem to matter how much money multinational entertainment corporations invest, the smaller, fan-driven outings consistently outperform theirs. The little ones might not always have the design slickness, but they make up for it with personality, character and heart.

If there is a lesson, perhaps it's that fans are often the best judges of what fans want. And for the first time, fans are capable of creating and directing the media which sustains them. This is a worrying thought for a lot people. The world-wide entertainment-industrial complex prospers through a web of spoken and unspoken alliances between the stars and those who package and present them. The stars know how to behave with the media and vice versa—it's rare that either side steps out of line. But once the fans take hold of the media, the game changes.

Fans don't care what the unspoken rules of behaviour are. They're not as controllable as the major media players. And they are—by and large—unconcerned with what they see as trivial, outdated niceties—you know, things like privacy and copyright. All of which suggests there will be legal brushfires across the Net for the next couple of years, as more official sites go up, and more entertainment lawyers fight to 'protect' their clients from fans illegally using their images and intellectual property.

Some of these breaches are simple and of no particular harm to anyone. They're just examples of the fans taking culture into their own hands, such as the **X-Files Fan Fiction** site, where X-Philes contribute their own stories to the eerie canon.

Presented on a non-profit basis, these stories are not exactly denying anyone a royalty, but it must be odd for X-Files creator Chris Carter to watch what people are doing with his brainchildren. By way of the most obvious example, the relationship between Mulder and Scully is ambiguous on the show, but in the fan fiction, the duo is clearly on heat.

> Slowly, Scully brought her hand up to caress the slight stubble along her partner's jawline. In mimic, Mulder did the same to her; his hand eventually running up into her hair as she leaned closer. Their breaths mingle together for what seemed eons until Scully gave a little nudge and their lips met. Electricity surged through them and both drew back in shock at the power and passion lying in that simple kiss . . .

On heat too, from the look of the exploding amount of fan fiction devoted to her, is **Xena: Warrior Princess**. Not content with swords and sorcery, our heroine apparently likes to come home after the cameras are turned off and relax with a jolly good shag.

> As I nuzzled against Xena's shoulder, the scent of campfire smoke, the long day's ride, and the well-aged leather commingled with the closeness of her hair and drove me boldly. I wanted her. I needed her. Desperately. My teeth bit into the bare hollow between neck and collarbone. I can still remember the quiet moan rising from her throat and the soul devouring sound of her voice when she asked me to stop.

There is fan fiction for shows no longer with us from **American Gothic** to **Batman** to the **Forever Knight**. There are more than 400 **Lois & Clark** stories alone. Some offer you the chance to display your completed work. Others, like the **Interactive Star Wars Story**, let you add little pieces to a constantly growing narrative.

The **Alt.Startrek.Creative Official Web Site** is a whole library of work from Net-drifting Trekkers. You can read from the collection of hundreds of stories based in the various Trek worlds. Taking things further than the X-Files folk, there is a separate adult section which features stories of your favourite Star Trek characters doing the wild thing with various inter-planetary (and interspecies) partners.

There's Kirk and Spock finding the meaning of true love: 'Throwing away his clothes, Kirk bent over the Vulcan and held his face in his hands. "Spock! Reach out for me!" Only waves of lust and desire surged through him . . .'

And there's Voyager's Captain Janeway's lust for her first engineer, the half human, half Klingon B'Elanna Torres: 'The more Kathryn thought about B'Elanna, the more she began to fantasise about her. "I bet she's rough." Kathryn liked that. Although she had never had sex with a woman before, the idea had always intrigued her. To touch and to feel another woman. To know exactly where to touch her, and for her to know exactly where to touch you. It was almost incredible. Kathryn realised that now she wanted to fuck B'Elanna more than anything . . . She thought more. How could she make this a reality? Of course! During shore leave, she would try to come on to her . . .'

There's also a crossover section, full of fan stories that prominently feature other fictional sci-fi characters, from **Dr Who** to the crew of the **Red Dwarf**. Look hard enough and you'll even find dear old Edmund Blackadder.

Given this licence, it's no surprise that in January 1997, Viacom, which owns Star Trek, announced it was going to clean up the Net, to attempt to shut down fan-based sites (of which there are hundreds). Its reasoning was that the fan sites, though they are almost all non-commercial, denied the company control of its own brand.

Jeff Rhind, who hosts the **Capt. James T. Kirk Singalong Page**, was one of the people who received Cease and Desist letters from Viacom laywers, asking him to remove all images, sounds, movies, script excerpts, and episode synopses. Rhind reprints the letter on a part of his site called the Wrath of ViaKhan, along with his responses and any progress in the case. He points out that he receives no money for his Web site, and actually spends his own money to maintain it, and that his site provides publicity for the Trek franchise

'We, as webmasters, love the craft of creating an engaging experience for visitors by providing a well designed site with frequent updates,' he writes to Viacom. 'Compliments and kudos steadily come in from all over the world for our efforts. A kind or encouraging word has been my only payment for a satisfied Web site visitor.

'Therefore, I have forwarded an invoice to your accounts payable department for the time covering my Web site's inception to the receipt of your letter, or approximately sixteen months, for the design, development, programming, implementation, and weekly maintenance . . .'

Viacom was not the first to take this line. Disney had been stamping out **Disneyland** tribute pages, and Twentieth Century Fox had been doing the same thing with Simpsons sites, both for months previously. The network also put the screws on X-Files and Millennium sites, causing an outbreak of **protest** across the Web.

This protest was echoed six months later when the copyright battle moved from film and television to music. In May 1997, Oasis's management company, Ignition, sent an e-mail message to hundreds of unofficial Oasis sites (via its own site, **Oasisnet**), demanding that they remove photographs, lyrics and sound clips. Site operators were given until 2 June to stop stealing from the band they claim to support. If they failed to meet the deadline, they were warned, legal action would follow.

A spokesperson for the band said bootleggers could take

photographs and music from these Internet sites and sell them as posters or CDs, which is not much of a case to answer. It's unlikely that a low-resolution Internet image could be blown up to poster size with any kind of useful picture definition. And as for live concert recordings, it's a lot easier to source them from radio, TV and the shows themselves.

Where the band did have a case to make was the problem with the circulation of leaked, unreleased material, a situation U2 faced in 1996 when songs from its *Pop* album were stolen and distributed on the Net. Ignition Management also rightly questioned the value of misinformation that was spreading about the Oasis album (then a work in progress) on various sites. What is the line, they asked, between acceptable fan discussion and malicious rumour-mongering? Is there a point where a Web site can be damaging?

Still, their approach was heavy-handed and failed to recognise the value in the sites. Appalled at the demands, some of the more responsible site folk responded by forming a group called **Oasis Webmasters for Internet Freedom**, citing the band's rebellious lyrics in their defence ('I'm free to do whatever I, whatever I like, if it's wrong or right, it's all right').

Jack Martin, the University of Kansas student behind OWIF, says the unofficial sites constitute what is defined under copyright law (US copyright law, at least) as 'fair use', in that they are non-profit and exist for what the law defines as 'purposes such as criticism, comment, news reporting, teaching, scholarship, research and similar activities'.

'The Oasis fan Web sites,' he says, 'are just for fun. Any fair-minded person will admit that the fan Web sites only help the band and do not deprive anyone with a financial interest in the band of any money. In fact, by generating more interest in Oasis, the fan web sites may well be getting those people more money.'

Following the fans' complaints, Ignition released a clarification, claiming that 'Oasis and the Official Oasis homepage have always encouraged fan pages'. 'However, there are a number of sites out there who, to be frank, we feel have taken advantage of the situation. In particular, a number of pages have been copying freely from the official homepage . . . [and] some sites have been posting large numbers of unauthorised sound and video clips without permission. It is this sort of behaviour we have to discourage.'

In June, the deadline came and went. Some sites began to close down (OWIF began keeping a Missing In Action list), but many others stayed open for business. Jack Martin posted an open letter to other site operators saying 'there is absolutely no reason to panic'.

'Ignition and Oasis Internet know that our pages are beneficial to Oasis exposure and record sales,' he wrote. 'They also know that if they take any type of legal action, the press will jump on the story. Just look how many stories were written just about the threat of action. The last thing Ignition wants is the headline "Oasis sues fan site owners" being published all over the world.'

As I write, there has been no legal action . . .

Meanwhile, who knows how many 14-year-old Web site builders have had fat, threatening legal letters arrive in their mailboxes? There's more than a little sledgehammer nut-cracking going on here. And the question really does remain of how much damage to the band these sites are doing? Some sites break copyright but are good, clean, imaginative fun.

Cindy Crawford, for example, has dozens of sites devoted to pictures of her, emanating from virtually every country on the globe. The best of these, **Cindy Crawford Concentration**, is a photo memory game which asks you to match Cindy

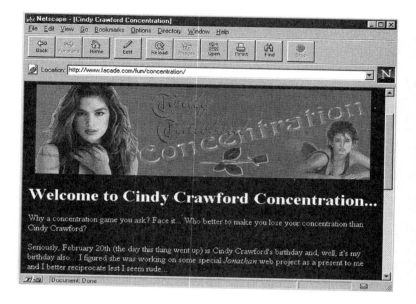

pictures on a board, two at a time, remembering where your wrong guesses were.

The excellent **Faces**, put together by Cory R. Gilbert, hearkens back to those childhood flip books that let you put the head of one animal onto the torso of another. The best use of Netscape's lame frames technology I have seen, it encourages you to build your own celebrity from the facial parts of others. Take Gillian Anderson's hair, Pamela Anderson's eyes and Jim Carrey's mouth and wham! It's Phyllis Diller. Add a little Sandra Bullock to a soupcon of Ronald Reagan and a jigger of Bob Dole and Voila! Mao Zedong.

The weirdest, least controllable and most fraught end of the continuum of fan activity is represented by recent goings on in **alt.binaries.nude.celebrities**. Here is the kind of place inhabited by the folk who are usually found thumbing through copies of *Celebrity Skin* in your newsagency. Somewhere around late 1995, fake nudes began to appear in the newsgroup post-

ings, celebrity heads pasted onto nude bodies by digital manip-
ulators. Some were grotesque and some were hysterical—one
artist went to great lengths in the creation of a shot of the
shipwrecked **Gilligan's Island** crew, with Ginger and Mary
Ann pretending to be nudists. Another created the picture of
Marcia Brady that all men of a certain age will recall having
wanted to see so much as children.

Mostly these fakes were pretty obvious, but some were
almost seamless. Some smarty even came up with a great name
for the practice: Frankenporn. And it was all in good fun,
though the stars in question would no doubt have been unim-
pressed. But in 1996, the stakes began to go up. People began
posting manipulated 'photos' of the likes of Cindy Crawford
and Pamela Anderson Lee (with a horse, in a scene that must
been cut out of Mr Ed), engaged in the kind of activities that
can't be reported here. Or sold over the counter.

Copyright, privacy, defamation . . . how many laws can you
break at once? It's almost enough to make you hope the Big
Guys will win. But not quite.

Web addresses

X-Files Fan Fiction
http://gossamer.simplenet.com/

Xena Fan Fiction
http://xenafan.com/fiction/

Xenerotica
http://members.aol.com/labrysxena/xenerotica.htm

American Gothic
http://members.aol.com/roxannep/agfanfic.html

Batman
http://www.missouri.edu/~c667778/dadadada.html

Forever Knight Fan Fiction
http://www.fkfanfic.com/

Lois & Clark
http://www.win.net/~lcw/fanfic/

Interactive Star Wars Story
http://www.ultranet.com/~abryant/

Alt.Startrek.Creative Official Web Site
http://www.cs.runet.edu/~sratliff/index/
http://aviary.share.net:80/~alara/

Dr Who
http://www.drwho.org/

Red Dwarf
http://smeg.com/

Capt. James T. Kirk Singalong Page
http://www.loskene.com/singalong/kirk.html

Disneyland
http://www.disney.com/Disneyland/

X-files and Millennium Protest Sites
http://www.yahoo.com/News_and_Media/Television/Shows/Science_Fiction_Fantasy_and_
Horror/X_Files_The/X_Philes_ Millennium_Protest/

Oasisinet
http://www.oasisinet.com

Oasis Webmasters for Internet Freedom
http://falcon.cc.ukans.edu/~jackm/OWIF.htm

Cindy Crawford Concentration
http://www.facade.com/fun/concentration/

Faces
http://www.corynet.com/faces/

Gilligan's Island
http://www.lookup.com/Homepages/58181/home.html

Marcia Brady
http://www.ttinet.com/mccormick/

Bandwidth and Balkanisation

WHAT do we want? Bandwidth! When do we want it? Now! Bandwidth. The word has a magical power for Netheads. In their mouths, it's more an invocation than a denotation. It's the solution for every problem, the answer for every question, the antidote to every snakebite, the bulldozer for every rainforest . . . sorry, getting carried away there. It's the universal cure, the new penicillin.

No matter what complaint you make, the response always seems to be a shaking of the head, a slight click of the tongue and a 'Don't worry. It'll be different when bandwidth increases.' The Net isn't fast enough? Don't worry, bandwidth will change that. Audio and video quality aren't high? Bandwidth'll fix it. You can't get the public interested in your online activities? Bandwidth will help.

What if . . . and this is just a thought . . . this magical increased bandwidth everyone is talking about brings, at least in the short term, more grief than joy? What if it creates as many problems as it solves?

We'll find out pretty soon. Phone companies around the world have been promising ultra-powerful cable modems since late 1996, at prices that will make them attractive to the few rather than the many, but you can bet the rates will head downwards. These devices are promising speed of access to the Net at a rate so much higher that it's hard to imagine. Meanwhile, 56kbps modems are becoming more widespread.

As these new modems achieve some kind of market penetration, we'll be facing modem lag. A significant proportion of the Net community will still be using 14.4kbps modems while, at the other end of the scale, another section will have 10 or 20 times the technological pull. Some will drive Ferraris, some Mini Minors.

Net commentators often talk about the growing worldwide gap between the info-rich and the info-poor. But the social calibration within the Net community is changing too, and few have stepped up to discuss the potential ramifications of this. Increasingly, it is apparent, we will also be seeing a gap between the rich info-rich and the poor info-rich.

How will these powerful modems affect packet flow? If a network is only as strong as its weakest link, are we heading towards a situation in which we find people with powerful, fat modems sucking hard on information that is stuck in the turnstiles on the other side of the world? Will the high-powered modems overwhelm the weaker ones?

Whatever happens technically, on the other side of the screen, we will be left wondering how to design Web sites for the different capabilities of users. There could, for example, be a growing economic divide. The real money could move away from the audience. The people who can afford cable modems, the richer end of the Net market, may well be sought after by advertisers. This could mean that the high-end sites will attract high-end advertising and high-end revenue. Indeed, they'll need to in order to finance the technological innovation that will make them so attractive.

I'm speculating here, but I see this leading to a situation in which sites pursuing the ad dollar push themselves upwards, more or less abandoning ordinary users. And yet, there will be fewer of these people to advertise to at the top end. The demographics of the Net will be split. Advertisers will be even more selective, more hesitant about dispensing their cash. One of the positive effects of the consistency of Net users to date has been that broad markets have been easy to define, easy to explain and relatively easy to sell. That will no longer be the case.

The result of this bandwidth fragmentation, at the very least, will be confusion among advertisers and site builders.

Many sites will be forced to take a schizoid view of themselves. At the moment, it is common for sites to have high and low bandwidth (or text only) versions. In future, the number of alternatives a site has to offer could multiply. Meeting the expectations of different users will add significantly to budgets.

This is a new problem for the media. Newspapers, radio networks and television stations, by and large, present one face to the world (okay, some papers do city and country editions, and some broadcast media cut local news bulletins into national networks). Audience members all look the same to them. But on the Net, we are no longer the audience. We are the users. And we are increasingly individual.

How long it will be before modem lag sorts itself out is anybody's guess. Sooner or later, most users will make the switch from coaxial cable to fibre optic because, well, they won't have much of a choice. But while we wait, the situation will only get more complex, fragmented further by the current browser wars.

As I write, there are four versions of Netscape Navigator being used by Net surfers. There are four more of Microsoft's Internet Explorer. While a majority of people are using the latest versions of the software, there are still significant numbers (around 40–50 per cent, if you add it up) of people using older versions. Many universities and corporate institutions, caught up in the Internet rush of 1995, are still using Netscape 1.1, the software that was loaded onto their machines when they first arrived in cyberspace. There are also people using IBM browsers, America Online browsers and a dozen other types of software (in admittedly minor numbers).

Until recently, the Web may have been a chaotic place but, technologically speaking, its users have been relatively consistent, accessing it with similar software and strength. We are in the middle of the Balkanisation of the Net. Now, we're going to have chaos at both ends. This is what bandwidth will help bring us. This is what our hunger for new versions of browsers is doing.

It may not be a problem in the end. But more than likely, this fracturing will cause fissures to spread across the surface of the Net. The more chaos we have, the more likely it is we'll be so frustrated that we'll want industry standards. We'll want simple answers. And the more that we want those, the more the ball moves out of the court of the user and into that of large hardware and software companies such as (but not only) Microsoft. We are, after all, a lot easier to conquer once we're divided.

I meet a lot of people who want to discuss censorship online and how to combat it. It's easy to get Net surfers to think politically about the legislation process and how it will affect their freedom of speech. It's much harder to get them to see that the politics of the virtual world don't end there. Every decision you make, which service provider you give your money to, which browser you use, is a political decision. Think carefully.

Shopping Online

'IT'S almost Christmas,' my editor said to me. 'Why not do a piece about shopping online, so that our readers won't even have to leave their houses to buy presents?' 'Great idea,' I replied.

'But let's not be half-hearted about it—why not spend some serious money, say, a few hundred dollars, to see whether the much-hyped online commerce actually works?' 'Great idea,' I said again.

'And why not use your own money while you're at it?' D'oh!

Two things had stopped me from blowing my hard-earned cash online to that point. The first was the issue of security. The second was my own stupidity. Credit-shopping for things you can't even touch when you buy them is unreal—almost too game-like to take seriously. I had visions of myself in clicking frenzy, ordering up thousands of dollars worth of rubbish, buying things I would never buy in a store, just because I liked the idea of buying them. Just because I could. 'Dammit, an inflatable elephant! I have to have that! It will go with my life-sized plastic horse!'

The stupidity, I had to accept, was something I couldn't do much about. One of the biggest dangers about Net shopping is always going to be the loss of the cause-and-effect feeling about it. Parting with your credit details by e-mail just doesn't seem as real as handing someone cash. It is, I'm assured by regular shoppers, easy to get carried away.

Security, on the other hand, was an issue I could deal with. It's the one thing, according to experts, that most scares off potential Internet customers. People are understandably fearful of parting with their credit card numbers in a medium they don't really understand. The Internet is still a little like magic

to most of the people using it, a little like what Catweazle used to call 'Electrikery'. It took a long time for people to lose the fear of divulging their numbers over the telephone and it will take at least as long for it to abate on the Net.

But really, security is a slowly dissolving problem. More and more sites are secured these days, encrypting credit card transactions. And more and more people are coming to accept that while the Net may not be a perfectly secure medium, neither are the other ones. There could be someone out there scanning your phone as you give the numbers during a call. There could be someone going through the skip bins behind your local shopping mall, looking for discarded credit slips . . .

I rang my local authorities, the Fraud Enforcement Agency of the NSW Police Service, and they told me that as far as they were aware, there hadn't yet been a single case in Australia of credit card fraud involving the Internet. It could happen, the nice man conceded, and was likely to happen at some point, but hadn't. Before I could hang up, he gave me a lecture about using the same kind of common sense online (stick to major retailers, think about who you're giving the number to) that you would offline.

So I take a deep breath and get over my fear. Then I find that making the decision to buy on the Net is not the hard part. Working out where to start is the hard part. At first, I thought that postage and packaging might be a bit of an obstacle so maybe I should shop locally. For me, that means Australian stores. Two jump-off indexes are **The Australian Shopping Mall**, where you can buy everything from Ugg boots to gourmet bush food, and **Australian Internet Directories Shopping List**, which lists online goods and services in more than 40 categories, from alcohol to videos.

Realistically, most Australian vendor sites have not passed the glossy brochure stage yet. You get to the bottom of the spruiking to find there's no way you can order anything over the Web. You still have to go to the store or phone them. As usual, America is comfortably ahead in this curve. Consult **Yahoo**'s selection of online products and services if you want to be overwhelmed. Find out where to buy an **Alien Embryo Key Chain** or an anatomically correct **Voodoo Doll**. Or, if you're lonely, why not buy a hand-crafted, male or female, highly realistic **corpse**—degree of decay yours to choose. There's even a guy who will, for US$15.99 (plus postage and handling), sell you real estate on the **moon**.

I spend about three hours wandering through this maze of sites. I'm in shopping mode now, determined to lose my commercial virginity. My hands are shaking with the desire to purchase something, my mind telling myself over and over not to be stupid. I realise after all this time has elapsed that I've been over-compensating and haven't spent a cent.

I take another deep breath and start my modest buying

binge in a safer, saner province, at **CD Now**, the oldest and best-known of the many online music stores. The site offers the latest in pop and classical music (it stopped counting the records in stock at 180,000), as well as videos (35,000 and counting) and games. How does it work? CD Now asks the shopper to create a new account, assuring you that it's in Netscape-secure mode before you have to hand over any details. After filling out their form, all you have to do is click on the price of any item to add it to your shopping cart.

Whee! We're away, running down the aisles and dropping things into the basket. I pick up the Leon Parker album, *Belief*, and the Tricky album, *Pre Millennium Tension*. Because I'm buying them when they were relatively new, they're on sale, at $13.46 and $13.96 respectively. I also grab the last Billy Bragg opus, the attractively titled *William Bloke*, and the American version of the first Crowded House album, because it has an extra track on it.

The bill comes to US$71.53, including postage and packaging (shipping to Australia is $10.51 for the first item, $2.29 each for the next five items and $1.80 each thereafter). They promise delivery within four weeks, but for a few cents more (67 cents to be exact), that comes down to six working days. I take the quick option and hand over my credit card number. The site e-mails confirmation.

Sure enough, two working days later, the delivery man is at my door. For $90, I have four new albums. If I'd gone to my local record store, it would have cost me $124, not counting the bus fare. And this is the first and biggest shock of online retail. A global business, it has different values for everyone who takes part. Depending on your exchange rates, you can pick up major bargains or cough up way too much. If you know what you're looking for, it makes sense to go to a site where it ought to be the cheapest. Just like the offline world, it pays to shop around.

Increasingly, by the way, it is also possible to listen before you buy. CD Now connects to **InterJuke**, one of a handful of Net jukeboxes, Web-based listening posts, which let you road test new and old records, with hundreds of tunes available, to reassure yourself that they're worth shelling out the cash for.

Anyway, I'm elated by my success with CDs. The spending rush is hitting me. I'm a magazine junkie, so I head off to the **Electronic Newsstand**, to browse the racks of 2,000 periodicals. What I want to find is *The Utne Reader*, a US bowerbird magazine of media gleanings that is almost impossible to get where I am, and when you can find it, costs $11.95 an issue. The Newsstand refers me to the **Reader**'s own site, which offers a six-issue surface mail subscription for US$28 or an airmail one for $50. I take the former. This way, it will take the same amount of time to get to me as it does to get to the few local newsagents who carry it, and I'll get each issue for $5.83. Half the price. Woohoo!

Feeling buoyed, I decide to throw caution to the wind and subscribe to **Internet Underground**, one of the only Web mags really having fun with the medium, but when I visit, its subscription facilities are down. Bummer.

Staying with the written word, it seems like it might be time for a little bookstore visit. There are more than 500 **booksellers online**, from the American-hosted but Australian-run **Bibliocity**, which deals in rare and collectable books, to locals like my favourite Sydney store, **Gleebooks**.

The biggest hyperbarn of all is another American, **Amazon.com**. One of the Web's most amazing success stories, it boasts more than two million titles in its warehouse. Like CD Now, it is not encumbered by the costs of retail, by staff and high rental store space. So most books in Amazon's virtual store are offered at a discount of 10–20 per cent.

I opt for a paperback copy of *The Evolution of Useful Things*, a book about the history of everyday artefacts by Henry Petroski ($10.40) and a hardback of Simon Schama's *Landscape and Memory*, for US$36 (it's around the $60 mark here). And before I leave, I spot a book by *Weekly World News* columnist Ed Anger, a man so far to the right that he'll be coming back round on the left any minute now. *Let's Pave the Stupid Rainforests and Give School Teachers Stun Guns and Other Ways to Save America* seems like such a good deal at $8.95 that I order two copies. I know what I'm giving myself this year.

Like CD Now, the Amazon site has a secure server. The site offers to giftwrap my purchases for a couple of dollars, with swatches of the paper available for viewing. If I wanted, I could even type in a message for the card. To countries other than the US, it's $4 a shipment plus a per book charge of $1.95. Delivery to Australia is promised in six to eight weeks. For $7 a shipment, plus $5.95 a book, I could have them here within a week.

I go for the surface mail option because the postage would otherwise cancel any savings I would make. I also figure that if the package takes six to eight weeks to arrive, I'll have completely forgotten I ordered the books by then, so it'll be a nice surprise. My four books, with postage and packaging, come to a total of A$95. If I had bought them here (assuming I could find them), they would have cost at least $20 more.

Video hunting next . . . sorry for being juvenile, but I've been waiting years for tapes of *Pee-wee's Playhouse* to hit the market. Pee-wee Herman's kiddy show, a huge hit in the US in the 1980s, never made it to Australian screens. Finally, in late 1996, they arrived. **MGM Home Video** now sells eight volumes, with two episodes on each tape, for a paltry $12.95

each. Boy, do I get depressed when I find out its ordering service only covers the US. The local service, **OzVideo**, says it offers close to 10,000 titles but Pee-wee isn't among them. Sigh.

It's getting hot. I loosen my collar and switch my thoughts to clothing. The prospect of buying something to wear on the Net makes me wonder about the whole nature of this type of commerce. Some shopping is transactional (you know what you want and what you'll pay—the Net offers ease of access), but a lot of shopping is leisure-related. I can't imagine buying a suit or shoes or a flashy shirt without trying them on first. But there are clothes I would buy online, I decide, staples such as socks and underwear. Best to think local again.

I find them at **Lowes**. The store, which has branches all over eastern Australia, has twigged to the idea that people will buy the things they already know. It offers simple clothes in simple categories, with free delivery Australia-wide for orders above $95. Under that figure, it'll cost you up to, but not more than, $6. In its Activewear section, I find a basic Hanes T-shirt for $14. Having saved $2 each on four shirts, I reckon that at worst, I'm $2 ahead. And that seems as good a point as any to declare the day a success before I feel the urge to build a golf course on the moon . . .

I have spent $276.50. I have saved, by my reckoning, $94. A couple of weeks later, Amazon.com sends me a little thank you present for shopping with them, a mousepad with a quotation from Groucho Marx on it. It's smart thinking, and the kind of act that is almost guaranteed to get the customer back in their door. But the gesture wasn't really necessary. My decision had already been made, the second I looked at those two figures. Some things are hard to argue with.

Web addresses

AAA Australian Shopping Mall
http://www.aaaaustralia.com.au/

Australian Internet Directories Shopping List
http://www.sofcom.com.au/Business_and_Economy/Products_and_Services

Yahoo
http://www.yahoo.com/Business_and_Economy/Products_and_Services

Alien Embryo Key Chain
http://www.alienated.com

Voodoo Doll
http://www.mja.net/yoodoovoodoo/

Corpses For Sale
http://distefano.com/

Buy The Moon
http://www.moonshop.com

CD Now
http://www.cdnow.com

InterJuke
http://interjuke.com/jukebox

Electronic Newsstand
http://enews.com

Utne Reader
http://www.utne.com

Internet Underground
http://www.underground-online.com/

Booksellers on the Net
http://www.bookwire.com/index/booksellers.html

Bibliocity
http://www.bibliocity.com

Gleebooks
http://www.gleebooks.com.au

Amazon.com
http://www.amazon.com

MGM Home Video
http://www.mgmhomevideo.com

OzVideo
http://ozvideo.com.au

Lowes
http://wwww.lowesaus.com.au

REMEMBERING THE HUMAN

Pregnancy and Your Computer

IN the family way? Up the duff? Got a bun in the oven? (feel free to insert your 1950s pregnancy euphemism of choice here)? If so, click on over to the **Olen Interactive Pregnancy Calendar**, a seriously cool piece of Web software which comes to us courtesy of Mollee and Michael Olenick of Minneapolis.

This kindly couple have put together a site which will generate a customised calendar for your pregnancy. If you're pretty sure of the date of conception, or even if you just know the date of your last period, all you have to do is feed the information in and the site will provide an explanation of what's going on inside your body today. Or next week. Or next month.

If, for example, you reckon you conceived on New Year's Day, then the due date of your child, according to the calendar, is 25 September. Around mid-March, about the end of the foetus's eleventh week, its bones will begin to grow—they'll harden later. Four months later, you'll find bub is already making grasping motions, sucking its thumb inside you ('Stop that! If I've told you once, I've told you a thousand times!').

It's a fascinating example of the kind of help and entertainment that the Web can provide for expecting mums and dads. No other medium would offer you the personalising option; well, not for free anyway.

The **Chinese Gender Prediction Chart** may be a lot less convincing, but it's fun too. This site claims that you can choose the sex of your child by following the directions set out 700 years ago on a chart found in a royal tomb near Beijing (Peking). 'The original copy,' the site says, 'is kept in the Institute of Science of Peking. The accuracy of the chart has been proved by thousands of people and is believed to be 99 per cent accurate.' It bases its predictions on the age of the mother and the month of conception, arguing, for example, that

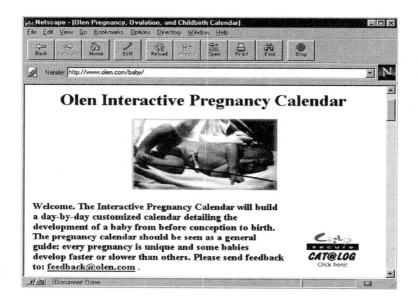

every 29-year-old woman who conceives in July will have a boy and every 34-year-old who conceives in September will have a girl.

Like the Olen calendar, **Ask NOAH About Pregnancy** has a similar breakdown of the nine months of pregnancy, but it doesn't automatically match up with your dates. Not to worry, because the NOAH site, a joint venture by a bunch of New York universities and libraries, is a comprehensive collection of gestation information, an attempt to create a convenient resource for expecting parents. There are sections on: family planning issues, pre- and post-natal care, possible problems and risks during pregnancy, and resource directions. Look around and you'll find everything from advice about the morning after pill to nutrition tips to explanations of how a cocaine habit will affect the unborn baby.

There are many other sites which function as pregnancy libraries—stopping off points for those wishing to educate themselves about parturition, including **The Pregnancy Place** and **Lynne's Ultimate Pregnancy Page**. **Cathy's Pregnancy Web Page** goes a step or two further by letting you download pregnancy shareware for tracking the pregnancy, planning for the baby and keeping online baby albums.

It also has its own gender prediction testing, in the form of a collection of old wives' tales: omens which supposedly indicate how things will turn out inside your baby's nappies. If the baby's heart rate is 139 or below, the site says, it's a boy. If the hair on your legs grows faster, you are having a boy. If your feet are colder than before pregnancy, you are having a boy. If you sleep in a bed with your pillow to the north, you are having a boy. If you refuse to eat the end of a loaf of bread, you are having a girl. If you're inclined to eat with a fork, it's a boy.

The list goes on, winding its way towards my personal favourite—a scientific test. Add one teaspoon of Drano to a small amount of morning urine. If it turns bluish yellow, you are having a boy. Greenish brown means a girl.

One of the most interesting things about the site is that besides offering directions to other online resources, Cathy shares her own birthing story, recounting the details of the arrival of her daughter Jordan. As you wander around the maze of pregnancy sites, you realise that this is a path a significant number of them head down. Having a child is obviously something so meaningful in the lives of so many people that they find themselves wanting to articulate their feelings, to talk about it, to tell their own stories. The Web provides the forum for them to do so.

Birth Stories, a sub-branch part of the mammoth **Childbirth.Org** site, contains well over 100 of these personal journeys, these tales of interesting entrances to the world. The range actually boggles the mind, the permutations seemingly endless, as individual as the people they involve. There are late, induced caesarian sections, homebirth twins, mothers unaware they were pregnant until labour, long labours, short labours, unassisted births and births involving almost every drug known to man. (NB: The site's collection of pregnancy links is enormous, and covers issues ranging from 'Preparing Your Dog for the New Baby' to 'Nose Bleeds During Pregnancy'.)

If it's the stories that most interest you, one of the quickest ways to find them is to make use of the **WWW Pregnancy Ring**. This WebRing (a group of sites that share connections to like minded others in the form of a circle, allowing the user to just click on the 'Next Site' button) was founded in July 1996 'to make it easier for people interested in pregnancy, childbirth, and infant care to find high quality informational sites'.

Some of these sites really make use of Web technology to invite you into their experiences. **My Baby Girl** followed the pregnancy of a woman who calls herself Teddy Bear, leading up to the birth of daughter Marina Ann on 22 February 1997. There are photos on site from the delivery room as well as a record of live updates. There is a sound file of the baby's heartbeat at birth, which will no doubt one day form the basis for a great dancefloor hit. There are ultrasound photos taken at six different points of the pregnancy. And there's a diary of the final two weeks before birth.

It's Just Another Baby tells the story from the other side. Christopher Rywalt, a first-time Dad-to-be, kept an online journal of his wife's pregnancy throughout the nine months, adding updates whenever he felt anything of interest had happened.

Share Our Miracle went down the interactive route, not only offering ultrasound photos of the foetus and a diary of its growth, but the chance for the Net user to predict the sex of the child (11,000 people guessed—slightly more went for the boy option) and suggest a name for it. The child in question, Halen Tucker Knapp, a boy, was born in June 1996. Both names came from Net suggestions.

Another couple has also been calling for Net assistance, for a child due about the time this book comes out. **Name Our Baby** is the catchy, simple, self-explanatory title of their site. They don't know if it's going to be a boy or a girl, but ask for all suggestions to please be of Hebrew origin. 'Here she is at 7 weeks old,' they offer by way of assistance for your choice, enclosing the ultrasound photo.

They could have just looked around. There are a number of places to go if you're looking for something to call the little one other than 'Hey you, yes you, Mr Stinky!'. **Baby Names**, created by sisters Jennifer Moss and Mallory Moss Lubofsky, is just one of the phone book-sized repositories of naming suggestions. It also runs a bulletin board for soon-to-be parents and name aficionados to get together and discuss the pros and cons ('Is Lazarus out of date?').

The **Utah Baby Namer** lists Mormon names from Aasta to Zya. And **Jellinek's Random Baby Name Chooser** picks from a list of more than 10,000 names. I asked it to choose three girl's names and it came up with Biddie, Rochella and Marika. Hmmm, could have done better than that myself. But like all random acts, I'm sure it's inspirational some of the time.

One last thing. If you're going to have a wired pregnancy, don't forget to build your **Birth Announcement** Web site. Yahoo lists a whole bunch of them. Why let your children make the decision whether to have a Web page or not when you can do it for them? Embarrass them from birth. Send their nude photos out to the world.

Web addresses

Olen Interactive Pregnancy Calendar
http://www.olen.com/baby/

Chinese Gender Prediction Chart
http://www.infocom.net/~newland/html/chinese.gender.chart

Ask NOAH About Pregnancy
http://www.noah.cuny.edu/pregnancy/pregnancy.html

The Pregnancy Place
http://www.preg.com/index.htm

Lynne's Ultimate Pregnancy Page
http://www.geocities.com/Heartland/5552/

Cathy's Pregnancy Web Page
http://www.telepath.com/canance/pregnancy/

Childbirth.Org
http://www.childbirth.org

WWW Pregnancy Ring
http://www.fensende.com/Users/swnymph/Ring.html

My Baby Girl
http://evansville.net/~tbear/baby/

It's Just Another Baby
http://www.westnet.com/~crywalt/pregnancy/

Share Our Miracle
http://www2.southwind.net/~wknapp/miracle/

Name Our Baby
http://supremeweb.com/tutor/baby/

Baby Names
http://www.babynames.com

Utah Baby Namer
http://www.geocities.com/Heartland/3450/

Jellinek's Random Baby Name Chooser
http://www.jellinek.com/baby/

Yahoo Birth Announcements
http://www.yahoo.com/Society_and_Culture/Birth/Birth_Announcements/

See also . . .

The Online Pregnancy Test
http://www.worldweb.net/~jcanterb/pregnant.html

'Why mess around with trying to fill some silly cup or aim for some tiny slip of paper, waiting for something to change colours. What is up with that, anyway? If you wanted to watch something change colours, you would buy a mood ring, right? No, none of that for you. Hey, it's the 1990s! Let's take advantage of the technology we have available to us! And now, your opportunity to determine your current condition! Simply click on the button below to determine quickly and efficiently your current reproductive status! Who knows—you might even get the right answer!'

Birthdays

WE'RE nothing. Nothing at all. Zip. Zero. Zilch. Nada. We come from nothing and we're heading back to nothing, on a greasy track with the brake drums malfunctioning. We're small and irrelevant and the only thing that stops us all spinning off into nowhere is, as someone much smarter than me once put it, our misplaced faith in gravity. Sigh.

I wasn't this depressed five minutes ago. Then I found myself here, at **World Birthday Web**. I know depression is not the effect the site was meant to have, but for some of us, a visit to this place is more like staring into the abyss than the Prozac experience it's intended to be.

Why? This is a Web site where people come to leave their anniversary details. It updates every day, a giant list of party animals, people happily commemorating the passing of another year. The lists for all 372 days of the year (all months go up to 31 here, including February) are online for you to trawl through.

It sounds harmless enough, if a little addle-pated. Then you find your own special day, a list of people who share it, with their e-mail addresses and, in many cases, links to their individual home pages. And suddenly, it doesn't feel so special any more. I was going to count exactly how many people have as much claim to 25 July as I do, but at around 75 I'd hardly made a dent and just seemed to lose the will. If you ever wanted to feel like nobody, this is the place to come, an interactive ego deflater. Anyway, if being born is so good, why do we celebrate getting further away from it?

The birthday list idea is replicated all over the Web. There are so many similar, smaller services out there that you begin to suspect the creation of them must be a standard assignment in HTML classes.

Like most things on the Web, it can get extraordinarily specialist. There's the **Country Birthday Page**, which houses 'birthdays and other trivia for over 850 country personalities'. Should you wish to send a card to a member of the cast of the sci-fi show **Babylon 5**, there's a site that will tell you when to do so. And of course, there is a **Sports Birthdays** site out there too.

Where Is Your Birthday In Pi? will search for your six digit birth date (month, day, year) in the 1,254,543 digit sequence of the number. **Ask Raymond** is just as stupid. Aping *Rain Man*, it pretends to be an idiot savant site. You tell it your birth date and it tells you immediately (depending on download time) what day of the week it was.

The **Encyclopaedia Britannica** has an online birthday calendar which provides a daily list of famous people who share your special day, with one-sentence biographies and links to more information. I share mine with film director Sidney

Lumet and Catalan architectural wizard Antonio Gaudi. Cool. You can also enter your birth year and take a look at who else of note was born then, or your approximate age range for a broader view. **Famous Birthdays** offers a similar service.

The **Birthday Calculator** rises above our narrow-minded concept of years and offers you the chance to calculate how old you are in days, hours, minutes, seconds. Calendar buffs can even work out how old they are in Gregorian years and months. While you're at it, you might as well swing by the **Death Clock** and see how many days, hours, minutes and seconds you have left.

There are all kinds of birthday-related sites on the Web. Most of them are thinly veiled (or entirely unveiled and immodest) attempts to get you to part with your money. There are sites flogging cards and flowers. There are delivery services, gift specialists, pretty much everything you'd expect offline transferred to the digital marketplace.

One curious development is the birthday Web site. The idea here is that, as a loving tribute, you have a site constructed in honour of the birthday boy or girl. You then e-mail the address to your loved one or friend as a surprise.

One of the many places which offers this kind of service is the **Birthday Greetings Page**. Here they will build a simple card/site for US$15. For another $20 you can sing *Happy Birthday* (or *Sympathy for the Devil*, they're not fussy) and have the sound file added to the site. And for another $10, they'll make a little guestbook for friends to leave salutations.

Of more interest (and it's free) for those of us whose memories do great sieve impersonations is the **Internet Reminder Service**, an automated e-mail secretary to remind you of those important dates. You just fill out a form and lodge it, and the Reminder Service will tap you on the shoulder 10 days before, even reminding you of the person you're meant to be recalling.

It does everything except remember the present, but that's no problem. You can get the gift at **Virtual Presents**. This dressed-up image library allows you to send a token of your esteem (well, a two dimensional, still-photo one at least) via e-mail. Its collection includes everything from fishing lures and bath beads to whitegoods, cars, diamond rings and pets ranging from the musk ox to the lion fish. I sent myself an elephant.

And if you really are one of those people who find birthdays a downer, try the storehouse for the lyrics to the **Birthday Dirge**, a doom-laden view of the anniversary, sung to the tune of Russian folk song *The Volga Boatmen*. The origins of the dirge are shrouded in mystery (or someone just forgot them), but the slow, heavy heart of it is unmistakable:

> Now you've aged another year
> Now you know that death is near

The verses, which go on for ages, have been cobbled together from various newsgroup postings and don't get any cheerier. So don't worry, there's always somebody out there who's more depressed about it than you are.

Web addresses

World Birthday Web
http://www.boutell.com/birthday.cgi

Country Birthday Page
http://www.wp.com/MillerCreek/birthday.html

Babylon 5 Cast Birthdays
http://skynet.ul.ie/~dowlingm/b5/b5birthd.html

Sports Birthdays
http://www.sportsline.com/u/birthdays/index.html

Where Is Your Birthday In Pi?
http://www.facade.com/Fun/amiinpi/

Ask Raymond
http://www.idiotsavant.com/raymond/index.htm

Britannica's Birthday Calendar
http://www.web.com/calendar/calendar.html

Famous Birthdays
http://205.199.95.66/~edog/bday.html

Birthday Calculator
http://www.parc.xerox.com/csl/members/spreitze/bdc/

Death Clock
http://www.speedoflight.com/techs/ray/death/

Birthday Greetings Page
http://www.webcom.com/getagift/Order_A_Birthday_Home_Page.html

Internet Reminder Service
http://www.novator.com/Remind/Remind.html

Virtual Presents
http://www.virtualpresents.com/

Birthday Dirge
http://www.lib.ox.ac.uk/internet/news/faq/archive/music.birthday-dirge-faq.html

Weddings Online

IF you've ever been on the wedding circuit, you'll have seen them lurking in the back pews, those little old ladies, related to no-one involved, who turn up to pull at the corner of their hankies and have a bit of a weep as the radiant bride swishes past. I've always thought bridespotting a rather sweet hobby. That wedding watchers can draw such simple joy from someone else's nuptials nurtures the soul. Then again, maybe I'm romanticising. Maybe they're all dangerous weirdo tulle fetishists.

Anyway, (I think) I'm glad to say that nowadays, the Web provides for the needs of bridespotters too. For many and varied reasons, mostly ranging between practicality and vanity, the online wedding album is becoming more and more commonplace, many of them major undertakings.

Wendi and Jason, for example, did the splicing thing on 27 December 1996. Their expansive wedding site contains all the details of the big day, with an attention to detail that can only be described as numbing. I now know that Wendi's shoes cost US$26 and where she bought them from. I know that their house, where the wedding was held, is an 'Arts & Crafts-style bungalow (built in 1911) on Beacon Hill, in Seattle'.

I know they designed the invitations themselves. I know they rented the reception chairs for 85 cents each (a bargain if you ask me). I know that the flower girl and ring bearer couldn't make it because of a snowstorm. I have seen the program and considered the musical choices: *The Bells of Dublin/Christmas Eve* by The Chieftains (perfectly suitable) for the bride's arrival, and *When You Wish Upon a Star* from the *Pinocchio* soundtrack (hmmmmm) for afterwards.

I have seen the photographs of the ceremony, read the script of the vows and also taken the time to peruse the IRC

transcript of the whole shebang—yes, the wedding was broadcast live on the Net, with blow-by-blow commentary from their friend David, for those who were unable to make it.

I feel *sooooo* enriched. I think I even wept once, but not because I was moved.

Tina Lee and Brian Wong were married in San Francisco in April 1997. A clock on their site counted down the days, hours, minutes and seconds until their wedded bliss (or whatever now approximates it) commenced. The site also contained introductions to each of them (a systems analyst and a chiropractor), photos, the story of the engagement, a special cartoon, maps to the various destinations and tourism information for those making the trip to join them. And, of course, there were also all the latest planning updates on the way to the altar, riveting announcements such as: 'We've finally found a baker.'

Some weddings, like this one, have already happened. Some are yet to happen. **Jennifer and Clay** are planning to swap rings about three months after this book is released. The couple did the boyfriend/girlfriend thing as children, but broke up and didn't see each other again for almost a decade (there's a kind of *When Harry Met Sally* thing going on here). Second time around, says Clay, it really was love.

Their very sweet site tells you where the wedding is being held, who's in the bridal party, and where the after-show festivities will take place. It offers travel and hotel tips, and even suggests what else you might do to make a weekend of it in the area.

The wedding site is an odd beast, and one that encapsulates some of the Net's polyvalent tendencies, being simultaneously public and private in its nature. The sites fulfil the private function of keeping the families and guests in touch with goings-on before and after the happy event. And on this level, take advantage of the Web's potential — we are now in a world where wedding photos don't have to be mailed or passed around. But these sites are also out there in the public sphere of the Web, attracting strangers and passers-by, people who enjoy reading the stories or are looking for advice and ideas for their own weddings.

Most wedding sites have guestbooks, many filled with con-gratulatory messages from strangers who have taken the time to explore the contents. And if you're thinking it's just the little old bridespotters getting wired, think again. All kinds of people leave their mark in these logs.

This interest in other people's marriage ceremonies has been a cash cow for women's magazines for decades, but it's always been a celebrity issue — it's never been as personalised as it is on the Web. Pennsylvanians Kimberley and Carl White, who run the **Way Cool Weddings** site, were the first to really spot the gap in the market.

'In June of 1995 we set out to create a simple wedding

page to give our guests some online information about us and our wedding plans,' they explain. 'The response we received from our guests as well as the Internet community was overwhelming. We fell in love with idea of sharing our special day with the world. This page was designed to highlight other couples who have created personal wedding pages on the Web.'

Their site is now a kind of clearing house for other online wedding sites, with a Wedding of the Week and monthly archives of all those tying the knot on the Net. Participants from Europe, the UK and Israel have made their way into the alumni list.

There are as many different types of weddings as there are people. Not all are hetero. The Net, of course, doesn't recognise prejudice. So **Adam and Sean** have a wedding page, as do **Greg and Matt.**

Not all are serious. **48 Hours in Las Vegas** is a journey, told in words and photographs, through one couple's attempt to harness the twin spirits of Elvis and Liberace to their nuptials. Dennis and Dana formalised their relationship last September. Dennis wrote his own, mysteriously beautiful vows, reprinted online: 'Dana, I have always loved your sweet sincerity, like the time when I gave you a 20-cent lacquered plaque of Barry Gibb that I found in some garage sale.'

See, there's a little bit of the poet in all of us. Should you want to put your own wedding experience online, there's even a site, **Internet Wedding Album**, that will help you do it — for a fee of course.

Web addresses

Wendi and Jason
http://www.slumberland.com/wedding/index.html

Tina and Brian
http://www.best.com/~suppis/wedding.shtml

Jennifer and Clay
http://www.claydough.com/wedding

Way Cool Weddings
http://www.waycoolweddings.com

Adam and Sean
http://www.sover.net/~sterling/wedding.html

Greg and Matt
http://www.xq.com/gregmatt/

48 Hours in Las Vegas
http://www.tezcat.com/~jalfrank/fehrs.html

Internet Wedding Album
http://www.just-married.com/

Sites for Left-Handers

TONY Bennett left his heart in San Francisco. Don McLean was left for dead on the road to love. The Pet Shop Boys were left to their own devices. Suzanne Vega was left of centre. When Elvis's baby left him, he found a new place to dwell . . .

Hmmm, I'm running out of cultural metaphors here and I still haven't found a good way to segue neatly from this introduction into a guided tour of Web sites for left-handers. While I carry on regardless, you might want to e-mail me if *you* can see the link.

We start our journey into the left experience at **Living in the Mirror**, which may well be the essential left-hander's home page. This lefty, E. Stephen Mack, has taken it upon himself to build a very impressive Web resource for those who would greet the world with a different handshake, if the world would let them.

'I experience anti-lefty bias,' Mack writes, 'school desks that are unusable, carrot peelers that are useless, power tools (such as skill saws) that are dangerous or even life-threatening, pens that smear and make my writing illegible, computer mice that cause hand cramps. Teachers in England tried to force me to write with my right hand when I was a child; I used to stutter, and perhaps that was why.'

Compiling a site which aims to make people confront left prejudice, Mack collects personal experiences of southpaws. But the prime value of Living in the Mirror is that it offers directions to dozens of other Web resources, from scientific and historical essays ('Creation of the Sinister: Biological Contributions to Left-Handedness', 'Primate Handedness and Brain Lateralisation') to lists of left-handed celebrities, left-handed fiction and poetry, left-handed humour, handedness surveys, and lefty home pages, societies and businesses.

The **WWW List of Left-Handed Celebrities** has lists of hundreds of sinistral politicians, writers, actors, scientists, artists and sports people. Those who are looking for common denominators will be interested to note that the line-up includes W.C. Fields, Joan of Arc, Jack the Ripper, Aristotle, Ronald Reagan, Elizabeth II, Robert de Niro and Beethoven. Make of that what you will. (While we're on the subject, I feel I have to mention that one of the other celeb sites, **Famous Left-Handers**, offers its site in English, French, Spanish and Pig Latin!)

Another strong resource centre is the **Left-Handed Universe**, available in English, Dutch and German. It attempts to put right (sorry) our biased view of all things by showcasing the contributions of lefties in various fields of endeavour. It disputes claims that southpaws die earlier because of clumsiness brought on by the fact that the world is not designed for them, looks at paw preference in animals and asks if the percentage of left-handers in society has dropped since medieval times. It explains exactly how lefties write differently, arguing that their technique is more refined, employing 'a much different, subtler movement . . . the subtlety of the left-hander's movements demand well-made tools. Use a pencil, a fountain pen or a roller ball, but leave the clumsy biro to right-handers.'

The site has a small but fascinating art section which disowns Picasso, despite the fact that he has often been nominated as a lefty, and looks at the role of the left-handed subject in art, from Michelangelo's David to Gabrielle d'Estree's famous sixteenth-century painting of two naked sisters, the one on the left delicately tweaking the nipple of the one on the right. With her left hand!

There's a bibliography of books devoted to leftist views (incidentally, there are more Web sites devoted to left-handers than to communism), a test to see whether you're left-handed or not, just in case you can't tell, and a section covering left-handed curiosities (from the Japanese bent against them to the fact that the percentage of dyslexics who are left-handed is slightly higher than the average).

The Left Side ('Did you know it's a known fact that left-handed people have a higher intelligence, better sex lives, and are a lot cooler?') makes a short case for lefty superiority. **Treker L's Left Handed Page** is another Left Pride venture, as is the opinionated writing of **Left Handers Do It Right**, while **The Lefty FAQ** answers a range of questions from 'Is left-handedness inherited?' (nobody is exactly sure) to 'What makes a bowling ball left or right-handed?' (slight difference in the relationship of the finger holes to the thumb hole) to 'Why are there more left-handed males than females?' (it may be testosterone related).

If you're looking for something a little less profound, the **Left-/Right-Handed Simpsons** (remember the Ned Flanders

Leftorium episode?) site analyses the propensity of the cartoon family to use either hand when necessary—left-handed one episode, right-handed the next—except for Maggie, who is clearly a lefty.

The **Top Ten List of Things that Annoy Left-Handers** is both humorous and serious, and includes the following: right-handed scissors, learning to drive and wondering why they built all the roads backwards; sitting at a desk three inches to the right of a right-hander and trying to write; the reaction you get from the salesperson when you ask if they sell left-handed potato peelers; and the ergonomic mouse—designed to fit comfortably in the right hand.

The Web being what it is (a giant shopping mall with some interesting bits in the basement) there are also plenty of opportunities for southpaw commerce. There are sites that will sell you left-handed **golf gear**, left-handed **computer keyboards** (the numbers are on the left) and left-handed **boomerangs.** There are specialist lefty **shops,** flogging books, gifts, kitchen and outdoor products, sports equipment, computer accessories, tools and stationery. And beer fans will note that there's even **The Left Hand Brewing Company.**

At this point in my excursion, winding further and further into places where I might be likely to spend money on stupid gifts for left-handed friends I'm not even sure I have, I did what I always try to do in places where my temptation gland will overrule my brain. I left.

Web addresses

Living in the Mirror
http://www.emf.net/~estephen/facts/lefthand.html

WWW List of Left-Handed Celebrities
http://stekt.oulu.fi/~mjh/lefties.html

Famous Left-Handers
http://www.indiana.edu/~primate/left.html

Left-Handed Universe
http://www.xs4all.nl/~riksmits/

The Left Side
http://www.ccds.cincinnati.oh.us/~razavir/left.html

Treker L's Left Handed Page
http://users.aol.com/trekerl/lefty.htm

Left Handers Do It Right
http://www.sdsu.edu/daztec/archive/1996/04/11/file008.html

The Lefty FAQ
http://www.cs.ruu.nl/wais/html/na-dir/lefty-faq.html

Left-/Right-Handed Simpsons
http://www.cyberspc.mb.ca/~davehall/leftrght.html

Top Ten List
http://www.cuug.ab.ca:8001/~pringleg/lefthand.html

Left-Handed Golfer
http://www.lefthandedgolfer.com/

Left-Handed Computer Keyboards
http://www.lefthanded.com/

Left-Handed Boomerangs
http://pd.net/colorado/howto/index.html

The Left Hand (a lefty shop)
http://silo.com/lefthand/

The Left Hand Brewing Company
http://www.lefthandbrewing.com/

Luddites

LUDDITE. It's a strange word, an insult to some, a badge of honour to others. Spat out by the technophiles, it's an accusation of guilt, a dismissal of those who would question the Brave New World theorising of the digital era. Its implications are clear. The person at which the epithet is hurled is considered an anachronism, desperately out of touch with reality, foolishly attempting to drive a wedge under the wheels of progress.

The original Luddites appeared in England in 1811. After knitters began to smash machines that made poor quality stockings at prices which undercut them, the movement grew quickly, with bands of weavers around the country storming cotton and wool mills. Ultimately, it was a futile resistance effort, but valuable points were made about quality of life and priorities.

Nowadays, those who wear the **Luddite** term with pride do so because of the overweening hype and hyperbole of the technological era. To them, the Net (and the computerisation of society) is a giant madhouse, with a locked door and a fluoro sign: 'Do Not Disturb — Myth Creation in Progress'. It's the Emperor's Entire New Wardrobe.

The most famous Neo-Luddites are, unsurprisingly, American, though there is also **Luddite** activity in **England**. The two best known of the Statesiders are a criminal and an academic: the **Unabomber** and author **Kirkpatrick Sale**.

Theodore Kaczynski, 53, was arrested in April 1996 at his secluded Montana log cabin, on suspicion of being the Unabomber who, as a weird form of publicity for his anti-technology campaign, had sent 16 bombs through the post in 17 years, killing 3 and injuring 23. The Unabomber's fame reached its peak in 1995 when major American newspapers,

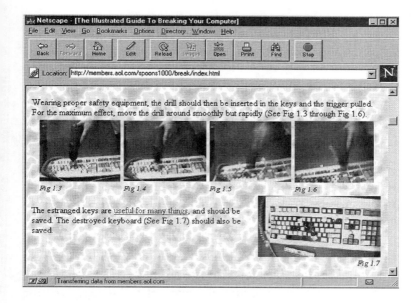

including the *New York Times* and the *Washington Post*, acceded to his demand that his rambling 35,000 word manifesto, **Industrial Society and its Future**, be published. It can be found in many places on the Net.

So popular is the Unabomber as a cultural anti-hero that his work has inspired a handful of **parody** sites, as well as a greater number of more serious examinations, such as **The Definitive UNABOM Page**, which has kept track of events, reactions and commentaries on the case.

Before Kaczynski was caught, Kirkpatrick Sale admitted that he and the Unabomber had more than a few shared feelings, though he stressed that he wasn't exactly happy to be sitting on the same side of some of those fences as a killer. Sale, patron saint of the Neo-Luddites, finds many similarities between the early nineteenth and the late twentieth centuries. He argues that the questions raised by the original Luddites remain unanswered, and that there were great **lessons** to be learned from their acts.

'Some may call [what the Luddites did] foolish resistance . . . but it was dramatic, forceful, honourable, and authentic enough to have put the Luddites' issues forever on record and made the Luddites' name as indelibly a part of the language as the Puritans'.'

The author of the book *Rebels Against the Future: The Luddites and Their War on the Industrial Revolution*, Sale made his symbolic point in a very public way in 1995. During a speech to 1,500 people in New York, he took a non-symbolic sledgehammer to an IBM PC. Verily, did he smite it.

'It felt wonderful,' he said afterwards. 'The sound it made, the spewing of the undoubtedly poisonous insides into the spotlight, the dust that hung in the air . . .'

Sale is regarded as a mortal enemy of technology fans for bludgeoning a machine to bits. *Wired* magazine took chunks out of him in an **interview** with Kevin Kelly. Me, I'm just jealous. I lie in bed at night dreaming of running over fields of computers in a tank. When has there ever passed a week in which we did not all think of speeding our own computer's demise? (Digressing for a moment, the **Illustrated Guide to Breaking Your Computer** isn't just a quick and dirty relief site. No way. It shows you how to do it so that the machine will actually *suffer*, demonstrating all the techniques necessary to make your own personal HAL beg for mercy as you squeeze the life from it. Give it none. What has it ever done for you?)

There have been others standing up against techno-hype. **Clifford Stoll**, a Californian academic who wrote the first hacker book, *The Cuckoo's Egg*, appeared to bite the hand that fed him when he published *Silicon Snake Oil — Second Thoughts on the Information Superhighway*. Stoll asked in that book whether the Internet could really provide a sense of community, whether it could really add meaning and depth to the education system, whether it could enrich our lives even a fraction as much as a walk in your local park or the smell of fresh-baked bread. Sure, he went a little over the edge in his arguments. His prose was 14 shades of purple. But, like Sale, he asked some pertinent questions.

And then there's critic Sven Birkerts, whose contribution to the debate is **The Gutenberg Elegies**, a homage to the printed word, to the smell, touch and out-of-body experience of the book. At the end of his tome, Birkerts rails against technophilia:

'The devil no longer moves around on cloven hooves, reeking of brimstone . . . he is an affable, efficient fellow. He claims to want to help us all along to a brighter, easier future, and his sales pitch is very smooth. I was, as the old song goes, almost persuaded. I saw what it could be like, our toil and misery replaced by a vivid, pleasant dream.

'Fingers tap keys, oceans of fact and sensation get downloaded, are dissolved through the central nervous system. Bottomless wells of data are accessed and manipulated, everything flowing at circuit speed. Gone the rock in the field, the broken hoe, the gruelling distances.

'"History," said Stephen Dedalus, "is a nightmare from which I am trying to awaken." This may be the awakening, but it feels curiously like the fantasies that circulate through our sleep. From deep in the heart I hear a voice that says "Refuse it".'

Too often in our society, we fail to recognise the value of dissent. We fail to understand that to get the best picture of ourselves, we should attempt to see through the eyes of our critics as well as those of our supporters. I'm kinda fond of the New Luddites. The more people who question the values and impacts of technology, the better it will have to be. And if nothing else, the Net would be a duller place without them.

Web addresses

Luddites
http://www.usu.edu/~sanderso/multinet/luddite.html

What is a Luddite?
http://town.hall.org/places/ludd_land/whatsa.html

New Luddites (England)
http://www.york.ac.uk/~socs203/luddites.htm

A History of the Unabomber
http://www.stardot.com/~hhui/unabomb.html

Industrial Society and its Future
http://www.hotwired.com/special/unabom/

Unabomber Parody Sites
http://www.yahoo.com/Entertainment/Humor__Jokes__and_Fun/Parody/People/Unabomber/

The Definitive UNABOM Page
http://owl.cs.umass.edu/~ehaugsja/unabom/

Lessons from the Luddites
http://www.ensu.ucalgary.ca/~terry/luddite/sale.html

An Article on Kirkpatrick Sale
http://www.microtimes.com/sale.html

Wired Interview with Sale
http://www.hotwired.com/wired/3.06/features/saleskelly.html

Illustrated Guide to Breaking Your Computer
http://members.aol.com/spoons1000/break/index.html

Clifford Stoll Home Page
http://www.ocf.berkeley.edu/~stoll/

The Gutenberg Elegies (excerpts)
http://www.obs-us.com/obs/english/books/nn/bdbirk.htm

See also . . .

Popular Luddite Magazine
http://members.gnn.com/RadioGuy/luddite.htm
Claims to be the online version of popular newsstand mag.
Sends up computer culture—a recent edition had a cover story
on Bill Gates doing a deal with Steven Spielberg's Dreamworks
for *Windows: The Movie.*

Luddite Purity Test
http://www.luddites.com/purity.html
'In a global effort to ferret out the Hated Geeks that walk
among us Faithful Luddites, we present the Luddite Purity
Test. Hand-tabulated by illiterate latch-key children in the
suburbs of Orange County, California, your answers will determine your true status in the coming Deindustrial Revolution
and subsequent Misinformation Age. Answer all the questions
below and then click on the button marked, "I hate submit
buttons".'

MEDIA MOVEMENTS

Where is the News Going?

AT seven minutes past midnight on the morning of 6 January 1997, Des Carne finished uploading and checking the material he was putting live on the **Deliverance** Web site in Alice Springs. There had been four hits on the site between midnight and seven minutes past—there would be many more as word spread of the new content.

By 4am, Carne says, the material on the site had travelled out to the rest of the world, jumped the bounds of the Web and replicated itself in other media. It was making its way back into Australia via international news wires, spreading like a virus. By breakfast, it was all over Australian radio.

Darwin doctor Philip Nitschke, with the help of Carne, had used the Net to announce the death of Janet Mills, the second person to take advantage of the Northern Territory's controversial euthanasia legislation.

Carne's additions to the pro-euthanasia site had been pretty simple. They included a media release outlining the circumstances of Mrs Mills's passing, a letter from her in support of the legislation, a request for privacy from Dr Nitschke and contact numbers for the National Coalition for Voluntary Euthanasia.

'We chose to use the Internet to release this information because we wanted to draw attention to the [Deliverance] home page,' Carne says, 'but also because we saw the possibility of using this new technology as an opportunity for publishing information ourselves, rather than relying on the traditional wire services.

'It was therefore a bit of an experiment, in seeing how quickly the story was taken up, and we are quite pleased with the result.'

Indeed, the first aim of getting the home page seen succeeded handsomely. In the days before the announcement, the site had been chugging along, doing minor business. Four or five people an hour would drop by to read some of the earlier material on Bob Dent, the first patient to use the legislation.

But as the story broke—and as the mass media, with a startled look on its face, revealed that it had broken first on the Internet—the figures began to climb. By 3pm on the same day, the hourly number was peaking at 170. Within 48 hours of uploading, almost 4,000 people had clicked their way through the Deliverance server.

'The interest exceeded our expectations,' Carne says. 'And if the Internet is thought of as the communications toy of the young, this is belied by incoming e-mail messages of support, which have included at least one [from a] person in her seventies.' The site has since added a guestbook, reprinting many of the comments.

But though the stats tell a fascinating story, the decision to self-publish the information is just as crucial, and in the long term, much more significant. It was the first local example of the Net being used to break a major news story. The Net has *been* a major news story before, but it has not been used to launch one.

Taking the Net option allows an element of control pre-viously unavailable to the people at the centre of events. For Nitschke, the Web cut out the middle man of mass media and allowed him to make his statement (and that of his patient) directly to the public.

Further, the doctor was able to make the statements with privacy, without being drawn into brawling about the issue of euthanasia—he discreetly directed all inquiries elsewhere. And he ensured that, at the very least, the Net-connected part of the public could read exactly what he wanted it to read, instead of a filtered or edited version.

In media terms, these little ripples may yet turn out to be

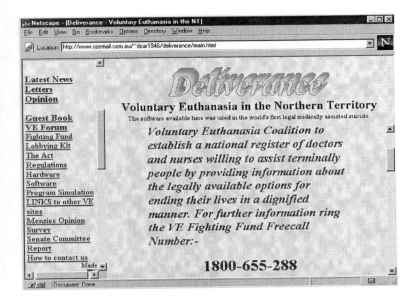

the start of waves. Certainly, it is easy to overlook the power shift that is implicit in Nitschke's actions. But that shift is profound. The media is no longer just something that is done to him; it is something he *does*.

The likelihood of more people taking control and using the Net to release information is as bankable as it is sensible. In March 1997, controversial author **Helen Darville** (formerly Demidenko) went digital. Having cut a swathe through the publishing world—she scandalised the book industry in 1995 with the identity games surrounding her first novel, *The Hand that Signed the Paper*, and was fired in early 1997 from a fortnightly newspaper column for plagiarism—the author moved to the one arena where almost anything goes. Darville uploaded part of a work in progress, *Past(s) Imperfect: Ancient Rome And/In Historical Fiction*, to her Web site, which is hosted by the University of Queensland, where she is a graduate student. 'It [*Past(s) Imperfect*] includes a sneak preview of my forthcoming novel and a major defence of the rights and roles of the historical novelist,' Darville explained. 'In many ways, this is the "official response" that people have wanted me to publish in the newspapers.'

In the introduction, the author wrote that 'I've been wanting to publish something on the Web for quite a while, and this . . . seemed the perfect way to do it.' Making use of Web technology, the essay, 'approximately 20,000 words in length' (it was actually just over 6,000), had hyperlinked footnotes and was interspersed with virtual reality photo tours of the Forum and a Pompeian taverna.

As someone who has batted with the mass media, which she felt distorted her views and words, Darville was a perfect candidate for the Web. It provided her with a chance to get her message to whomever was inclined to listen.

The increase of this self-publishing, self-publicising trend will change at least some of the ways we gather and use information. Certainly, people in the newspaper office I work in — a surprisingly unwired lot, by and large — who had never previously given a fig about the Net suddenly wanted to know how to get connected when the Deliverance story broke.

You could sense a note of panic about their future. For the first time, news was going on where they couldn't see it, touch it or own it. And though newspapers will continue to be needed to package and interpret news events for us, you could see that behind their eyes questions were starting to form about competition and the increasing complexity of the media landscape.

Those questions pushed closer to the surface when, on 28 February, the **Dallas Morning News**, one of the best online newspapers, decided to break a story about the supposed jailhouse confessions of Oklahoma bombing suspect Timothy McVeigh on its Web site instead of in its paper.

'We put the story on the Web site,' the *News*'s Ralph Langer

explained at the time, 'because it was, in our view, extraordinarily important, and we got the story finished this afternoon
and we felt we ought to publish, so we did.'

It was inevitable that one of the online papers would take
this approach sooner or later. And we can expect more of it.
The Web release created a buzz around the story which was
followed next day by the expanded newspaper version, with
the background and context of the event. Eyes all around
American were turned towards Dallas. It was the smartest
marketing the paper had probably done in ages.

It was a decision which also showed that forward-thinking
media companies are in the process of coming to terms with
that fact that they are information providers, that their future
involves not just the jobs they have had in the past, but a
number of possible hybrids of their services. A Web site makes
a great adjunct for a newspaper. Many of the staff and much
of the resources can be shared. But the Web offers the power
to transmit news with more speed and ease of access than any
other medium. It begs to be a live news medium, like radio.
Understanding the nature of time-related media is where the
challenge will lie for the old school.

But back to the little guy. Since Janet Mills's death, the
Deliverance site has not been inactive. Not only has it been
releasing more and more information, letters from terminally
ill patients who wish to die, analyses of policy and debate,
updates on further voluntary deaths, but it has also been using
the Net to combat the media. It challenged the reporting of
Mills's death in *The Australian* newspaper, alleging bias in its
coverage of events, on its own terms and without having to
keep it under 200 words to keep the editor of the letters page
happy. Sure, Deliverance doesn't have the same kind of audience as a major newspaper, but the Web has given it a voice
and a forum it previously lacked.

And if that seems to be about moving at least a little power back into the hands of the individual, then it's worth noting that another area of Deliverance has included a downloadable Senate lobbying kit, which allowed the user to campaign for the euthanasia legislation by automatically faxing any and every Senator in the country with a form letter of support. Power to the people. Dead or alive.

Web addresses

Deliverance
http://www.ozemail.com.au/~dcar1946/deliverance/

Helen Darville
http://www.uq.edu.au/~enhdemid/

Dallas Morning News
http://www.dallasnews.com

The Content Business

FEW Web sites have received as much comment and criticism as **Slate**, the news magazine funded by **Microsoft** and run by Michael Kinsley, an editor with credentials as long as a basketballer's arm.

Slate was launched in June 1996 with predictable fanfare. But what was most interesting was not the site itself, but the size of the storm that immediately brewed around it. The Web zine was praised, dismissed, queried, exalted, buried and exhumed, all within the first few days of its existence. And yet it survives, a testimony, among other things, to the staff's thick skin, to their ability to persevere under intense scrutiny and criticism.

The reason *Slate* received such a level of attention is simple. It represented, and became emblematic of, a major shift in Web (and media) culture. Until late 1995, Bill Gates wrote off the Internet as nothing more than an interesting diversion. But then, realising his mistake, he threw his juggernaut company into a breathtaking U-turn, aiming its full might squarely at the online world. A crucial element of that turn was the decision to not only change tack, but change business.

In the last couple of decades, many electronics giants like **Sony** have eaten their way another step along the food chain, moving from hardware into software, buying the record and film companies that provide the material for the machines they have always made. After years of making delivery systems for other people's content, Gates decided his company would make the content as well.

Suddenly, major computer companies were connecting apple with noggin and deciding to wade into the content business. 'Eureka!' they all seemed to be shouting, slapping their collective foreheads. 'It works for Rupert. We've gotta

87

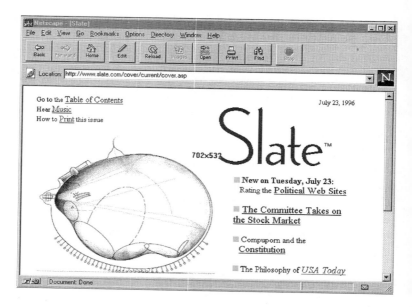

get a slice of that action.' There's barely a telecommunications company in the world that doesn't now think of itself as a funky Web zine publisher. And most of their output is erratic at best. It's almost as if they think content is just a lever you can pull, a switch you can throw. You can see them thinking that, heck, since they built the restaurant, they must know how to cook better than anyone. They built the highway—they must be good drivers.

But it just isn't that simple. **IBM**, long happy to be a hardware and infrastructure provider, found out just how difficult and fractious content could be with its official Atlanta Olympic Games Web site in 1996, which crashed and burned with all the spectacle of a fireworks display. There were wounded carrier pigeons bringing the results to the world faster than its service. It took up to 36 hours for some race results to make their way to the Web site—the time lapse originally promised had been less than a minute. Since the

Olympic problems, and the bad press that resulted, IBM has visibly retreated from Web content, keeping a modest amount on its own site, but not overplaying its hand or promising too much. Wounds are still being licked.

Slate made, and still makes, a fascinating case study for students of media. Kinsley played a risky, bold marketing card at the time of its launch by stating in his opening editorial that most of what is out there in cyberspace is crap—'there is a deadening conformity in the hipness of cyberspace culture in which we don't intend to participate', he wrote. No arguments from me on the assertion, but for many Netophiles, those were fightin' words.

Slate's clear intention was and has since been to be a Web equivalent of upmarket brainfood magazines such as the *New Republic* and *The Spectator*. It adopted a patrician tone and design aesthetic (its maroony brown look is reminiscent of gentlemen's clubs and leather upholstery), and has striven for intellectual credibility, upholding traditional journalistic values. Constructed along the lines of a magazine, it has a pithy briefs section up front, with news, gossip and upper-drawer scuttle-butt. Half a dozen feature articles reside in the middle and if you make it through to the back, you'll find arts reviews, columns, diaries, poems, musings and letters pages.

Slate challenges the idea that Net surfers have criminally short attention spans, that they can't or won't read more than 200 words. It challenges the idea that the Net has no room for serious, sober journalism. It challenges the idea that a looser, more conversational form of language is the key to Net publishing. And I have to say, even though Bill is bankrolling it, I have always quite liked it. The magazine invites interesting writers to have their two cents' worth, and doesn't beat all the usual media drums. *Slate* offers quality. It's worthy. It's smart. And it has plenty to read, unlike most sites.

But it ain't working. Because, and this is what the argument has boiled down to since its beginning, it just doesn't make a lot of sense in terms of the medium. *Slate* is a Web zine in serious denial, an attempt to graft offline publishing logic onto the online world. The user navigates it page by page. It even carries a printout button which allows you to convert the whole thing to paper, so you won't have to bother with that annoying old Net. Its simple linearity denies the nature of online media. Its static feel ignores the potential for textual and graphic exploration. It uses almost none of the Net's publishing advantages. And if Kinsley doesn't think what's out there on the Net is much chop, people asked why not show us what can be done with the medium's strengths, instead of refusing to acknowledge them?

Slate ultimately retreats from the creative bandwidth. It goes beyond a misunderstanding of the Internet — it almost displays a kind of contempt for it. Even the name hearkens back to a pre-Gutenberg era. Maybe this refusal to play by the rules will be *Slate*'s strength. Maybe it will succeed because it argues that really, nothing changes. Maybe its very contrariness will help it to stand out from the pack. Maybe, but I wouldn't bet on it.

Meanwhile, **MSN,** Microsoft's latest attempt to build a virtual empire, works on a set of principles in many ways almost perpendicular to those in operation at *Slate*. It too brings an offline rationale to the online world, but a very different one. The interesting thing about MSN is that it argues, as many big business sites are now arguing, that the best model for the Web is television.

The company is one of many working on plans to integrate computers with television. The first Web-capable TVs hit the market in time for Christmas 1996 in the States, and slowly spread around other markets in 1997. The major players are convinced that the Web will achieve a much higher market penetration if it is sold as part of the friendly TV, rather than the scary computer. Of course, if they're right, the Web will become schizophrenic. A TV-based browser will require distance viewing. Most people using the television are a couple of metres from the screen. Most using their computers are not.

The MSN site presents itself in much the same way a cable network would, as a series of six specialist channels, with what it likes to call its 'shows' (it launches and cancels sites in seasons, following television methodology) spread about on each.

America Online and PointCast have also begun to organise their sites along channel lines, and both Yahoo and Excite have indicated they will follow suit. What all of them are hoping is that the familiarity of the television model will make it easier to attract both audience and advertisers.

But, as **Salon**'s Scott Rosenberg pointed out, MSN's channels aren't real channels at all. You could just as easily, he said, call them menus or bookmark lists. And rather than participating in the glorious breadth and depth of the Web, MSN's channels 'attempt to narrow and control users' experience'. MSN is one of the few sites dedicated to keeping you on it, to making sure you don't surf anywhere else. You *can* break the boundaries of the site and venture out, but only if you click on the tiny 'Internet toolbar' icon and know what address you want to type into the space it provides.

'It's almost too obvious a point,' Rosenberg wrote in *Salon*, 'but apparently it bears repeating: The more the Web is like TV, the less we need it. TV already does a pretty effective job of delivering what Net content people call "broadband multimedia information and entertainment" to the home, and most consumers already own the hardware. What sells the Internet to newbies is its promise of things TV can't deliver: "many-to-many" communication via bulletin boards and e-mail; interactive services that go beyond catalogue shopping; quirky content unavailable on TV's limited number of channels; specific, accurate information that's there when you need it, whether it's sports stats, stock quotes or plane-ticket availability . . .'

MSN puts its eggs firmly in the multimedia basket, betting that a range of interactive gimmicks and gadgets will draw in an audience more certainly than anything else, despite the fact that e-mail and simple chat options are still the most popular uses of the Net. Who knows, its gamble might even be the right one. Quality is not always what gets you over the finish line in this age of marketing, hype and financial muscle. Ask Beta video. Ask Apple computers.

But more than likely, this commitment to a model we already have will bring it unstuck. A clear example of the futility of this thinking comes from one of the cornerstones of the MSN service, its commitment to online news, as evidenced by its joint cable channel/broadcast/Net venture with American network NBC, cannily titled **MSNBC**. In the Australian version 'Putting a TV in your PC' is one of the pithy catchphrases. And this they do, with a **Vivo**-driven screen popping up to show an MSNBC newsreader rolling through today's headlines. It's putting a TV in my PC, but a 1950s one, not a 1990s one. It's a case of right technology, wrong idea. To add a news bulletin to the site is to abandon what is beneficial about the Net, its interactivity, its speed. You can't decide what to hear or see yourself. You have to sit there in front of your computer, like a stoned puffin, and wait for the newsreader to get around to the part of the bulletin you're interested in. Isn't that what is wrong with TV already?

There *are* many reasons to enjoy MSN. For one thing, the site hosts that pernickety cartoon character **Duckman**'s online chat outing, with monologues, interviews, mystery guests and various other sardonic shenanigans. It's the official home of

Hollywood gossipmongers *Entertainment Tonight*. And it's also the online ground zero—thanks to a smart deal—for *Star Trek* information and merchandise. But these reasons are difficult to get to, positives overwhelmed by negatives.

Because most of what is on MSN is unavailable to the regular surfer—you have to join, and fork over your credit card number, to gain access. So far, only porn sites and highly specialised sites have been able to charge successfully for membership on the Web. Now MSN, a mainstream, highly public entity, has its hand out again—a tactic it tried during the Microsoft Network experiment. It may only be asking around $10 a month (it's hard to tell—the site doesn't actually tell you what the fee is until you've joined), but that's a lot of money if you're happy with what you're getting elsewhere for free.

A year after *Slate* began, despite its detractors, it's still going strong. It wasn't able to go through with its planned subscription charges, but it's still there and still pumping out great words. MSN, on the other hand, was haemorrhaging workers within a few months of its opening, shutting down sites within its site. This may well turn out to be perfectly normal streamlining, a company constantly realigning itself with the market, but the Microsoft watchers are taking bets . . .

Web addresses

Slate
http://www.slate.com

Microsoft
http://www.microsoft.com

Sony
http://www.sony.com/

IBM
http://www.ibm.net

Salon
http://www.salonmagazine.com

MSNBC
http://www.msnbc.com

Vivo
http://www.vivo.com

Sydney Morning Herald
http://www.smh.com.au

Duckman
http://www.duckman.com

The Future of Radio is Here Already

HUMORIST **Harry Shearer** is a media renaissance man. Apart from his regular gigs with Spinal Tap (as bass player Derek Smalls), *The Simpsons* (as the voices of half a dozen characters, including Montgomery Burns *and* Smithers), and *Slate* Web zine (as a columnist at large), he also hosts a weekly radio show, syndicated around America.

Le Show is a wry, funny, crisply starched look at the failings and foibles of contemporary life Stateside. Until now, the chance to pick it up has been one of the joys of travelling to that country. But, of course (why didn't I think to look for it sooner?), it's out there on the Web, archived every week with loving care. Sure, it crackles, pops and clicks a little bit, and occasionally sounds like it's coming from a radio playing at the end of a long and echoey corridor, but it's at least marginally better than the alternative. Which is not hearing *Le Show* at all . . .

Newspapers have been stampeding towards the Net since late 1994. Radio, thanks to developments like **RealAudio**, is following suit, and not just in *Le Show*'s archival sense. Drop in to **AudioNet**, the hub of Internet radio, for proof. There's an awful lot to listen to.

In September 1996 Dallas radio station KLIF used the fat bandwidth of AudioNet to broadcast live, continuous radio for the first time on the Internet. **RadioNet** had been on air longer (it broadcast from July 1994 to October 1996), but operated on Sunday mornings in California, interviewing movers and shakers in the digital world.

The Net broadcasting idea has more than just caught on — there are now well over 100 stations accessible through the site. Winding across the Net dial, you'll find everything from classical to country to news and talk, sports, rock and religious radio. There are live stations broadcasting from the US, UK,

China, Hungary, Greece, Argentina, Hong Kong, Italy, Portugal, Colombia, Switzerland, Malaysia (in English, Tamil and Bahasa) and Australia.

The first thing you notice, if you take the time to drift around, is that the world really is shrinking. In less than an hour of site hopping, I took in some rabid religious radio from America's deep south ('Bacteriological warfare will be used against the US at some point soon. I think you can see the writing is on the wall. I think the CIA has a hand in this...'), a couple of popular songs from 2FM Ireland, and some spirited rhythms from FM 92.1 Cada Dia Mas, coming to me live from Buenos Aires. Many of these sites not only allow you to listen to their broadcasts live, but to backtrack through archives of programs you missed. As they increase in bandwidth and power, they will also offer multimedia radio hybrids, perhaps showing clips during the songs.

What will it be like if the trend continues? What if we'll soon be able to listen to thousands of radio stations via the Net? How much joy will that bring to expatriates, immigrants and travellers? Or even just the curious?

And how much pain will it bring to local stations? Because licences have been so expensive, kept that way due to a lack of space in the frequency spectrum, what will happen when space is no longer a problem? What will happen when those multi-million dollar licences become worthless, when they buy station owners no more access to an audience than anyone on the other side of the world would have?

Digital radio, just around the corner (its launch is planned for Europe in late 1997 and Australia late 1998), also blows up the spectrum. It will be able to deliver thousands of stations via satellite, offering CD quality.

Things are moving fast. It is theoretically possible right now for every radio station in the world to make itself available

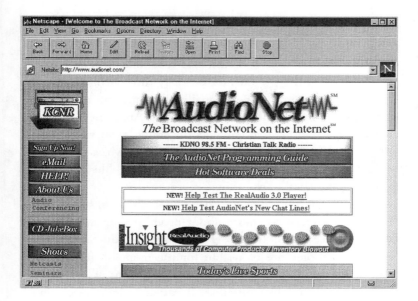

over the Net to anyone who would call up the site to listen. In the same way that newspapers have seen their opportunity to become global specialist information providers, radio can and probably will find niche markets it has never had access to. If I were living in another country and had the chance to listen to news and talk radio from home while I worked, I'd certainly take it up.

So, the next couple of decades will be an interesting time for the medium. Actually, I reckon radio is well suited to survive and prosper in the digital age. It is such an immediate, localised medium that the inevitable availability of a multitude of other stations will probably not make too big a dent in the mainstream audience share. Niche fragments will break off and follow their own interests, but what most people use the radio for—weather, traffic, local news and a familiar voice—will remain constant.

All this, of course, is just speculation right now. The technology has a way to go yet. Even using the newest version of the Real Player, with a Pentium-driven machine and 32-bit sound, many of the stations, particularly those broadcasting on 14.4 modems, sound either appallingly tinny, or like they're transmitting from a submarine under the Antarctic ice. Many of them recall nothing so much as the sound a car radio makes when you drive under a thatch of telephone wires. You could wedge your head into a goldfish bowl and bury it in the backyard and you'd hear things more clearly.

My rule of thumb seems to be that music-based stations are, for the most part, more about promise than achievement (the classical stations offer Net sounds that only Stockhausen could love). Some are okay, but for the moment, it's safest to stick to the talk, unless you have an ISDN line.

Still it's all tantalisingly close. If cable modems catch on in the next year or two, I'm predicting it'll all fall into place quicker than most people would believe. Then again, judging by the enormous quality difference between sites you'd expect to be of a similar standard, the network chain is only as strong as its weakest link. Cable modems could just make it easier and faster to pick up inferior sounds.

None of these problems is stopping anyone getting ready for increased bandwidth though—the Web broadcast is an idea that has extraordinary momentum. The logic seems to be that the creases will be ironed out, so you might as well be ready to jump when it happens. At the moment, **Timecast** is the other major player on the broadcast block. A spinoff project from the Real folk, it offers you the chance to compile a personalised daily audio news briefing. The site collects bulletins from the various news, sport and entertainment services, and allows you to subscribe based on your own hierarchy of interests.

Like AudioNet, Timecast also offers a guide to the live

stations on the Net, as well as a seemingly endless list of the sites using Real in some form or other. This is worth checking out just to get a handle on the breadth of the use of sound on the Net.

You'll find zines, catalogues, rock bands, audio books, history briefings, ski reports, interviews, poetry readings and all manner of business and entertainment-related ideas.

Just a few that attracted my attention were: **Aotearoa Good Morning**, a library of New Zealand birdsong; **CDNOW's Internet Jukebox**, which offers hundreds of albums for you to sample (AudioNet has a similar, if a little less interesting, service); **Movie Tunes**, a site which plays soundtracks; and **David Bowie**'s official site, which he has used in recent times to launch a single, *Telling Lies*, and to offer a birthday present (for his own 50th, in early 1997) of six unreleased tracks to Web-based fans. Bowie has said he plans to continue releasing Web-only material, as a way of getting more complex, difficult songs to the public, the kind of tracks that record companies might have cold feet about releasing.

Timecast, in association with LA's House of Blues, has also launched **Live Concerts**, which allows you to listen to shows from the Neville Brothers and John Hiatt. AudioNet has an archive of concerts on its site too, from the Bay City Rollers to silverchair. **iMusic**, one of the largest music sites on the Net, has its own on-site radio station (which lets you vote on its playlist) as well as an archive of live songs from Web concerts featuring acts such as Garbage and Ben Harper. The sound on the radio and the recording of the Orbital concert, in particular, is up with the best I've heard on the Web.

And if that's all too funky for you, there's always **The Polka Channel** . . .

Web addresses

Harry Shearer
http://www.harryshearer.com

RealAudio
http://www.realaudio.com

AudioNet
http://www.audionet.com

RadioNet
http://www.radionet.com

Timecast
http://www.timecast.com/

Aotearoa Good Morning
http://www.gen.com/bigjude/BIRDSONG/Goodmorning.html

CDNOW's Internet Jukebox
http://interjuke.com

Movie Tunes
http://www.movietunes.com

David Bowie
http://www.davidbowie.com

Live Concerts
http://www.liveconcerts.com/

iMusic
http://www.imusic.com

The Polka Channel
http://www.AudioNet.com/pub/q-net/q-net.htm

Web TV

IMAGINE, for a moment, a world in which **Melrose Place** plays something like this:

Alison: 'But Billy, you know I always wanted to fi . . . (freeze frame and sound for 16 seconds) . . . nd my lost mother.'

The camera swings jerkily across the room towards Billy, stopping with only his nose in shot. Twenty-two seconds later, the rest of him appears. He speaks, but his lips seem to have all the synching skills of Kung Fu film actors.

'I know Al . . . (freeze) . . . ison. I have her . . . (freeze) . . . address. Here it is.'

He hands Alison what appears to be a piece of paper. Although, taking into account the size of the screen we're looking at and the low resolution of the image, it could actually be an aardvark. Or a moose . . .

Such is the reality of much of Web television for those of us on standard connections. At least during peak hours. Web television? **First TV**, the Internet-only television network, has been on air (now there's an expression that has to go) since the middle of 1996, broadcasting its raft of programs to the waiting world. Launched by American technical magazine company CMP Media, its grand plan is to build itself up as the first and foremost provider of Net-only television programming.

Others may broadcast live from events, or repackage cable and free-to-air material, but First TV guarantees it's all new and all of their own making. The site clearly hopes to capture a slice of the fledgling market now so that as the bandwidth ramps up and Net television delivery becomes more feasible, it has a ready-made audience and a reputation as a pioneer.

Using a plug-in called **VivoActive**, First TV provides streaming video to the visitor, who can choose bandwidth

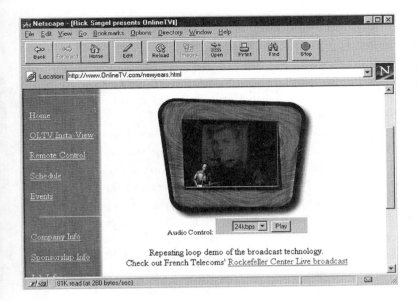

options: high (ISDN) and low (the rest of us poor schmucks). Streaming video, for anyone who has ever sat through the interminable downloads required for most video on the Web, is a blessing. It comes down the pipe in sequential pieces, which then play in order. You don't have to wait for the whole file to make it to you before being able to see any of it.

But even though Web TV is an idea with plenty of potential, for the moment the whole thing is as frustrating as it is exciting (hmm, there's a slogan just waiting to become the Official Net Motto). The screen is about the size of a business card. The images are pretty spotty. And in the jerky stakes, at 10–12 frames per second, the cup is either half full or half empty, depending on how you feel about these things. But whichever side you fall on, you can't exactly imagine one of your friends saying 'Hey, let's all go around to Bob's place and watch the final on his incredibly small, erratic screen.'

The video feed from First TV can be paused at any point, though why you would want to when it already pauses so often is another question. Most of the segments are around the three-minute mark (about 500k). In my experience (this will differ among service providers), they take about twice that time to make it through the pipe.

Unless, and this is a big unless, you do it between the hours of midnight and 9am, when there is a lot less traffic out there. In the middle of the night, the feed just spews through the modem as the Net Lord intended. The rest of the time, it's like the Melrose experience described above. Except that it ain't Melrose we're seeing. Exactly what is showing on Web television? Wait for it . . . Wait for it . . .

Yep, shows about the Web. Sigh. *Fresh Click*, First TV's main offering to date, is a series of segments which you're meant to watch individually, in your own order, piecing them together into a coherent program. There's a news bit, a women's interest bit, a Web tour bit (linked to the **Net Guide** site), interviews with Net personalities, site operators and critics, and reviews of game sites. The footage is presented in a stylised television set which, oddly enough, looks more like a 1930s radio.

The first thing you notice, when you get beyond the novelty of it all, is that people who design Web sites should not be given cameras. The shooting of the clips is amateurish (in any shot, at least one of the people will have no discernible facial features) and the lighting is best described as hopeful. If First TV are going to take the TV part of their name seriously, they need to hone a few skills.

The other thing is that there's no disguising the fact that people sitting around talking about the Net is a pretty dull use of moving pictures. The sooner that Net publishers and broadcasters realise that self-obsession is not the basis for a successful cultural putsch, the better off we'll all be. So much of what is on the Net is about the Net. And most people visiting couldn't care. They just want to know where to find the football scores. Or the stock market index. Or something that will make them laugh.

Anyway, *Fresh Click* has two modes of attack. It's either a snappy monologue, which would have worked just as well in audio or text, or it's a comfy chat, and quite frankly, when you're trapped in download limbo, the inanity of the chatter is all the more irritating (memo to Beth from Net Guide: I do not care about your freckles).

At this point, the smartest thing to do is click on the More Videos icon at the bottom of the main page and check out the site's small but attractive collection of art videos, such as Julia Swenson's appealingly odd *Pineapple Princess*, the adventures of a girl and her tropical fruit. Need I say more?

First TV has been joined by a handful of other fledgling networks, including the **Internet Television Network**, which uses a different software, the **VDO Live Player**, to achieve similar results. The Network is actually more of a library, with hundreds of special interest videos available for perusal in a number of categories: health, business, the world, the environment, sports, the home, fashion, travel, family, entertainment, computers, science and public affairs.

InterneTV, a Net video pioneer which began in 1995 at KVR-TV, a student and community television station at the University of Texas, makes use of both Vivo and VDO. It offers a selection of music videos on demand (a small, but interesting collection), film trailers (all the **Troma** films) and shorts, and also broadcasts some live events.

ITV Net, another of First TV's major competitors, uses VDO, Vivo and the Real Player. ITV has five channels, pumping a diet of culture, comedy, music, sports and films. It has a greater range of material available than First TV, but a less coherent sense of itself, presenting more like a library than a network. As with First TV, service is dependent on time of day and strength of modem.

Online TV is a newer addition to the market, which claims to be 'uniquely positioned with original content'. It has been in development through 1997 and was expecting to be broadcasting regularly from about the time this book was released, using Java software already incorporated in browsers.

'Our goal is to give 24/7 service with a variety of content on our one channel. OnlineTV will go to multiple channels in the next 12 months as content is developed and obtained. We intend to divide into channels that have their own domains and can have their own identities. Examples of secured domains for specific programming are: MusicTV.com, MovieTV.com, ScifiTV.com, AlienTV.com and LatinTV.com.' Watch the space.

Keep an eye, too, on the **World TeleVirtual Network**, 'still in the experimental stage', promising to launch its raft of content sometime soon. 'Social justice, political awareness and environmental balance will be our guiding principles. WTV.net will provide live and recorded shows that are unavailable in any other medium. We will be sending virtualcasts to millions of people at a level of honesty and directness never before seen. While the technology is fairly primitive compared to standard television, we will provide contents unavailable on the Internet and certainly never seen on conventional TV.'

If you just can't wait for Net technology to catch up, you can always go see what's on ordinary television. **TV Live** offers the chance to get frozen frame grabs of exactly what is going to air now from more than a dozen cable and free-to-air channels in the States. You just click on one, from Court TV to the Sci-Fi channel, and the site lets you see what others are already seeing elsewhere. Why is it that every time I do it, I always seem to get ads?

Web addresses

Melrose Place
http://www.melroseplace.com/

First TV
http://www.first-tv.com/index.html

VivoActive
http://www.vivo.com

Net Guide Live
http://www.netguide.com/

Internet Television Network
http://www.intv.net/

VDO Live Player
http://www.vdolive.com

InterneTV
http://www.internetv.com/

Troma
http://www.troma.com

ITV Net
http://www.itv.net

RealVideo
http://www.real.com/

OnlineTV
http://www.OnlineTV.com/

World TeleVirtual Network
http://www.wtv.net/

TV Live/Live News
http://www.users.interport.net/~mnw/liveview.htm

Anti-Advertising Sites

THE much discussed V-chip seems like an okay idea to me. Built into your TV set, it would detect and block violent programming by reading a signal embedded by the networks. That way, people who don't want to be assailed by blood and guts could opt out, without limiting the choices of those who do. It makes a sort of sense, even if it is a distraction from the real problem—the media doesn't make people violent, their upbringing does.

What excites me about the V-chip, though, is that it could well be the harbinger of a new era of consumer power. If you think about it, the possibilities are endless. I dream of the D-chip, which would automatically detect and block Ted Danson. Or the W-chip, capable of blanking out any program which starts with the words 'World's Funniest'. Or the G-chip. Three words: no more golf.

More importantly, if we have a V-chip, could the all-important, media-shaking A-chip be too far behind? Couldn't some backyard wizard come up with the TV equivalent of that which Axel Boldt invented for the Net: a way to kill ads?

In 1995, Boldt released **WebFilter** (it was originally christened 'No Shit', but he wanted to see it taken more seriously), an ingenious program which strips ads out of Web pages.

'You have probably noticed how many popular Web sites that offer cool stuff sooner or later inevitably turn to advertising,' he explains on his site. 'They are very welcome to do that, of course, except if they try to place their shit on my computer screen. Instead of placing the ads on a separate page and linking to it as "A word from our sponsors" or "Advertising", the ads are usually gifs that I'm forced to download because they appear in the middle of the information.

'I don't recall having rented out any of my time, bandwidth, screen real estate or brain capacity to anyone; so I decided to do something about these ads and filter them out of the Web: that's what WebFilter does.'

For Boldt, and for many others, the distaste for advertising is a principle thing. And while we may have had no real way to fight ads in other media, short of our refusal to pay attention to them, advertising dissent can be heard loud and clear on the Net. A living embodiment of Newton's first law, the medium has seen the rise of anti-advertising voices, balancing the new marketing philosophers.

Fans of the English comic *Viz* will be glad to know it has an online presence. One of the things **Viz Online** has done is taken a specific, and aggressive, anti-advertising line of attack. 'In my view,' explained editor Chris Donald in 1996, 'every advertising executive in the country should be thrown on to the dole queue. In an ideal world, there'd be no advertising. We never advertised *Viz*. A good product is an advertisement for itself. Any artist who devotes their talent to advertising other people's products is a prostitute . . .'

To make its point, the site includes a selection of the spoof ads the magazine has been famous for, as well as examples of real anti-ads the *Viz* design team concocted for local concerns when they were just starting out.

'I'm a Luddite,' Donald said. 'Until a year ago, we didn't have a computer in the office. As far as I was aware, the Internet was just a big electronic postal system for sad bastards like Stephen Fry seeking pen pals. When we realised how seriously the advertising industry is taking it, we thought we ought to have a go. It's time the whistle was blown on these powder-snorting, pony-tailed, overpaid charlatans.'

The **Gallery of the Absurd** is much less vitriolic in its tone, but has a similar effect in the long term. The American site is a rest home for bad ads, stuffed with 'little bits of popular culture'. And though it all looks like satire, everything is actually real. There's the magazine ad for Pounce—'Treats for Cats with Tartar Control 'cause Cats Don't Brush!' And the one for the line of McBaby kiddie clothing. And the one for the Cordless Super Massager, a fine example of advertising euphemism—the photos of the item look suspiciously like something else . . .

Another gallery, this one of **Advertising Parody**, is the work of an American agency, no doubt hoping a little reverse psychology will do the trick on us—'Hey, we hate ad agencies too, that's why you should bring us your business.'

'Did you ever have one of those days where you were sick of advertisements?' the site asks, no doubt rhetorically. 'Lame ads, dumb ads, ads that exploited everything from women to bald guys. Well, we did! [And we're in the business!] So it was natural for us to say "Let's create a site on the Internet where everyone could take a potshot at the Ads From Hell, the ads we all love to hate".'

These industry folk have turned their skills to anti-ads, to versions of the real deal which use the same techniques to present the truth instead of the hard sell. Some they have designed themselves, some they've borrowed from other sources for their collection.

One of those prime sources is the **Adbusters** site, an online ambassador/agitator for a Canadian magazine of the same name which specialises in **Culture Jamming**, the attempt to use the media's power against itself, to 'jam' the signals that blanket society, then reconfigure and rebroadcast them.

The Adbusters site introduces itself with an apposite quote from Marshall McLuhan: 'World War III is a guerrilla information war, with no division between military and civilian participation.'

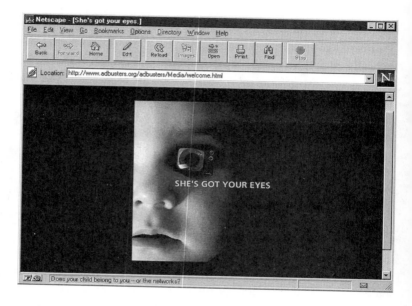

'Our goal in creating this site is to turn that grey or beige number-cruncher in front of you into the most versatile activist tool ever reckoned with,' it proclaims. 'For the potential to be realised, culture jammers have to learn to work with the resources they have at hand without worshipping or fearing the mediums of communication. We must strive to be spiders, stepping quickly and lightly, rather than flies caught up in the gluey gossamer of the irrelevant hype on the World Wide Web.'

Adbusters sets out to satirise advertisers, whom it describes as 'polluters of the mental environment'. It funds what it calls 'uncommercials', provocative spots for television (which can be watched on the site) and 'subvertisements' for magazines.

An example is a recent fashion ad, which features a nude model, bending and grunting, apparently performing some kind of exercise routine. As you get used to the rhythmic sounds and motions, the camera pulls back to show you what she's really doing, dry-heaving above a toilet bowl. The slogan? 'The beauty industry is the beast.'

Television networks, unsurprisingly, have refused to screen uncommercials, afraid of upsetting their other advertisers. So Adbusters has been taking its case to the courts, trying to argue that the refusals constitute a denial of free speech rights. So far it has been unsuccessful, but it continues to try.

Through a series of articles, suggestions and sponsored events (29 November is the annual Buy Nothing Day), the Adbusters site encourages us to be more critical of the media we consume, to consider the values and messages within. It offers us some powerful advice: you really don't really need governments and new technology to be your own screening chip.

Web addresses

WebFilter
http://www.math.ucsb.edu/~boldt/NoShit/

Viz Online
http://www.viz.co.uk/

Gallery of the Absurd
http://www.nlci.com/users/royal/absurd.htm

Gallery of Advertising Parody
http://www.dnai.com/~sharrow/parody.html

Adbusters
http://www.adbusters.org/adbusters

Culture Jamming
http://www2.sva.edu/readings/Culture-Jamming.html

The Fine Art of Parody

IF you can't beat 'em, mock the hell out of them. This would seem to be the *raison d'être* of the Web's growing ranks of satirists. As soon as a site achieves any kind of prominence these days, you can bet that its parody won't be far behind. Spoof sites have become an increasingly visible part of Web culture since the arrival, in late 1995, of **The Squat**. The grandaddy of Web parodies (and probably still the best of them) The Squat took, and continues to take, a scalpel to the hit cyber soap **The Spot**, ridiculing its style as well as its content, beating it at its own game.

The Spot, for those of you who have been in jail, is an Aaron Spelling-style soap opera centred around the lives and loves of a handful of spunky twentysomethings who share a big old Californian house with their dog. It's bright, snappy, easily digestible and crammed with attention-seeking happenings.

The Squat, on the other hand, is about four go-nowhere losers—Cleitus, Val, Earl and Woody—who share a trailer home with a horse in Nothingsville. Created by Josh Hancik, Lynn Kyle, Georges Saab and Greg Zguta, the four online journals chronicle the lives of the characters, which are based around bingo, getting drunk, watching TV and sacrificing as many brain cells as possible in the shortest amount of time.

An excerpt from Woody's diary (12 August 1996) gives a pretty clear picture: 'It just ain't right for me to be gamblin' all the time, seein' as I don't win no more. Nothin' fun 'bout binga when you ain't the one hollerin' and receivin' the payday in cash. So now is the time fer me to change my thinkin'. I figger there's got to be sometin' else fer me. Earl got his country singin', Cleitus got his manager-type job, Larlene is ridin' that bull, and Val—well, everyone know that she kin jest have anything she want 'cause the people is scared of her. Mebbe it's time fer me to find mah callin'. Mebbe I should go to thet school. Mebbe I should go get some pork rinds . . . I'll be back.'

The irony of The Squat is that it has often looked like it will outlast The Spot, a high budget venture which never actually made the money everyone predicted it would—the company went into bankruptcy at the start of 1997. The site is still running, and time will tell if it can stay on its feet. Even if it fails, it has been incredibly influential, as has The Squat in its own way.

Microsoft's (and why not check out **Microsnot** while we're on that subject?) controversial Web zine *Slate* is another outing which has inspired its share of comic alter egoes. Slate got under the skin of surfers from its unveiling in early 1996 for its Old Media attitudes to New Media, its staid design, and the holier-than-thou philosophies spouted by editor Michael Kinsley.

It didn't take the Web community long to answer. First off the rank was **Stale**, which got the design right all the way down to the inclusion of a crappy theme song. It also included a sharp and often savage derailment of the *Slate* methodology, orbiting around a long and comprehensive send-up of Kinsley's introduction to the magazine.

'At first we wanted a name that would reflect that dedication to originality, a name that would capture our unique style, our fresh vantage point, our singular opinions. A name like the *New Republic*, the *New Yorker*, the *Weekly Standard* or *The Economist*. Strangely, these were all taken and we ended up with STALE.'

Stale has been joined more recently by **Sleight** (really a home for online humour writing which has nothing more in common with *Slate* than basic design principles) and the much

more incisive **Stall**, which links to *Slate* under the heading 'Check out a lame parody of Stall'.

Stick your head above the parapet and you'll get shot at. **Suck**, a site which specialises in acidic, take-no-prisoners demolition jobs on Web culture (its motto is 'A fish, a barrel, a smoking gun'), is another that has inspired joke clones, including **Molt** ('a server, a domain name, and a crappy attitude').

'Don't get us wrong,' Molt writes. 'We like reading the scribbles of the many self-appointed arbiters of taste found infesting the Web underneath so many metaphorical refrigerators, bottom-feeding off of other people's efforts, eating their left-behind crumbs while complaining about both the bad taste and small portions. Some of our best friends are scavengers.'

Hmmm. Think about that. Here we have a site (Molt) which is a parody sending up its subject (Suck) for living off the creative efforts of others, while it's doing exactly the same thing. And I'm doing it to both of them. Is this confusing or what?

If a straight send-up isn't enough for you, try the **Suck Drinking Game**, which lampoons the site by pointing out its clichés. And while we're here, it's worth noting that there is even a *salon des refusés*, **Suck Harder**, a sub-Suck site built specifically for cast-offs, for the things that Suck won't print. As **Yahoo!**'s index notes, 'if you don't get published by Suck, maybe you should have Sucked Harder in the first place'.

Suck's mothership, **HotWired** (the zine was started in a back room by two HotWired employees), comes in for a Web pasting as well, courtesy of **Underwired** and **HayWired**.

Yahoo!, of course, cops its knocks in the form of, among others, **Yecch!!!** (a well-presented, funny and useful collection of links), Dutch satire **Hatchoo!** ('De eerste Internet Parodie van Nederland'), **Yippee!** (a search engine obsessed with He-Man and Weird Al Yankovic), and **YoPet!** (a searchable directory of pet home pages).

Then there's my personal favourite (for no other reason than the cheap gag of the name), **Net'N'Yahoo!,** a hoax site: 'Press Release 1.7.1996: SILICON VALLEY—World Wide Web giants Yahoo and Netscape announced a surprise merger and relocation today. The new firm will move to Israel and call itself Net'n'Yahoo.' Boom tish!

Another hoax comes to us in the form of the snifftastic **RealAroma,** which takes its shots at **RealAudio**: 'With the RealAroma Drive, and RATML (Real Aroma Text Markup Language) you can share smells in real time, over the Internet, with olfactory buddies all over the globe. Because all smell conversion is done locally in the RealAroma Drive itself, bandwidth requirements are extremely low and even users of embarrassing 14.4k baud modems can enjoy the odours you concoct.'

Tech culture zine **C/Net** (**C/Not**) and juggernaut news site **CNN** (**CN...Not**) get poked in their ribs by their alter ego sites, while **Same Site of the Day** makes fun of the dozens of self-appointed cool site awards: 'Soak it up! Yes, for your browsing enjoyment, it's the link to the same place it was yesterday!' In a similar vein, there are a handful of **Bottom of the Web** fake awards sites, including at least one **Australian** one.

The Blue Ribbon free speech campaign of the Electronic Frontiers Foundation has inspired a rainbow of other activists: the **Green Ribbon Campaign** ('Stop Bill Gates!'), the **Avocado Ribbon Campaign** ('Ban The Stupid!'), the **Brown Ribbon Campaign** ('Support Less Crap Online!'), the **Grey Ribbon Campaign** ('For the Rights of No Good WWW Pages'), the **Invisible Ribbon Campaign** ('More nonsense in the electronic world') and the **Puke Green Ribbon Campaign** ('Dedicated to the ending of all that is pointless and moronic on the Web', no doubt starting with itself).

And last but by no means least, there are plenty of **Netscape** parodies out there, from the silly (**Netape**, which is chimpanzee-obsessed) to the rude (**Nutscape**—you can guess the rest) to the intensely personal (**Nedscape**, a fantastic homepage for Ned Lily, designed in brilliant style).

Oddly, given the copyright rumblings elsewhere on the Web, there has been little legal action in the parody area. Maybe imitation really is the sincerest form of flattery.

Web addresses

The Squat
http://www.thesquat.com

The Spot
http://www.thespot.com

Microsoft
http://www.microsoft.com

Microsnot
http://www.microsnot.com

Stale
http://www.stale.com/

Sleight
http://members.aol.com/Sleight1/index.html

Stall
http://c3f.com/stall/

Suck
http://www.suck.com

Molt
http://www.joesapt.com/cmp/molt.html

Suck Drinking Game
http://www.stardot.com/~lukeseem/suck/

Suck Harder
http://www.theobvious.com/harder/

Yahoo!
http://www.yahoo.com

Yecch!!!
http://www.yeeeoww.com/yecch/yecchhome.html

Hatchoo!
http://www.xs4all.nl/~control/index.html

Yippee!
http://www.awod.com/gallery/rwav/ctyner/

YoPet!
http://www.hisurf.com/yopet/

Net'N'Yahoo!
http://www.reshet.com/atar/netnyahu/

HotWired
http://www.hotwired.com

Underwired
http://www.covesoft.com/underwired/

HayWired
http://www.geocities.com/SiliconValley/2582/haywired.html

Real Audio
http://www.realaudio.com

RealAroma
http://www.realaroma.com/

C/Net
http://www.cnet.com

C/Not
http://www.bcpl.lib.md.us/~dbroida/index2.html

CNN
http://www.cnn.com

CN . . . Not!
http://guerrilla.com/cnn/default.htm

Same Site of the Day
http://www.pnx.com/falken/samesite.html

Bottom of the Web
http://www.halcyon.com/cbutton/bottom95.htm

Bottom of the Web (Australia)
http://www.csu.edu.au/faculty/commerce/account/bottom95/bottom95.htm

Green Ribbon Campaign
http://www.datacomm.ch/~chris/ribbon/rib.html

Avocado Ribbon Campaign
http://www.mindspring.com/~rickwood/elf/

Brown Ribbon Campaign
http://www.mtsi.com/~osiris/litter.html

Grey Ribbon Campaign
http://www.ifi.uio.no/~klausw/GreyRibbon.html

Invisible Ribbon Campaign
http://stud1.tuwien.ac.at/~e9126408/invisible.html

Puke Green Ribbon Campaign
http://www2.gvsu.edu/~munsont/pgrc.htm

Netscape
http://www.netscape.com

Netape
http://www.bcpl.lib.md.us/~dbroida/netape.html

Nutscape
http://www.spwa.com/jupiter2/nutscape.htm

Nedscape
http://home.nedscape.com/

BELIEF AND DISBELIEF

Skeptics, Debunkers and Dissenters

THE spectrum of human belief seems to have broadened considerably in the last decade or two. These days, when a new acquaintance lets slip that he or she believes we're all descended from an ancient race of dirt-worshipping Neptunians who colonised this planet because of the attractively high nitrogen content of the soil, you're meant to be sympathetic.

You're meant to tilt your head meaningfully to one side, as if to say 'Well, that's a proposition I'm going to dedicate some serious thought to.' Instead of just punching them in the face, the centuries-old preferred option.

In our live-and-let-live, tolerant society, it's now okay to make up your belief system as you go along. You used to be a Catholic or a Protestant. Now it's whatever gets you through the night. And whatever you can remember the next morning. Some people still cling to organised religion. Some believe in money. Some believe in what are loosely (and less and less meaningfully) called alternative lifestyles.

And some believe in any of the myriad of millennial weirdnesses which are spreading like little viruses through our culture. As *X-Files* creator Chris Carter is fond of pointing out, 3 per cent of Americans believe they have been abducted by aliens. An even larger percentage of Australians believe that, whatever the question, Ray Martin has the answer. Truly, we live in freaky times.

And as I'm inordinately fond of noting, the Net is playing an increasingly significant part in the spread of kooky ideas, providing forums for the dissemination of previously marginalised viewpoints, fuelling the fires of superstition, conspiracy and ignorance.

But not always. **The Skeptic's Dictionary** is a one-man quest to shift a little of the balance back in favour of empirical,

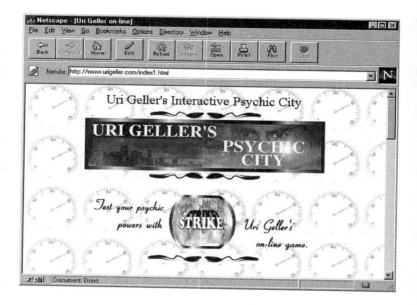

rational thought. Robert T. Carroll, a Californian philosophy teacher, is spending his spare time compiling an archive of refutation material, a one-stop shop for people who want to arm themselves for battle with believers or just find other viewpoints on some of the belief-related issues of our time.

Carroll holds a palm up to those who put their faith in 'God, ESP, the Easter Bunny and pyramid marketing schemes', to those mired in 'the supernatural, occult, paranormal and pseudoscientific'. His message is simple: 'Enough is enough'.

'The only thing infinite is our capacity for self-deception,' he writes on the site's home page.

His exhausting work-in-progress 'book' has more than 170 chapters so far, some only a couple of paragraphs and some into thousands of words, dealing with subjects as disparate as reincarnation and the Roswell incident, false memory syndrome and the faces on Mars, dowsing and dianetics.

The Skeptic's Dictionary is free of all Net whizzbangery. Nothing moves, nothing flashes, nothing changes colour. There aren't even any pictures. It's text all the way but, like the **Urban Legends Archive**, is proof that even on the Net, good content will beat good design.

Carroll began growing the Dictionary in 1994. He notes that 'The Skeptic's Dictionary is probably one of the first books written expressly for publication on the World Wide Web'. He says he was attracted to the idea that it would be free to anyone who had access to a computer and modem. The site now has more than 15,000 visitors a month.

The author is not just stirring or looking to be an intellectual killjoy. He doesn't simply deny the validity of his subjects. Some of his pieces are dismissive, but others explore both sides, giving ground to the believers, at least enough to keep a debate going on.

And it's not as if he simply loves the sound of his own voice. One of the best things about the site is that it links to other resources, on and off the Web, on both sides of the argument.

After pulling *The Celestine Prophecy* to pieces, he offers links to sites that defend and deify the book, like **The Celestine Prophecy Home Page**, as well as those which don't, including one with the snappy title of **Why I Hate The Celestine Prophecy**. For every **Uri Geller**, there is a **James Randi**.

'I thought of the book as mainly a resource for people trying to find skeptical literature on occult, supernatural and pseudo-scientific matters,' Carroll says. 'I intended to restrict my recommended readings to skeptical literature. I wanted a one-sided, biased text, to counterbalance the seemingly endless material on the other side. I've kept to that plan for the print recommendations, but I've included a lot of links to non-skeptical WWW sites.'

The site has hundreds of links embedded within its page, but the biggest growth area has been reader feedback. Carroll posts the brickbats and bouquets for his thoughts at the end of each chapter.

'I post a list of the top ten hits each week,' he says. 'The two most popular entries have been on Amway and mind control. The first entry I had on Amway was a tiny little thing that focused on a report I read in the *Wall Street Journal* about some guy who was trying to bring Amway to Poland. I found it amusing. I found the idea of multi-level marketing somewhat suspicious, but it was not a very strong interest of mine.

'I was bombarded with mail from Amway "devotees"—I can't think of a more appropriate word. The response seemed to me so disproportionate to what I had written that I had to investigate further. I then posted a much more detailed and extremely more critical article on Amway, as well as articles on multi-level marketing schemes and on pyramid schemes. The mail has not stopped. I have posted comments on the Amway article that amount to about three times the length of the article itself, which is one of the longer Dictionary entries.'

There are no plans as yet to make The Skeptic's Dictionary a 'real' book, but if you can't afford to wade around the site online, you can download the current version for free. It may not change your beliefs, but at least you'll have to work out why you hold them.

Web addresses

The Skeptic's Dictionary
http://www.dcn.davis.ca.us/~btcarrol/skeptic/dictcont.html

Urban Legends Archive
http://www2.best.com/~debunk/

The Celestine Prophecy Home Page
http://www.maui.net/~shaw/celes/celestine.html

Why I Hate The Celestine Prophecy
http://www.science.mcmaster.ca/csc/moylek/cp/

Uri Geller
http://www.urigeller.com/

James Randi
http://www.randi.org/

See also . . .

Skeptics Society
http://www.skeptic.com

One stop shop for skeptical resources on the Net, worth more than 100 useful links to Net debunking. It includes *Skeptic Magazine*, a quarterly digest of the activities and research of the Skeptics Society.

Jesus Gets a Web Site

In 1996, I wrote a newspaper column about the spread of Web sites that purport to be cyberspace's very own versions of **Hell**. For my troubles, I received a bunch of well-meaning letters and e-mails from Bible believers, many suggesting that Satan had plans to flatten out my soul and use it as wallpaper in his downstairs bathroom.

Perhaps, they said, I could render this eventuality slightly less likely by giving some coverage to sites about Christianity. I politely declined. I'd gently mocked the sites about Hell. To take a similar attitude to sites about Heaven or Himself would be inviting problems into my house. There are still a lot of people out there who don't see the funny side of **Monty Python**'s *Life of Brian*. And most of them seem to know where I live. Besides, the last time I plugged the word 'Jesus' into the **AltaVista** search engine, it told me there were 789,189 documents matching my request. Yipes!

Then I stumbled across the **Jesus Home Page**. No, really, I did. I'm not making this up. It had to happen — pretty much everyone and everything seems to have a home page these days. Why should a deity be any different?

'My name is Jesus Christ,' the site proclaims upfront. 'Welcome to My home page! I work as the messiah for a major world religion — it's called Christianity. However, when I'm not at work I like to "surf the Net". So I've finally made Myself a Web page.'

This Jesus (something inside my head tells me that it's not the real one, although you never know — and while we're following that thought, would you want to be God's ISP when he couldn't get a free line?) even has an e-mail address. Write to him at *jesus316@aol.com*. His attractive site features a 'photo' album (a handful of rather nice reproductions of classic paint-

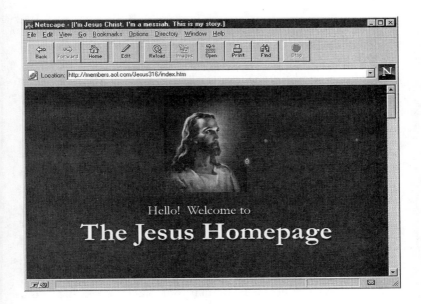

ings), which He bills as 'a selection of wonderful colour pictures of Me, My family and My friends'.

Dig a little further and you'll find some personal information: 'I'm a Capricorn (12/25), and, yes, I am single. My interests include carpentry, public speaking, fishing and catering. I was born in Bethlehem, but I grew up in Nazareth (see map below).'

The site offers you the chance to be saved online merely by filling out and submitting a form. And there's a collection of wacky messiah links: 'My roadmap to the most tacky Jesus-related roadside attractions on that nutty thing we like to call the Web.'

From here you can head off to visit an FTP site for the entire Bible, but only if you want it in **Pig Latin** (the real **Bible** can also be found online, fully searchable and in several readable languages). The book of Genesis begins thusly:

1:1 In-ay e-thay eginning-bay Od-gay eated-cray e-thay eaven-hay and-ay e-thay earth-ay.
1:2 And-ay e-thay earth-ay as-way ithout-way orm-fay, and-ay oid-vay; and-ay arkness-day as-way upon-ay e-thay ace-fay of-ay e-thay eep-day. And-ay e-thay Irit-spay of-ay Od-gay oved-may upon-ay e-thay ace-fay of-ay e-thay aters-way.

There's also reference to a site which draws out the eerie similarities between the lives of **Jesus and Elvis**. Another finds strangely compelling links between **Jesus and Windows 95**. Jesus, it says, started life as a carpenter. Win95 turns perfectly good computers into furniture. Jesus was remembered for protecting the weak. Win95 has weak memory protection. And so on.

Another, the **Miraculous Winking Jesus**, is a Web miracle, a line drawing which may or may not bat an eyelash at you. 'On April 23rd 1996,' the site owner says, 'this picture of Jesus miraculously winked at me. Many other people have claimed to have seen this picture of Jesus wink and have had plenty to say about it. My only hope is that millions will be touched by this miracle.'

Blink and you'll miss it.

Really, the control knob of the satire on the Jesus home page is turned down pretty low. It has fun with the concept of the messiah, takes the odd name in vain and makes its share of mildly tasteless jokes, but there's nothing cruel or spiteful or savagely anti-Christian about it (you can find that stuff elsewhere on the Web).

It's actually rather benign. And for this reason, the most fascinating part of the site is its reader feedback section. As you may expect, most of the responses tell you more about the responder than the site itself. And my, don't a lot of people have kooky hangups these days.

The reader missives fall into four categories. These are: believers appalled by the blasphemy; people who can't tell if it's serious or not (sadly, this group is well represented); disbelievers who roar with laughter; and, perhaps most interestingly, believers who find themselves having a good old chuckle as well.

More than one writes in to offer thanks, with explanations usually to the effect of 'you have enhanced my relationship with Jesus by forcing me to look at him in a different way'. There's even a congratulatory epistle from a Lutheran Reverend, simple and to the point. 'God does have a sense of humour!' he insists.

Let's hope so.

Web addresses

Hell column
http://www.smh.com.au/computers/content/960528/current/columns/960528-columns2.html

Monty Python
http://www.pythonline.com/

AltaVista
http://www.altavista.digital.com

Jesus Home Page
http://members.aol.com/Jesus316/index.htm

Bible in Pig Latin
ftp://ftp.netcom.com/pub/ea/earl/lble-bay/lble-bay.html

The Bible
http://www.gospelcom.net/bible

Jesus vs Elvis
http://www.infidels.org/library/humor/jesus_vs_elvis.html

Jesus and Windows 95
http://www.cs.bgu.ac.il/~omri/Humor/JesusVsWin95.html

Miraculous Winking Jesus
http://www.fastlane.net/~sandman/jesus/

See also . . .

The Bastard Son of the Lord Home Page
http://www.trog.com/jesus/

A much, much less reverent site.

Santa Claus

HE'S the Elvis of childhood. Huge. Fat. Overly gifted. Immortal. Reclusive. Prone to wearing outlandish costumes. The subject of uncorroborated sightings. Loved by millions the world over . . .

He is Santa Claus. And like Elvis, he also has many, many sites devoted to him. Go searching sometime. You won't believe how *cuuuuuute* the Web can be.

There are sites that allow you to calculate the **Months, Days, Hours, Minutes and Seconds Until Christmas**. There are places like **The Santa Site,** 'the merriest place in cyberspace', where you can read recipes from Mrs Claus, catch up on the yule traditions and get your own personal sneak peak at Santa's naughty/nice list.

How have you been this year? Just type in your name and read Santa's judgment. I entered 'Heidi Fleiss' and got the following reply: 'Nice, but several naughty marks. Was very good yesterday, so it's nice to add another mark in the nice column. Needs to pick up toys better, and help keep things neat at home.' Santa clearly needs a better researcher.

Santa's Workshop, which arrives with five language options, is folksy almost beyond belief: 'Mrs Claus and I are so happy that you could take a couple of minutes out of your busy schedules to stop by for a visit. If you have a second, maybe you could share a glass of ice-cold milk and some freshly baked chocolate-chip cookies. Or maybe you'd prefer a fresh scone and a cup of hot cocoa. Mmmmmmm I can smell the scones in the oven and the cocoa simmering on the stove right now.'

There's a terrific library which boasts the original Christmas story, a history of Christmas, related traditions, 'Everything You Ever Wanted To Know About Santa' (actually it didn't tell me any of the stuff I *really* wanted to know), as well as stories and poems. There's also a live chat option on site.

If you have a yen (or a dollar), you can **Talk To Santa.** If your PC has a sound card and a microphone, you can download a piece of Net phone software and really talk to the fat — sorry, differently weighted — guy when he's not working on toys. Or working out on the Tummy Trimmer. For $5, the site will send a letter from Santa to your loved ones.

Staying high tech for a moment, the official **Santa Claus Radio Station** broadcasts each year from its Finland home, beginning transmissions in early December.

The old-fashioned souls among you might want to just write Santa a letter. **Santa's Helpers US Workshop** is one of many sites that offer you the chance to do so. It also has Christmas stories and facts, and a collection of festive poems and songs.

It gets into hot water only when it suggests that 'the original Santa Claus, St Nicholas, was born in the ancient southeastern Turkish town of Lycia early in the fourth century'.

Santa's origin and current location seem to be topics of some debate on the Net. **Santa's Home in Iceland** explains that 'once upon a time, when Santa was riding the skies and looking for a quiet place to stay, he saw smoke rising from the middle of the Atlantic Ocean. It was an island called Iceland and the smoke was not smoke at all, but pure, white steam. At first he thought it looked a lonely place, but was he in for a surprise! It was inhabited by elves, trolls and a few friendly people, and steam was coming from everywhere: mountains, hot springs, pools and lagoons. He knew that this was the right place to live and built his home on a mountain near a little town called Hveragerdi.' Of course, the fact that he was a Bjork fan didn't hurt.

Until recently, there was a site arguing that Santa 'is from Norway, and not Finland, the North Pole or anything similar. Santa Claus lives in a Norwegian town called Drøbak, and although his toolshed is a bit "out-of-town", he's got his very own Post Office there to receive the thousands of letters he gets from children all over the world.' Maybe someone called their bluff.

We've Found Santa Claus attempts to prove that he's 'living and laughing in San Jose, California'.

The **Santa Claus of Greenland Home Page** maintains that 'Santa Claus lives with his family and his helpers somewhere in Greenland. Nobody knows exactly where. He has chosen to live in Greenland because he loves the magnificent scenery and the tranquillity of the clean and unspoilt environment in Greenland. The ideals of Santa reflect the people and culture of the Greenland nation. No one represents our hopes for peace and harmony between nature and mankind better than Santa Claus and his environment.'

Yeah, right. Like Santa isn't the ultimate expression of consumer capitalism. Like rich kids don't get expensive toys and poor kids don't get cheap ones. Santa may be many things, but he isn't a tree hugger. Or he wouldn't give so many books.

There's also a substantial amount of conjecture on the Net about the practicalities of getting the Santa job done. **Santa's MH–2600 Cyber-Sleigh prototype** offers blueprints and engineer's specs on the sleigh, which is supposedly made of an alloy, a combination of adamantium, mithril, and the previously unknown vibranium. According to this site, the sleigh uses a form of forcefield propulsion to move with little or no friction. If you don't believe it, check out the footage of the sleigh obtained from a military spy satellite in late 1996.

Tracking Santa Software attempts to answer the question of just how the Alexei-Saylesque Fat Bastard gets around so fast. It's a downloadable program which features a world tracking map, satellite tracking view, a customisable destinations list and a lot of the usual songs and Christmas messages.

Last but certainly most, **A Technical Analysis of Santa Claus** answers a bunch of very important questions. It throws away ideas of mysterious alloys and force fields and looks at cold, hard facts.

It points out, with copious research as backup, that reindeer can't fly, that Santa visits 378 million homes, at 822.6 visits per second (taking time zones into account), and that at such a speed, with such a payload (the site estimates 214,200 reindeer would be needed to pull a sleigh holding a one kilogram present for each child), the entire team would be almost instantly vaporised.

'If Santa ever did deliver presents on Christmas Eve,' it concludes, 'he's dead now.'

Can't argue with science.

Web addresses

Months, Days, Hours, Minutes and Seconds Until Christmas
http://christmas.com/apps/daystil

The Santa Site
http://www.claus.com

Santa's Workshop
http://home1.gte.net/santa/

Talk To Santa
http://www.thunderhead.com/santa/

Santa Claus Radio Station
http://www.nettiradio.fi/test/santa/saneng.htm

Santa's Helpers US Workshop
http://wl.iglou.com/info/santa/letter.html

Santa's Home in Iceland
http://santa.smart.is:82/

We've Found Santa Claus
http://www.1earth.com/santa/

Santa Claus of Greenland Home Page
http://www.greenland-guide.dk/santa/default.htm

Santa's MH–2600 Cyber-Sleigh prototype
http://christmas.com/sleigh-stats.html

Tracking Santa Software
http://www.cyberhighway.net/~citius/santa.html

A Technical Analysis of Santa Claus
http://www.mit.edu:8001/afs/athena.mit.edu/user/a/v/avondale/Humor/
ChristmasHumor/HTML/SantaAnalysis.html

Digital Angels

I accept that I'm probably going to be in the minority here, but wasn't **Highway to Heaven**, with Michael Landon as the everyman angel, a fabulous TV show? Critics rave about how groundbreaking **Seinfeld** is, but they forget that *Highway* had God manifesting as a stuntman and supporting character in almost every episode. How innovative is that?! It's a blot on our culture that He never got an Emmy nomination.

I wouldn't like to assert that it was a direct consequence, but angels have had great press in the last few years. They've been the subject of a major cultural resurgence, which appears to have started more or less at the same time that Landon hung up his TV wings. Angels are big business nowadays, even if they are mostly in the kind of shops where you spend your

time swatting away wind chimes and wondering what died to make that awful incense smell.

The **Index of Web Residing Angels** got my hopes up— maybe, I thought, they have a significant presence on the Net too. After all, if you follow the logic of Net philosophers and theorists, we may all be angels here, disembodied spirits roaming the digital ether.

In reality, the site is more of an art gallery than a phone book (more of that later), a handful of paintings of the winged ones, pasted together from other Web galleries (with credit and links of course). Its bright moment comes with its cheeky postscript—the last painting is one of 'the greatest angel', Lucifer.

But there are a surprisingly high number of angelic sites out there. **The Holy Angels**, a classification and examination of the many types of angels, does tend to go on a bit—if it's definition you're looking for, better to skip to **The Skeptics Dictionary.**

Angels on the Net describes itself as 'The World's Largest & Most Dynamic On-Line Resource for the Angels', but it doesn't say how many actually use it. It contains stories, pictures and 'angel music' (sadly, the Devil still has the best tunes). It also offers 'an environment for companies and individuals to advertise themselves and a vehicle to be found by the people who they want to sell their product or service to'. Or to put it another way, 'we may have higher aspirations, but we also have our hand in your till'. The site even charges to link to others. Golly, that's angelic. It's also a consistent theme as you travel the Angel Web—just try to keep the sites out of your pocket.

In the Angels Minimall, you can buy literature, art (mmmm, airbrushing), sculptures, pendants, meditation tapes and T-shirts—among many other things. On the Angel Resource

Page, you can locate an angelic CPA or an angelic insurance salesman.

There is some content: a bunch of stories, a letters page, readers' drawings and some background material, but nothing with a sense of humour, and absolutely no jokes ('Halo halo halo, what's going on 'ere then?')

Cherub's Home Page features another gallery of pictures, as well as information on various branches of angel activity, art, books, angelic discussions and more. The most interesting things it points to are sites dealing with angel contact (the more spiritual version of alien abduction).

Angels: Stories, Encounters, Adventures, Products and Services is a catchy name for a site and a great acronym (ASEAPAS). It gets down to the nitty gritty of presenting actual encounters with angels, recollections of those who say they have conversed with the winged ones.

Take the case of Wendy Davies, who was driving back from visiting her mother in Calgary when she heard the voice of her dead father coming from the back seat, telling her to slow down because there was a radar unit ahead.

'It startled me. I hadn't noticed that I'd been going ten kilometres over the limit. In the silence that followed I convinced myself the voice had just been my imagination. I saw no evidence of radar up ahead. A few moments later I distinctly heard my father say, "It's over the next rise. The Mounties have one car pulled over." As I crested the next small hill, I saw an RCMP radar unit with one car pulled in behind. Just as he had said.

'"Dad? Is that really you?" "Yes girl, it's me. I know you're not sure, so when you get to Red Deer, pull in for gas at the first Husky station you see. When you're ready to go, you'll see a Mountie car driving east one block over." Of course it happened exactly as he'd said. Since then my father has talked to me often.'

Right.

If you're looking for **Angel Links**, they're not hard to find, and another good place to start is the **Angel Times**, an online version of an American magazine celebrating everything with wings that isn't a bird or a panty liner.

'The magazine is a place to share their stories about angel visitations, communications, and healing experiences,' it says, 'in a supportive, non-denominational environment. Our contributing writers, columnists and story subjects range from Christian to Jewish to Native American to Hindu, and come from all over the world.' 'Angels appear to all people, regardless of culture or religion,' explains Angel Times publisher Linda Vephula.

Varian's Angel Dreams is an angelic appreciation society, with quotations of interest to angel fans, a collection of poetry and lyrics, some more artwork, downloadable angels graphics and links to more than 20 sites flogging angel products, like **Angel Wings**, which specialises in jewellery, textiles, clothing, gifts and greetings, and **Lasting Impressions**, which offers a customisable screensaver and angel computer magnet. There's even an **Angel Yellow Pages**, which keeps track of the whole angel industry. At present, it's only available in hard copy, but you can order your copy online.

Me? I reckon **Charlie's Angels** is enough for anyone.

Web addresses

Highway To Heaven
http://members.aol.com/cadetteel/htoh.htm

Seinfeld
http://www.nbc.com/entertainment/shows/seinfeld/

Index of Web Residing Angels
http://www.wfu.edu/~matthetl/sunrise/angels/angels.index.html

The Holy Angels
http://www.ocf.org/OrthodoxPage/reading/angels.html

The Skeptics' Dictionary, Angels
http://wheel.ucdavis.edu/~btcarrol/skeptic/angels.html

Angels on the Net
http://www.netangel.com/

Cherub's Home Page
http://ourworld.compuserve.com/homepages/Rodway/

Angels: Stories, Encounters, Adventures, Products and Services
http://www.intouchmag.com/angel.html

Angel Links
http://www.imperium.net/~philbb/angels2.html

Angel Times
http://www.angeltimes.com/

Varian's Angel Dreams
http://members.aol.com/dreamweavn/angeldreams/

Angel Wings
http://www.mcn.org/a/angel/

Lasting Impressions
http://www.islandnet.com/~last/

Angel Yellow Pages
http://www.lynxu.com/angeltimes/yellow.html

Charlie's Angels Home Page
http://clever.net/wiley/charliea.htm

See also . . .

Decapitate an Angel
http://www.halcyon.com/maelstrm/angel.html

Not to be forgotten. A Web game for everyone who wants to book a one-way afterlife ticket. Just point and hack.

The Loch Ness Monster

YOU'D think, with the hundreds of Webcams in use around the globe, that someone would have found something interesting to look at by now. But no, it's just peaceful vistas, office scenes, skylines, and cute but pointless gimmicks like decaying plates of **Spam** ('SpamCam: the page that seeks to answer the question: is Spam organic?').

Why hasn't someone pointed these cameras at subjects that might actually be worth wasting download time on? Like KFC headquarters, where we could read over somebody's shoulder and finally discover what the secret herbs and spices are. Or university faculty desks, where we could read the questions before having to sit the exams. Or Winona Ryder's dressing room.

Actually, the most obvious missing Webcam is the one that ought to be pointed at Loch Ness. Wouldn't it be cool if we could all search for Nessie, at any time of the day or night, without leaving the comfort of our nerd dens?

People travel around the world to stand on the shores of the loch, with the crumbling remains of Castle Urquhart behind them, and gaze across the dark, still water, hoping for a glimpse of something that might resemble a plesiosaur, a giant baguette or a Japanese midget sub. Really, some canny punter should have set up Live Nesswatch by now.

It's not as if there aren't plenty of Nessie sites out there. The principal site and virtual habitat of the creature is **Nessie on the Net**. It goes close, offering a daily video scan of the lake, a few seconds of the camera crawling across the surface, looking for our reptilian throwback friend. But it only updates once a day—not often enough for serious study.

'Many people have poured scorn over numerous sightings of Nessie,' the site says. 'You must decide the truth.' Never one to resist a challenge, I clicked through its gallery of proof. The first photograph is supposedly of 'Nessie's hump as it just breaks the surface of the water', but it looks almost exactly like an old tyre to me. The second photograph 'clearly captures the long trunk of a monster as it stretches out of the water'. If that's 'clearly', then my understanding of the concept of 'muddy' needs to be worked on. I've seen lamingtons that look more like monsters. The third pic is meant to be a shot of Nessie cruising along the surface of the loch. Frankly, the cobbled together monster from the 1971 episode of *The Goodies* was more convincing.

But that's no loss. There's plenty of other ways to occupy yourself on the site, beginning with its database of important sightings of the creature, dating from 1527 to 1995. (Note to self: Nessie and Elvis have never been photographed together. Is that significant?)

Among many other things, Nessie on the Net encourages you to join the fight to save the castle from tourism redevelopment plans. They're obviously worried—all those coaches, tartan salesmen and shouting holidaymakers are bound to frighten Nessie away. You can also check out the Highland Picture Gallery, listen to one of the author's two cows having a bit of a moo (why not?), and join the Monster Fan Club. Or chat in the Highland Blether Bar—swap a sighting story or two ('I saw Nessie picking up a sixpack from my local drive through bottle shop').

A more controversial area of the site, Nessie Is Alive, for some reason immediately brings to mind the Monty Python parrot sketch. 'Nessie may be shy,' it says, 'but she's not dead!!!' Yes folks, she's just resting.

Strange Magazine's Nessie Page is another excellent source for information on the monster. 'At the age of 63,' it says in a tone usually reserved for the discussion of the Queen

Mother, 'Nessie has lost none of her charisma. She often appears in advertisements (usually selling beer and spirits), is the object of sonar searches of the Loch, and/or is exploited by public relations people cashing in on her ability to attract the international mass media. And there are new sightings of the old girl every year.'

The site points out that if Nessie is proven to exist, British bookmaker William Hill faces a payout of more than £1 million (A$2 million). Really, compared to her value as a tourist attraction for Scotland, that's small change.

The magazine collects information on the sightings, searches, photographic and film evidence of Nessie's existence, as well as the people who have attempted to debunk or promote her legend. And if that whets your appetite, it has special sections devoted to other famous water monsters: Nahuelito, the Patagonian Lake Monster; Champ, the Lake Champlain

Monster; Sweden's Lake Storsjön Monster; and Ogopogo of Canada's Lake Okanagan.

The **Sea Serpents** site follows that lead, spreading its oceanic net even wider as it catalogues all manner of sea beastie legend. It also offers a free Loch Ness Monster screensaver.

'The waters of this planet go mostly unexplored,' it argues. 'It is very easy to hypothesise that we have not come close to cataloguing all the creatures that dwell in these waters. There has been many a sailor who has told stories of seeing strange creatures while on the high seas. Are these just ramblings or are they actual eye witness accounts of creatures yet unknown to science? The giant squid was thought of as a creature of myth and legend until recently, when scientist found corpses of just such a creature. Many of these "sea serpents" descriptions are similar to creatures that are thought to be extinct. The coelacanth was thought to be extinct for 70 million years until it was discovered alive and well in 1938. The fish is no longer on the extinct list. If this fish could survive all those years undetected, why can't other prehistoric giants have done the same thing?'

Canada has its own faction of the Nessie watchers. **Loch Ness Monster!** offers a poetic defence of the Nessie legend. **Lore of the Loch** assays both sides of the does-she-exist-or-doesn't-she argument and offers the chance to add your own theory (the butler made her). **Ness-Scape** has sonar pictures of what it claims is Nessie's lair as well as a recent pic of the gal herself (another floating tyre), a news service and some attractively unconvincing fakes.

On the more critical side of the fence is our old friend **The Skeptics' Dictionary**. And **It's a Fake** takes on the most famous Nessie evidence of all, the 1934 'Surgeon's Photo'.

Even if it is a fake, my hopes are not daunted. I think it's time we got a Webcam out there, and took it in turns to mount a 24 hour surveillance on the loch. I'd be willing to give an hour of my working day occasionally, sitting at home seeing through the camera lens. We could get a roster going.

Wednesday. 1am: Darkness

1.30am: Darkness

1.45am: Wait, I think I see something . . . nope. It's only my reflection on the screen . . .

Web addresses

SpamCam
http://www.fright.com/cgi-bin/spamcam

Nessie on the Net
http://www.scotnet.co.uk/highland/index.html

Strange Magazine's Nessie Page
http://www.cais.net/strangemag/nessie.home.html

Sea Serpents
http://www.serve.com/shadows/serpent.htm

Loch Ness Monster!
http://www.ccn.cs.dal.ca/Heritage/FSCNS/Scots_NS/Loch_Ness_Monster/Nessie_llk.html

Ness-Scape
http://www.glencass.demon.co.uk/

The Skeptics' Dictionary, Nessie
http://www.dcn.davis.ca.us/~btcarrol/skeptic/nessie.html

It's a Fake
http://psg.com/~ted/bcskeptics/ratenq/Re6.4-Fake.html

The Kooks Museum

IN the introduction to her 1994 book, *Kooks—A Guide to the Outer Limits of Human Belief*, author and crackpotologist Donna Kossy recalls envisaging that it would take 30 years of serious study to write her magnum opus.

'I pictured myself hunched over crumbling manuscripts and antiquarian books in the life-long pursuit of solving the mystery of kooks,' she wrote. 'My office would be in a corner of a "Kooks Museum", located in a crumbling industrial area, accessed by climbing a rickety stairway.

'The museum would be one large room crowded with ancient perpetual motion devices, glass cases containing diagrams and manuscripts providing solutions to the World Riddle, bookcases overstuffed with self-published tomes, and filing cabinets bursting with the ephemera of fevered visionaries . . .'

Things rarely work out the way we picture them. The book took a fraction of the time expected, and while her office is in a corner of **The Kooks Museum**, an exhibition space crammed with oddities that have been brought to us by life's intellectual fringe dwellers, that museum doesn't actually exist anywhere but on the Net.

The Web site, like the book, is a fascinating ride across the bumpy terrain of left-field thought. But where the book is a finite, closed-off archive of material, the Web site is an ongoing project, a dynamic, hyperlinked document, to my mind one of the top ten sites out there. And I really do mean *out there*.

The Web, ultimately, is the perfect place for this kind of exercise. It used to be that if you had an interest in weirdness, you had to scour the back ends of obscure magazines, hoping to find advertisements for outlandish products or theories, all available cheaply by mail order. The Web's potential to act as collective soapbox, as virtual street corner, means that more and more of those people who would once have been handing out pamphlets on street corners are now moving their act to the digital domain, saving themselves massive mimeograph bills.

Kossy is not dismissive of those with highly unfashionable ideas. She attempts to juggle open-mindedness with scepticism. Her site and book seek to examine the ways in which thoughts marshal themselves, the ways in which ideas survive and prosper in society. By studying outcasts, she wants us to consider where our own beliefs come from, and why we cling to them.

The museum curator admits 'a great affection' for the people she profiles. Being assigned kook status, she says, is purely a matter of perspective, socially and historically. By way of example, she points out that geologist Alfred Wegener (1880–1930), who came up with the theory of continental drift, was regarded as a nut in his day.

It works both ways. People presumed to be kooks in previous centuries are sometimes now seen as geniuses. And people presumed geniuses in their own time can later be found out to be something else. Only a century ago, phrenologists (those possessed of the belief that your mental powers could be determined by the shape of your skull) were as respectable as psychiatrists are today.

Kossy lovingly catalogues the lives and times of all kinds of kooks, from harmless, loopy pamphleteers and soapboxers to armchair scientists, hermit philosophers and the extremists: zealots, hatemongers and conspiracy theorists.

There are those who are convinced that: Einstein was utterly, inescapably wrong; the earth is hollow; that the path to enlightenment involves trepanation (drilling a hole in your head); the Anglo-Saxons are the real descendants of the Jewish tribes; horror author Stephen King actually killed John

153

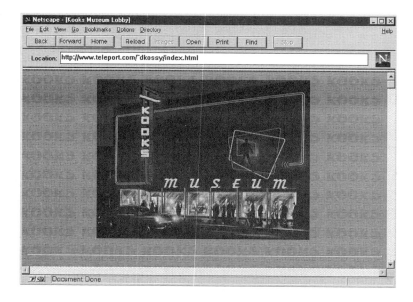

Lennon; goat glands will cure the world's ills; and much, much more. Just when you think it can't possibly get any more bizarre, it trumps you.

Like the Urban Legends Archive, the Kooks Museum is a place that you drop into expecting to while away a few minutes, but find yourself hooked and still digging away hours later.

And also like that site, it achieves its end purely on the strength of the material, by its vision and content. There are few bells and whistles, few of the tricks and games that many short-attention-span Net explorers expect.

Which is not to say that it's not well laid out. The visitor arrives in the museum's lobby and is offered a choice of areas to browse: the Schizophrenic Wing, Conspiracy Corridor, the Hall of Hate, the Library of Questionable Scholarship, the Gallery of the Gods, the Solution to the World Problem Exhibit, the Hall of Quackery and Monuments to Kookdom.

There is also an enviable selection of links to the many flavours of Web kookdom (the Wider Wonderful World of Kooks), a couple of art galleries and a gift shop (book outtakes, postcards, pamphlets, tapes, and research tools like the Kooks Book List and Database). And tucked away in the corner, as promised, is the curator's office, in which Kossy posts occasional thoughts and essays.

The other thing that's interesting about the Kooks Museum is that, in my case at least, it's more evidence that the Theory of Increasing Returns actually works. That theory, which sounds pretty dumb on paper, has it that the more you give something away, the more people will buy it.

It suggests that people develop relationships with products and their creators. If you tape a CD from a friend, and you fall in love with it, you will buy your own copy of the disc. Or if not that disc, then the band's next one. Or one of its relations. Either way, your cash will eventually find its way to the creator. The more people who find your work for free, the more people there are who will buy it.

If that's still not making sense, think of Netscape. Think of Microsoft. An awful lot of people have pirate or copied software on their hard drive. Millions of us are ripping off Bill Gates and yet he's worth $30 billion, or whatever it was at the last count.

It's a theory that other publishers have begun to put into practice. William Mitchell made his **City of Bits** available on the Web, with extra material and thorough hyperlinking. Mark Dery did a similar thing with **Escape Velocity**, making much (but not all) of the book available, with annotations and links. Each of those books has done very well, despite its availability to surfers.

I bought Donna Kossy's *Kooks* book because I loved the Web site so much that I wanted some kind of permanent record, something made of good old-fashioned atoms. Despite all the theories that the Net will kill publishing, it was the Net that made me want to go out and buy a book. Hopefully, the Net made you want to buy this one. Now how kooky is that?

Web addresses

The Kooks Museum
http://www.teleport.com/~dkossy/

City of Bits
http://www-mitpress.mit.edu/City_of_Bits/index.html

Escape Velocity
http://www.well.com/user/markdery/

See also . . .

Eric's Web Crackpot Page
http://www.voicenet.com/~eric/crack.html

A fabulous roadmap to the oddball delusional elements of the Web. From believers in miracles to flat earthers to paranoiacs to those who believe their brains are being controlled.

Tweaker's Crank Depot
http://www.kook.com/crank/

Another list o' Web loons.

The Internet Quackery Directory
http://www3.edgenet.net/jrk/crackpot.html

'Providing us all with discourse on anything from individual empowerment to superluminic velocities, the Web is host to thousands of dedicated crackpots, some of them quite convincing.'

BAD BEHAVIOUR?

Why We Have the Whole Idea of Censorship Wrong

WE used to sleep safe in our beds, secure in the knowledge that our cultural borders were sealed and protected. The various censorship bodies, working with customs officials, could stop whatever material was deemed to be socially harmful getting to us. Boats and planes could be searched. Crates of books, magazines or film prints could be confiscated.

And though, to some extent at least, that appearance of security has always been an illusion—illegal material has always found its way in—it has been a comfortable illusion, one that most people seemed happy to live with. But now it's fading. And here's an example of why.

In late 1994, Australian customs officials seized copies of the book *E is for Ecstasy*, which were headed for a Melbourne store. Brought to its attention, the Australian Office of Film and Literature Classification followed through and banned the book. *E is for Ecstasy*, by English journalist Nicholas Saunders, deals with the history of the designer drug, and details both its benefits and side effects. It includes tips for new users and first hand accounts of the E experience.

The book was banned in Australia (though it is widely available in Britain and Europe), for the simple reason that it encourages people to take the drug, which is illegal. A year later its follow-up, *Ecstasy and the Dance Culture*, was also banned.

These bannings, of course, are entirely ineffectual when it comes to distribution via the Net, an arena over which no one government has sovereignty. So I can sit down and read *E is for Ecstasy* at my computer. Thanks to Saunders' generosity, the book is available in its entirety on the Internet. In fact, there's

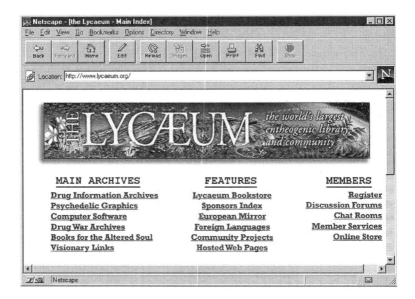

an extraordinary wealth of drug-related information out there on the Web, of the kind of first hand reporting that the public has little access to.

Encyclopaedic libraries such as **The Lycaeum**, the **Hyperreal Drugs Archive** and the Drug Reform Co-ordination Network's **Online Library of Drug Policy** offer more information than has ever been easily available to the consumer, and much of it is outside the usually acceptable limits of publishing. There are numerous accounts of drug takers, chemical breakdowns of various pharmaceuticals and annotated collections of media stories (usually beat-ups) about drugs and drug-related deaths, as well as directions to all manner of other resources. These are not banned. How could they be? They don't actually exist in Australia. They haven't been made into books and sent here. But I can access them more easily than I can access something at my local bookstore.

And even if they were made into books and banned here or in Britain, America, Venezuela or Vietnam, they would still be in the same boat as *E is for Ecstasy*, available as electrons rather than atoms. There are free speech fighters out there who see it as their duty to bring us this material. Saunders' book is one of the many linked to by **Banned Books Online**, a site which is dedicated to making available that which has been previously denied. Its contents range from *Fanny Hill* to *Ulysses* to *The Origin of Species*, the Koran and *Little Red Riding Hood*, more than 30 works which have either been banned or under serious threat. Each of them is stored for our perusal.

On the one hand, I find this reassuring, evidence that governments and the media cannot always tell us what to think. But there's no doubt that the same Net freedom that allows this, and makes us old-fashioned, libertarian-leaning folk feel nice and warm, also allows material that chills the blood.

Holocaust-denial material, for example, can be found in many places on the Net. A search based on the word 'pedophile' quickly turned up the *Pedosexual Resource Directory*, a site which makes a pseudo-scientific claim that 'intergenerational consensual pedosexual' relationships are perfectly normal. Presented in English, German, French, Dutch and Danish, this extensive site carries no pornography of either the written or pictorial kind, but fulfils a purpose just as insidious. It seeks to present a respectable face to the world for paedophilia. It functions as a kind of online library and support group for those the rest of us would call child abusers.

Personally, the site makes me extremely uneasy. I wouldn't ban it, because I don't think you can claim to be a tolerant society unless you tolerate views that aren't yours (and I also believe it's better to have people out in the open where you can see them, rather than sneaking around behind your back), but even if I wanted to, there's not an awful lot that could be done.

Let's try another example. One afternoon, I found myself wondering how easy it would be to get a recipe for a home-made pipe bomb. Apart from the allegedly constant spectre of child pornography, most of the Net's bad press has come from its reputation as a place to go to find out how to blow people up. So how hard is it to get that kind of information? Well, I typed 'pipe bomb' into the **AltaVista** search engine at 2.23pm.

The site told me that it had so many possible matches that if you laid them end to end, the sites would circle the moon a few times on their way to your house. The first site on its list that looked like it might actually tell me what I was curious to know, the charmingly titled How To Make Pipe Bombs, was nothing more than a dead link. I kept scanning. By 2.29, a total of six minutes after I began (and you know, traffic seemed pretty slow at the time) I was reading about how I could make plastic explosives from ordinary, everyday household bleach.

I was at a site called A Cookbook, derived from the famous Anarchist Cookbook (which also turned up pretty quickly when searched). A Cookbook is run by someone without the brains to spell 'Molotov' but with enough nous to put together and publish on the Web a How To manual for anyone considering a career based on the kind of skills they don't teach at school.

The site offers advice on how to make counterfeit money, get away with credit card fraud, pick locks, make bombs from many different kinds of easy to get substances, destroy cars, vandalise schools and phones, jam police radar and many, many other highly anti-social activities. The level of detail is high, and includes phone numbers and addresses of places, in the USA at least, where further information and materials can be sourced.

Another site, the Terrorist Handbook, offered even greater detail on buying explosives and propellants, acquiring chemicals and the use of household ingredients for other purposes, as well as step-by-step recipes for more than a dozen different kinds of explosive device. It had intricate explanations of fuse and delay devices, the kinds of casings and containers that should be used and even explosives safety tips.

Again, nobody shipped that material in my direction. Nobody smuggled it in. Nobody that my government has jurisdiction over is printing or circulating it in any physical form. Regardless of how we may feel about any of these books or online 'resources', the ease of access to such material, banned or not, is evidence of a crumbling of those safe and secure borders we have believed in.

So what does it all mean? Well, if you listen to a lot of people, it just means we have to get tougher, ban harder, and other various vote-winning strategies that don't actually make any practical sense. Basically, the time is fast approaching when we will have to rethink the whole philosophy of censorship. The platform it is built on, the idea that information can be managed and controlled by external, distant authorities, is looking increasingly shaky. Banning is a simple solution for simple times, and we're not in simple times.

I'm not saying that governments should give up classifying and censoring completely, that the gates should just be thrown open to everything, to things like child porn, bestiality, sexual violence, things the majority of citizens agree are unwanted. But it's important to recognise that old methods like this will have more to do with principle than practicality. They just won't be enough in this new age. The dam is breaking and a couple of governmental sandbags will not be enough to stop it.

Even if, through some kind of international diplomatic miracle, the majority of the countries of the world reached consensus on communications policy, there would always be some who refused to take part. Which means that there would always be a few who held out as censor neutral countries, as data havens. And on the Internet, it would only require one of those to exist to make sure this material is easily available to all. There is another option for governments, of course. They could just shut down all the phone and fibre optic lines. Some days, I wouldn't miss them at all.

So what should we be doing? Well, if we are to have censorship at all, we must broaden our understanding of the whole process, and achieve a more wide-ranging and multi-faceted form of address than the current one. We must come to terms with the basic truth that the point at which information can be blocked is more likely to be reception than transmission. The responsibility of governing what we see is going to move, more and more, from the State to us, to the individual. We're going to have to stop expecting the State to protect us.

So, any discussion of censorship ought to start from the premise that people *will* have access to information. The question that should be asked then is: assuming people can get to this material, what is an appropriate societal response? There is a role for government to play here, but it's not the one the government wants to play. The answer is one word. And in the days of the rise of economic rationalism and the corresponding fall of social responsibility, it is a word that is not in fashion. It is this: education.

We must all be helped to understand and deal with the images and the ideas that we are increasingly bombarded with. It is the job of schools and parents to prepare us for the information era. We have moved from being a culture of the written word to a culture that is at least equally visual. We must be taught in schools to understand the image as we are taught to understand the word. We must be equipped to comprehend the difference between fantasy and reality.

We must be brought up to be adults, capable of dealing with good and bad, capable of distinguishing between the two, and capable of making our own choices. We must be taught how to respond to these kinds of information, what to do with them, and how to fight them. Because anyone who thinks that legislation, on its own, is the solution is fooling themselves.

Web addresses

I'm saved from the moral question of whether or not to reveal to you the addresses of these sites, the paedophile and bomb resources in particular, because they rarely last long in the same place. These sites tend to server hop—they are built for speed, not for comfort. They're usually single files, or just a few, the kind of thing that can be folded up and dropped into a briefcase for a quick escape when the Feds knock at the door. Beyond that, just because I accept that some sites exist, and believe we shouldn't deny their existence, it does not also follow that I feel we should encourage everyone to access them. Therefore I have chosen not to include the Web addresses of some of the above sites. I realise this is a futile, token gesture—a search engine will find them quickly enough—but it's a gesture I feel I have to make.

E is for Ecstasy
http://hyperreal.com/drugs/e4x/

The Lycaeum
http://www.lycaeum.org/

Hyperreal Drugs Archive
http://www.hyperreal.com/drugs

Online Library of Drug Policy
http://www.druglibrary.org/

Banned Books Online
http://www.cs.cmu.edu/People/spok/banned-books.html

AltaVista
http://www.altavista.digital.com

Cheating for Fun and Profit

IF you're reading this on Highway 17 in South Carolina and you're nearing the Ashley River bridge, slow down. The place is apparently notorious for its speed traps. Sure, you can't see the motorcycle cops—they're probably hiding behind the bushes near the Holiday Inn. And remember, the speed limit on this stretch of road is 40 miles per hour—usually, they book anyone whose speedo is touching 45 . . .

Halfway around the world, somewhere on the Hume Highway in New South Wales, about five kilometres south of Marulan (former home of The Big Pavlova), there's a worn patch in the median strip on a right-hand curve, big enough for a police car to park, pointing in either direction, and hit you with a radar gun on the way past. It's a regular hangout for the highway patrol, so be careful when you're in the area.

How do I know these things? Well, apart from the fact that I have driven every road on Earth, and most of them twice, I've been browsing through the notes in the **WWW Speed Trap Registry**, a site started in February 1995 'to reduce the number of speeding tickets resulting from speed traps'.

The WWWSTR is a contribution-based archive of places where police radar units hang out waiting to catch law-breaking motorists. Its library covers all 50 states of the USA as well as 20 other countries, including Australia, Canada, France, Germany, Iceland, Israel, Malaysia, New Zealand, Switzerland and the UK.

Despite the obvious and perfectly reasonable conclusions to be drawn, the site maintains in its ingenuous disclaimer that it 'is *not* a tool to undercut the efforts of law enforcement. The Registry is a resource to help drivers know where they might encounter speed enforcement so they can adjust their speed to the conditions.'

It goes on to say that some police authorities would actually approve of its existence, because it encourages people to slow

down, bypassing the fact that it only encourages this part of the time, and by implication, encourages breaking the speed limit during the rest. Of course, from the police point of view, every place mentioned on the site could just be one place less they'll have to keep their eyes on . . .

Once again, the Internet offers a way for people around the world to get together and share information, creating the kind of database that previously would never have been available to us. And while you might have certain moral problems with the content of the database being built, you'd have to admit that as an example of the potential of the technology to help people, to do what other technologies can't, it's a pretty good one. Its whole is so much more than the sum of its parts.

Even more morally doubtful is the **Evil House of Cheat**, whose cheeky subtitle is 'What subject are you gonna pass today?' This site, for high school and university students, offers more than 8000 essays for the visitor to download, in 40 categories. They all carry grades received, dates of submission and explanations of what level of schooling the author is at and where the essay was handed in.

But it isn't as easy as just point and click. You have to join the essay swapping club. The site requires a password for entry, which you can obtain via two paths. You can send Jens Schriver, the curator, an essay of your own, or you can link to his site from yours. If you do either of these things, you'll get access to 1600 essays. If you want to see the rest, you'll need to fork out $10.

Visitors can get a peak at the database though, at a handful of essays with names like 'The JFK Assassination' (a 16-year-old's history effort which was graded at 95%), 'Showgirls and Present Day Gender Role Construction' (a 20-year-old's sociology essay which scored 90%) and 'Huntington's Disease' (from a 22-year-old med student, with a 100% grade). If what you need isn't on site, you can post a request. More than half a million people have visited the site since 1995.

Schriver is not at all coy about the purpose of his site. If you have complaints, he says in the site's FAQ, don't bother passing them on. He's heard them all before.

The brain behind **Cheater.com** thinks in a similar way. The author, who claims to be a normal high schooler just out to help other students, has put together a well-designed site that works much like the House. The user is asked to provide a report up front—hey, if you're complicitous, you can't complain. Doing so accords you membership rights to the club and access to the other reports available online, growing like the House of Cheat, by more than a thousand each month.

The person who built **The Source**, an online essay dump that houses more than 250 student efforts, positively revels in his task.

'Welcome to the Source, your one stop shop for all your "official" school business. The fact is that school is a terrible waste of time, and we students in today's information age do not have the time to write lengthy school papers. This site is a common meeting ground where students from around the globe can pool their resources and defeat the teachers.'

Others try to hide behind the same sort of rationalisations that the Speed Trap Registry goes for. Erin Carlson, the creator of the **Absolutely Free: Online Essays** site, which offers about 20 essays for public use, says that 'although I offer free essays and term papers on the Web, I do not suggest that students use this resource as an alternative to doing their homework. If a student were to copy and turn in one of these free essays, then he or she would be committing plagiarism'.

She points out the dangers of plagiarism, warning that it could lead to zero grades, a permanent blot on the student's records and possible expulsion from school or university. So why has she put the site up? She dissembles.

'I feel that writing essays and term papers is a very good way to improve your mind. However, there is nothing wrong with getting ideas from other people's work. Different perspectives on the same topic is wonderful if you want to write a quality paper. Even an idea on what to write about can be helpful.'

Though Evil House of Cheat is the biggest, there are plenty of others, from **Other People's Papers** to **y ME Reed?**, freely distributing the work of others, mostly for fun, but also for profit. **Ivy Essays,** for example, specialises in admission essays to colleges, business and law schools, discreetly available to Net users for a small fee.

Student Gorilla Tactics takes a broader view of the education system and the various ways of manipulating it, offering tactics for writings essays in extreme haste, with a library of online references to help you find appropriate sources and quotes to make your work look more impressive. It also contains a list of ways to finagle an extension from your teacher or professor, and advice on cramming for exams. None of the material actually suggests you cheat, but it does encourage you to cut more corners than a clothing factory.

Yahoo lists more than 80 sites which will tell you how to cheat your way through various **computer games**, but my favourite Web cheat is a more unique one. **Top Secret Recipes** is a site which presents recipes for well-known, commercially successful products. Here you can find the ingredients and directions to make things that supposedly taste exactly like: Kentucky Fried Chicken, McDonald's Big Macs, York Peppermint Patties, Sara Lee Cheesecake, Bailey's Irish Cream and Mars Bars, among many others.

Site author Todd Wilbur (who has published two books on the same topic, which can be ordered onsite via its link to the **Amazon.com** bookstore) has spent years in the kitchen attempting to clone brand name products, working overtime to recreate the exact flavours of synthetic ugliness. Despite the fact that making your own convenience foods is by definition pointless, he has persevered and compiled a library of recipes, which he's making available on the Net at about the rate of one per month.

'Designing a Web site is kinda like making a Big Mac,' says Todd. 'You gotta stack things on in just the right order and use just enough special sauce.' And cheat a little.

Web addresses

WWW Speed Trap Registry
http://www.nashville.net/speedtrap/

Australia Speed Trap Registry
http://netspace.net.au/~smack/speedtrap/speedtrp.html

Evil House of Cheat
http://www.CheatHouse.com/

Cheater.com
http://www.cheater.com

The Source
http://idt.net/~levin/

Absolutely Free: Online Essays
http://www.elee.calpoly.edu/~ercarlso/papers.htm

Other People's Papers
http://www.OPPapers.com

y ME Reed?
http://www.geocities.com/Athens/4169/

Ivy Essays
http://www.ivyessays.com/

Student Gorilla Tactics
http://www.islandnet.com/~tactics/

Game Cheats
http://www.yahoo.com/Recreation/Games/Computer_Games/Cheats_and_Hints/

Top Secret Recipes
http://www.topsecretrecipes.com/

Amazon.com
http://www.amazon.com

The Internet Death Row

THERE are places you can go on the Internet that you'd never go in real life, experiences to be had that you would never choose to have offline. There are shoulders to be rubbed that would never be rubbed in the real world, thoughts to be shared with people you would never meet, never find yourself in conversation with.

By way of example, Dean Carter is a Death Row inmate at San Quentin in California. His **Dead Man Talkin'** site broadcasts to the world the feelings and thoughts of a man awaiting his execution. Here, you can see the world from his perspective. You can go, safely, to a place you'd hope to never find yourself.

Part of San Francisco radio host Alex Bennett's site, Dead Man Talkin' is a collection of columns from Carter (he hasn't filed for a year now, but the material doesn't go out of date). The columns are sent by mail—Death Row inmates aren't exactly wired—to Bennett, who uploads them to the site.

'I do not intend to discuss my case because that is not why I have agreed to do this page,' he said in his first column. 'I would not feel comfortable using this forum to try and focus attention on myself, I am not the issue here. What I do feel is important is I give you a perspective of the Death Penalty, the justice (or "just-us", as a wise man once said) system, life in prison and hopefully I can give you a reasonably coherent account of what it is like from where I sit.'

Carter also replies to letters sent by people who have come across his work on the site.

'Yes, I think that I am afraid of dying,' he wrote back to one woman. 'I think that most people are. But I don't dwell on it. I don't know what I will feel if the time ever comes to be executed and hopefully I will never find out.'

Carter's words humanise his situation. They allow us to empathise, if not always sympathise, with someone for whom good news would just be getting more of his life to spend in jail.

He has been joined in his outreach exercise by **Bill Noguera**, an inmate a few tiers down in the same prison. Noguera doesn't express himself through his words. Rather, he communicates via his pointillist art, his pen and ink stippling. It's a painstaking, time-consuming artform—works often require hundreds of hours to complete—but Nogeura is not exactly deluged with better offers of ways to fill in his time.

'During the many years I have been on Death Row, I discovered that I had artistic skills,' he explains. 'I am a self-taught artist and have found many new worlds through my passion for art.

'I cannot begin to express in words what life on Death Row is like, but through my drawings I am able to visually describe it. I spend most of my days drawing. It helps transport my mind and spirit to a place where there are no bars. A place where I feel safe.'

In his time inside, Noguera has worked for a college degree in criminal justice and a paralegal certificate. Some of his education has been funded by the sale of his art. Only one of the works exhibited online is directly related to Noguera's position: Last Words, a visual attempt to cope with the inevitability of death.

The rest of the works, however, tell us just as much about his life. They're yearning pictures of children playing, horses in stables, women with wind in their hair—all concerned with freedom, desire and the small pleasures of life denied to prisoners.

The themes recur in the works of other prison artists, like **Stephen Dubov**, a lifer whose journals, drawings and sculpture photos can also be found online. Other examples can be perused at **The Voice of the Prisoner**, a site dedicated to the art, poetry and letters of men and women sent up river.

Online zines like **Voices from Prison** and **Inner Voices** (obviously, there's not a lot of titles to go around in jail) present poetry and creative writing from behind bars. Similarly, **Writings from Death Row** 'is a public forum for death row inmates', a chance for them to have their writings presented to the Net public.

Of the four who have, to date, taken the option, three rail against the justice system. The fourth writes about health risks, about the overabundance of sodium and potassium in our diets. Clearly, being in jail leaves you with a lot of time to think.

It leaves you with a lot of time to write too. But a lack of people to write to. IRC isn't an option, but the Net is as good a place as any to hunt for company. **Penn Pals** is a classified ad/matchmaking site for prisoners, offering brief biographies, with photos, of inmates of both sexes looking for mail and/or visits. For $20, a prisoner can get a listing. You can e-mail them for free.

Last but self-evidently not least, **The Final Word** is another collection of the thoughts of Death Row denizens, but only the last thoughts. The site is a small (but perfectly formed) collection of last words, of final quotes from those whose lives are about to cross the finish line.

The home page, which has a picture of a plug being pulled, hints at a little gallows humour, which is evident in most of the entries, from the intentional (one convict says he'd 'rather go fishing') to the accidental (another observes, in the period before the injection takes effect, 'I'm still awake'). Would you do any better?

Web addresses

Dead Man Talkin'
http://monkey.hooked.net/m/hut/deadman/deadman.html

Bill Noguera's Paintings
http://monkey.hooked.net/monkey/m/hut/conart/bill.html

Stephen Dubov
http://www.dubov.com/

The Voice of the Prisoner
http://clickshop.com/prisoner/

Voices from Prison
http://www.hartnet.org/ctpas/CPA/voices/front.html

Writings from Death Row
http://www.comedywriter.com/wri1.htm

Penn Pals
http://www.pennpals.com

The Final Word
http://w3.one.net/~tdaniels/parting.html

Virus Myths, Pranks and Hoaxes

THE penpal Greetings virus has been one of the great Web myths of 1996/97, a part of its folklore. If you receive a message headed Penpal Greetings, the story goes, you should delete it with undue haste. You should never, never read it. If you accidentally open the e-mail, it is said, all manner of unpleasantries will most certainly befall you. Hidden inside, according to the mythology, is 'a dangerous Trojan Horse virus' capable of not just crashing your hard drive, but erasing everything inside your machine. Hell's bells!

And that's not all. Not content with merely annexing Poland, the virus will then move forward across Europe, automatically replicating and mailing itself to every address in your computer mailbox. Who in the kingdom will be brave enough to stand up to it?

Of course, the whole thing is a hoax. Rob Rosenberger, on his excellent **Computer Virus Myths Home Page** (an absolute Must Bookmark), dismisses the whole Trojan Horse idea with nothing but the bare hands of his logic:

'Reading an e-mail message does not run it nor does it run any attachments, so this Trojan must be self starting,' he writes. 'Aside from the fact that a program cannot start itself, the Trojan would also have to know about every different kind of e-mail program to be able to forward copies of itself to other people.'

Rosenberger also points out that we have heard this story before (perhaps Helen Darville wrote it), beginning with the notorious **Good Times** virus, which crept into Net consciousness in November 1994.

The original hard-drive-trashing, system-flushing, leaving-the-lid-off-the-toothpaste Trojan Horse virus, Good Times has spawned a number of illegitimate offspring—Death69,

Deeyenda, Irina, Join the Crew and Valentines Greetings, to name but a few.

Penpal is merely the latest in this dishonourable line. Rosenberger points out that despite the paranoia and hype about viruses (much of which, he notes, plays rather too neatly into the hands of the anti-virus software companies), there have so far been no known e-mail viruses, no known HTML viruses and no known Java or ActiveX viruses. So there.

His Virus Myth home page, and others such as Charles Hymes's **Don't Spread That Hoax**, do what they can to dispel the virus panic that seems to grip the Net community at regular intervals. Both contain archives of virus-related material, proving that in many cases, viruses are the urban legends of the digital city (the **Urban Legends Archive** certainly stakes its claim on them).

But as always these days, the truth seems to be of little solace to most people. Everyone I know is white-knuckle

scared of viruses—when it comes to these spiteful little programs, we are hysterics, hypochondriacs.

Even though most computer viruses are like a case of mild
flu (irritating but not too difficult to deal with), we're convinced they're all Ebola, about to make our machines bleed
from every orifice and keel over dead.

Like the serial killer, the computer virus has become an
archetypal bad guy, a pop culture icon, an emblem of our times
(Stephen Hawking once said it might also be the closest we
have come to the creation of life). Viruses are culturally sexy.
They're fun. My sick friend Chris has taken to typing the
words 'Penpal Greetings' in the subject line of his e-mail
messages.

'A virus contained in this e-mail is currently impregnating
your girlfriend,' his last epistle began. 'It may be too late. You
will have to be quick to stop it moving on to devour your beer.
By the time you get to the living room, it will be occupying
your favourite chair and smoking a cigarette with its feet on
the table . . .'

Clearly, they have slipped free of the bonds of reality and
become something much bigger and more powerful. For this
reason, anti-virus sites (the **Electronic Frontiers Foundation**
houses a hoaxes archive on its site as well) are not just handy
for detecting and defeating our own idiocy. They play a valuable function in the social record of computing, as places where
the legends of this domain are kept.

Rosenberger and Hymes are curators, historians busy col-
lating an important part of the folklore of the digital world.
This place is brimming with lore, with myths, pranks and
hoaxes. Some of these hoaxes are annoying **chain letters**. Some
are dangerous scams and frauds, baseless get rich quick
schemes (check out **Internet Fraud Watch**) which constitute
serious Net abuse.

But others are more benign. **April Fools on the Net,** for example, bills itself as an archive of Net humour, and notes that 'April Fools postings and e-mail are a fine online tradition'. The site has yearly round-ups going all the way back to 1984, as well as a list of its top 20 April Fools' pranks.

This list includes minor gags like the 1996 Usenet newsgroup posting which explained (and convinced many people) that the Internet had to be closed down for cleaning for a day because it was a leap year, as well as larger scale japes such as the phoney 1994 press release which insisted that Microsoft had clinched a deal to buy the Catholic Church.

'We expect a lot of growth in the religious market in the next five to ten years,' Chairman Bill was quoted as saying. 'The combined resources of Microsoft and the Catholic Church will allow us to make religion easier and more fun for a broader range of people.'

There is also an online collection of fake **Macintosh** press releases for spurious products, from the caffeine manager to the Macintosh toaster ('an 80-megabyte hard drive, a 25-megahertz bus, and two slots for bread').

But if you're really interested in the accumulation of Net culture, perhaps the best place of all to go is **Cyberlore Central**, a library of links and resources on everything from emoticons (smileys) to acronyms to Net humour to 'stupid user' stories to hacker jargon. If it has ever sounded like technobabble, it's here.

Web addresses

Computer Virus Myths Home Page
http://www.kumite.com/myths/

Good Times Virus Hoax FAQ
http://users.aol.com/macfaq/goodtimes.html

Don't Spread That Hoax
http://crew.umich.edu/~chymes/Hoaxes/Think.html

Urban Legends Archive
http://www.urbanlegends.com

EFF Hoaxes archive
http://www.eff.org/pub/Net_culture/Folklore/Hoaxes/

Chain Letters
http://www.eff.org/pub/Net_culture/Folklore/Chain_letters/

Internet Fraud Watch
http://www.fraud.org./

April Fools on the Net
http://www.2meta.com/april-fools/

Macintosh April Fools
http://www.astro.nwu.edu/lentz/mac/humor/april-fools/home-af.html

Cyberlore Central
http://www.pass.wayne.edu/~twk/cc.html

Random Hatred

THE Web, as we know, brings people together. There are always others like yourself out there to be found, communities of taste, belief and obsession, no matter how obscure the common link. For example, I recently came across a site for people who are interested not just in tattoos in general, but in **Soviet Prison Camp Tattoos**. Obscure enough for you?

This trainspotting specificity can be one of the Web's joys, as long as it's your predilection that is being matched. Or, as it turns out, being *not* matched. Demonstrating its capacity for the Newtonian opposite reaction, the Web also brings together people who *hate* the obsessions of others.

A guy with the charming and singular name of Grum has been scoring well since the start of 1996 with his **I Hate Silverchair** site, which is little more than a statement of loathing with a few 'movies' (slide shows of line drawings) depicting himself in the act of tragically cutting short the band's career. If you dig deeply enough, you'll find that Grum doesn't really hate the band that much. His page is intended mostly as an outlet for his own fun—silverchair are handy targets for his derision.

I know our mothers told us all that 'If you can't say anything nice, don't say anything at all', but sometimes, the Grinch in you just wants to come out. Sometimes, there's fun to be found in hating other things, even if you like some of them (hey, a change is as good as something or other). So why stop at silverchair?

The **I Hate 'Alternative' Music** page seems to hate *everything* at first glance, but then you realise that the guy who runs the site is a prog rock fan (there are recommendations that you listen to Pink Floyd, King Crimson and Emerson, Lake and

183

Palmer), so there goes his credibility. He does have a great page of links though.

Sticking with music for a moment, the **I Hate Oasis** site offers a series of reasons (none too convincing) why the Gallagher brothers are worthy of your distaste, ranging from 'They think they are better than the Beatles' to 'Liam is a monkey'. The **People Against Alanis Morissette's Music (PAAMM)** make a similar case, though sadly, they stop short of comparing the Canadian warbler with other primates.

The **No Yanni Organisation (NoYo)** is a perfectly rational group of abolitionists looking for your membership. The **Official Hootie Sucks Home Page,** even though it has no content to speak of, is hard to argue with—the principle is perfectly sound. Ditto the **I Hate the Macarena** site.

David Hasselhoff is the Antichrist (and I Have Proof) is a great site which draws out the gobsmackingly obvious (how did we miss it?) Biblical evidence that *Baywatch* is a portent of Armageddon. You don't believe it? Read those passages again.

Revelations 13:1. 'And I stood upon the sand of the sea, and saw a beast rise up out of the sea.' Hmm, who could we be talking about there?

Revelations 13:5. 'And there was given unto him a mouth speaking great things and blasphemies.' The following, according to the site, are some of Hasselhoff's recorded blasphemies: 'I'm good-looking, and I make a lot of money', 'There are many dying children out there whose last wish is to meet me' and 'I'm six foot four, an all-American guy, and handsome and talented as well!'

Along the same 'they are not who we think they are' line is **Bert Is Evil**, a site which makes a case against a previously lovable, if anally retentive, **Sesame Street** character. The site, 'brought to you by the letter H and the CIA', claims it has the goods on Bert's dark side.

You'll find 'photographs' of Bert with Hitler, Bert taking Ernie to a nudie bar and Bert at Daley Plaza, Dallas, in November 1963. There are revealing 'interviews' with Ernie and Kermit, as well as 'intercepted e-mail correspondence' between our foam friend and Jeffrey Dahmer. See the site now. I'm sure the Muppet lawyers will be trying to shut it down soon.

Still on the subject of children's programming, the Web-based **Jihad to Destroy Barney** (aka 'B'harnii the Hell Wyrm') deserves your support and is a gateway to a whole slew of dino hunting sites. But the purple horrorsaur isn't the only major icon causing displeasure. Surprisingly, there's a **Marilyn Monroe Hate Page**. It's in Brazil and it's run by a guy who thinks 'she's just the stereotype of the woman to be hated. So nice, so cute, full of smiles and kisses and singing "happy birthdays". Damn, just look at her!' I suspect he has some emotional issues to sort out.

Though popular culture is perhaps the easiest thing to hate, because we're surrounded by so much of it, it's not the only thing out there attracting anti-fans. Who could go past the **I Hate Mayo** page, which warns that 'mayonnaise, like hollandaise, was invented by the French to cover up the flavour of spoiled flesh, stale vegetables, rotten fish. Beware the sauce! Where food comes beslobbered with an elegant slime you may well suspect the integrity of the basic ingredients.'

School children around the world should draw succour from **The Calculus Hater's Home Page.** Then there's the **Why We Hate Arsenal** site, a thoughtful examination of the question by Tottenham Hotspur fans.

Finally, though I suspect I'm missing whole continents of loathing and disgust by stopping so soon on my search, there is geek hatred. No, not hatred of geeks, hatred by geeks. It's hard to avoid the dozens of twisted, angry **anti-Microsoft** and, to a lesser extent, **anti-Apple** sites out there.

And of course, this being the Web, there is the inevitable **I Hate Frames**, as well as the **I Hate My ISP** site. Oh and let's not forget the short and simple **Why I Hate the Web**, a *Hot Wired* article by Tim Bray, which reminds us what we forgot to hate in the first place.

Please nurse, can I take the silverchair record off now? My temples are throbbing . . .

Web addresses

Tattoos from Soviet Prison Camps
http://ezinfo.ucs.indiana.edu/~birkene/prison.html

I Hate Silverchair
http://www.iap.net.au/~grum/main.html

I Hate 'Alternative' Music
http://www.geocities.com/SunsetStrip/7633/ih8alt.html

I Hate Oasis
http://home.earthlink.net/~Other/

People Against Alanis Morissette's Music
http://www.islandnet.com/~pholden/paamm/original.html

No Yanni Organisation
http://www.peoples.net/~maxs/noyo.html

Official Hootie Sucks Home Page
http://www.olywa.net/junkman/thc/nohootie.html

I Hate the Macarena
http://www.cyberport.com/~carl/hatemac.htm

David Hasselhoff is the Antichrist
http://www.indirect.com/www/warren/baywatch.html

Bert Is Evil
http://fractalcow.com/bert/bert.htm

Sesame Street
http://www.sesamestreet.com

Jihad to Destroy Barney
http://www.ntr.net/~sheridan/jihad/

Marilyn Monroe Hate Page
http://www.africanet.com.br/~nailbomb/mm/

I Hate Mayo
http://www.nomayo.com

The Calculus Hater's Home Page
http://www.psyber.com/~jacob/math/calculus.html

Why We Hate Arsenal
http://www.sys.uea.ac.uk/recreation/sport/thfc/history/odds/arse.html

The Anti-Microsoft Page
http://www.wsu.edu:8000/~tmuller/antims/Anti-MS_homepage.html

Why I Hate Macintosh
http://students.vassar.edu/~alchen/htmls/anti-macintosh.html

I Hate Frames
http://web2.airmail.net/atapaz/www/frames/

I Hate My ISP
http://squashed.roach.org/base/hate.html

Why I Hate the Web
http://www.hotwired.com/wired/3.10/departments/bray.if.html

SEX CRAZY

Sex Chat

SAMANTHA is 32. She lives in France and has what she considers to be a normal job as a financial administrator. From her point of view, she says, she leads a pretty normal life. She's married, has been for a few years. She loves her husband. His bedroom prowess isn't anything to write home about, but the marriage is not exactly in trouble.

Her own sexual resume has been wholly hetero but, she admits, she has occasionally wondered what it would be like to make love to someone of her own sex. She has gone no further than privately discussing with herself the possibility of actually doing it one day, if the right situation arises. But it's not that important, Samantha says. If it happens, it happens.

In conversation, she seems vivacious, honest and refreshingly down to earth, the kind of person you might want to meet. At first contact, there's nothing that would strike you as different about her, that would mark her out in the crowds of people hanging about the thousands of online chat rooms. But if you take the time to get below the surface, you might find out that Samantha has a strange hobby.

She likes to come to the Internet to be raped.

And she's quite happy to admit it, protected, of course, by Net anonymity. How did she arrive at this point? Well, the first time Samantha tried cybersex, she says, somewhere around the middle of 1996, it was really only because she was bored and curious. She recalls feeling totally clueless at first, unsure of what would happen, what she wanted and where she would end up.

'But it was even better than I had imagined,' she insists. 'My first chat was with a girl, and it was fabulous. It was a total surprise. I was dominated and abused . . . and I loved it!

'I've done things here on the Net that I would NEVER do

191

in real life. I never thought I would go as far as I have. I've been pulled by the hair, tied down on a bed, whipped, raped, peed on. I've had every orifice filled at the same time. I've been publicly stripped. I've been treated like a slutty whore . . . '

You can almost hear her shaking her head as she reels off the list. 'You can let your imagination go on the Net,' she says by way of simple explanation for her behaviour. 'Any fantasy is allowed and the thing is, you can do it all safely.' It's no surprise, she says, that people want to use the Net to explore the outer limits of their psyches. If you can keep your head on your shoulders, the risks are low.

What are we talking about when we say cybersex? Well, if you've never visited them, there are chat rooms on and off the Web where people congregate to type messages on the screen to each other, publicly flirting, sparring, teasing. When two people find what they want in an online partner, they generally switch to a private version of the same thing—both type, but they are the only ones who can see the messages.

In this situation, one on one (sometimes one on two—couples often type together), they then construct their fantasies, swapping comments and building their own little virtual worlds, housed entirely within their brains, a shared mental, virtual world. And while they type, they masturbate. It's simple.

So who are they, the tens, perhaps hundreds, of thousands of people doing it right now? A pretty diverse bunch, if my travels through the cyber-swamp are anything to go by. Horny young men and women, single mothers who can't get out of the house much and turn to the computer for companionship, lonely people, bored wives and husbands doing it with and without their partner's permission (and often with each other), kids sneaking in . . .

Some behave as they would in any other social arena. Some pretend to be other people, switching personality and/or

Netscape - [L'Hotel Chat]

File Edit View Go Bookmarks Options Directory Window Help

Location: http://chat.magmacom.com/lhotel/hotel.html

Welcome to the exquisite L'Hotel Chat, a five star hotel located on the coast of Monaco.

Document: Done

gender. Some play-act elaborate scenarios. Some just talk dirty. And some don't even do it at all. Take the case of Nikki, a 30-year-old Texan who likes to watch people dancing the dance in sex chat rooms, but has never felt the urge to join in. 'I like sex like I like basketball,' she says, 'one on one, and very actual, not virtual.' A neat answer to be sure, but when I ask what she's doing hanging around a chat room, she disappears.

Why do sex chatters do what they do? Why is it such a popular pastime? Fortunately the medium being what it is, many people in chat rooms are willing to talk openly about their lives, about the parts of themselves they don't show other people. After all, they can part with their most intimate secrets with complete privacy. They can get as weird as they want.

And they get very weird very quickly. I once met a guy who liked to pretend to be a 78-year-old woman and talk young men into initiating cybersex with him. I'm not sure why he wanted to do that (I'm not sure I even *want to know* why he wanted to do that), but the option was there for him. I have seen people pretending to be everyone from the Devil to Tom Cruise to Othello to Princess Leia (could have been worse, could have been the wookie). I have seen people pretending to be horses, dogs, cats, cartoon characters and inanimate objects.

Obviously, the chance to be someone or something else is a significant part of the appeal. If you listen to those who like to wax philosophical about cyberspace, the implications of this kind of chat are profound. This shape shifting, they say, is our soul breaking free from the prison of the body. They say that the ability to be genderless, bodiless, weightless, defined only by your own imagination, is a form of electronic liberation. They say that the ability to slip the bonds of reality can help us all to learn about ourselves. So it is that gender swapping has been a major part of Net sex from the beginning (see page 202).

Some believe this non-body-defined self is more real anyway. In her book, *Life on the Screen*, Massachusetts Institute of Technology academic Sherry Turkle dismisses the concept of the 'unitary self'. She argues that we are made up of lots of different selves, personae that react to different situations in different ways. Online, our selves are more discrete. We change to suit our surroundings, our gift being able to move between these selves. Some people, of course, do this better than others.

Samantha says her fantasy life is ultimately that and only that. A fantasy. She claims to be able to corral and control her online persona, to keep what happens on the Net from spilling over into reality. She maintains that her Net activities provide a form of release unavailable to her elsewhere. And hurt nobody. And though she has on occasion gone so far that she has scared herself with the violent and explicit nature of the words coming out of her fingers, 'the thing is, I have managed to realise and accept I have such fantasies. I've thought about what happens to me on the Net a lot. Everything I do stays here online. If it has a long term effect, it is only in that I know myself a lot better now. I've had to confront and accept things.'

It's hard to know what to make of Samantha's online experiences. I find it difficult to stop myself being judgmental when confronted with fantasy imagery so bold, so brazen, so ugly. But one of the things you learn if you talk to the people using the Net as a sex aid, is that the machine has a habit of reflecting the user. Net sexuality is fluid, chameleonic, whatever people need it to be at the time. Its manifestations are limited only by the imaginations of those using it. And humans, it has to be said, are bizarre and complex creatures.

Samantha's situation is not, as it turns out, an uncommon one. A lot of people admit to using the safety of the Net to explore the darkened corners of their sexualities. Chrissy, an English university student, has similar fantasies to Samantha: 'I've found that I like to be talked to in explicit terms. I like being degraded, which is something I hadn't delved into in reality.'

Others seem much purer by comparison. Eva is a 21-year-old American student whose boyfriend, Mike, lives hundreds of miles away, at a university in another state. They've been apart for almost a year and meet online every night, mainly because it's so much cheaper than phoning each other.

'This works great when it works,' she says. 'But it's not anywhere near the real thing. I feel sorry for the people who come here just for sex. There's no real togetherness. It's not real—it's a dream world. If you're into fantasies, that's fine. But exploring your fantasies is a healthy part of a real relationship. Here you could think you are making love to a god/goddess and the person in front of the corresponding computer could be the same sex, a real cow, a maniac . . .'

'I'm here because I miss my girlfriend,' says Peter, a German high school student. 'She lives far away right now. I pretend I am with her when I talk to these people. It's all I can do to keep sane from missing her so much, ya' know? I'm a good decent person. Most people that come here are. It's just that we can release a whole different side of ourselves that we don't want society to see . . . we can be what WE want to be . . . and have fun.'

Peter says he masturbates regularly while in chat rooms, but always thinks of his girlfriend while he's doing it. (This is another common cybersex behaviour—people say 'Oh, well, it's not like you're being unfaithful, so it's completely OK.')

'The cybersex can get *really* involved here, almost to the point where you feel you are there. You do have to have an imagination though, a good one.'

'It's odd,' say Mark, an Australian who won't give any details about himself, beyond saying that he has online sex almost every night. 'But when it's really good, it's almost like an out of body experience. It's difficult to come to terms with. You feel like you have to settle back into your body afterwards.'

Samantha says the scariest thing that has happened to her in sex chat rooms was not degradation, but love, an emotion apparently not so easily compartmentalised. It happened once, and strengthened her resolve to keep the real and the virtual rigidly separated.

'I had a kind of a love affair. I fell in love. I really don't want to talk about it. At the time, the feeling was very strong, and it did bridge the gap between dream world and real world. That was really hard—I felt it was almost making me go insane . . .'

This is the point where cybersex gets tricky for some people. Some find their worlds blurring whether they want them to or not. Some, on the other hand, actually want it to happen—they're actively looking for a partner this way. For both camps, cybersex brings with it a lingering question of what comes after, of whether the boundaries between the real and virtual worlds should be broken.

It's very easy to like someone you meet in cyberspace. You don't have to deal with what they look like or their annoying personal habits and mannerisms. You don't have to wake up next to them. It's easy to convince yourself that this character, which is half a conjuration of the other person's mind and half of your own, is actually really interesting.

So many online couples, people who have played with, teased and tweaked each other's Net selves, make the decision to meet up. Even though the odds are stacked heavily against it being a positive experience, they go ahead and do it. Some do it surreptitiously, one on one, and some do it very publicly. Some sex chat rooms even have conventions, where regulars can meet in public, in the safety of numbers, and put faces to the names of people they've been virtually bonking.

For the occasional couple, it has to be admitted, the result is all champagne and roses. The media has been a sucker for Internet marriage stories, regularly trotting out footage of couples who met on the Net and travelled thousands of miles to be together. But for every story of success, there are dozens of others of love gone wrong, sometimes horribly wrong.

'Let's just say I hope he rots in hell,' is Cheryl's response to a request for her to tell the story of the man she flew all the way from the remote Canadian backwoods to Washington to meet, after falling for him in a chat room. 'I kick myself over that meeting every day! What an idiot I was!'

The relationship started off like many. The guy, she says, seemed different to other chatters. He was smart, funny, attentive. He made her feel special. And she had nothing better to do, living in a small town with a shortage of acceptable men.

The Net was her escape into a bigger world, a place with different kinds of people.

Before long, the pair had moved from the chat rooms to the phone. She found out he was more than a decade older, and married. But although a little voice inside her spoke up, she decided to ignore it. She says she was overwhelmed by his attentions. He sent flowers to her work, called her all the time.

'On the day I flew to meet him, I was totally exhausted,' Cheryl recalls. 'My plane was late, so I missed my connection and had to sit in an airport for two hours waiting for another flight. I guess I was nervous more than anything, but I made sure people knew where I would be — I had my bases somewhat covered.

'Truthfully, I had no expectations. It certainly wasn't as though I planned on running away and moving down there to be with him. I mean, we were worlds apart in age and likes and dislikes. I think the main reason I went was . . . loneliness. And just getting too caught up in this world, not leaving it at the computer when I log off. I lost myself and who I was for a while.

'He picked me up at the airport and we drove to the hotel. It was well after midnight. We checked into the room and went to sleep. The next morning was different, but I have to admit the sex was nothing special. The cybersex was better than the real sex. He was very different to the way I had pictured him. There was awkwardness. It just wasn't there, no spark, no nothing.'

They did what most people would do in the circumstances. They had breakfast, spent the day sightseeing, eating and drinking, making polite conversation. He was, Cheryl says, always a perfect gentleman. But she knew she had made a mistake. Not an awful, dangerous mistake, just a sad, stupid one.

'I found myself staring off into space a couple of times when I was with him. He would ask what I was thinking. I said nothing, but all I could think of was cold, cold Canada. We had sex twice and that was it. Basically I couldn't wait until the time came for me to catch my plane home.

'I learned my lesson: don't meet anyone off line again. What really got me was the fact that he didn't have enough guts to tell me he didn't want to talk with me again. He just disappeared. Nothing. It left a real bitter taste. I'm real gun shy right about now. It has even affected me in real life. I look at guys differently now, lump them all together as assholes and jerks. I was burned badly, but I have no one to blame but myself.'

Caroline had a different experience. A woman in her 30s, like Cheryl, from the south of the USA, she has a husband, two children and says she can be found looking for a virtual companion most nights. She didn't fly to meet her cyberlover. She met him in her home town, with the approval of her husband.

'We had started out bantering . . . just talking, then we started seeking each other out when we signed on. We talked about everything and found we never ran out of things to talk about. It came up in conversation that he was going to be in my city for a couple of days on business and we decided to meet.

'I told my husband that I wanted to meet him and he said "Okay" (her husband knows and approves of her online activities — 'he enjoys the benefits', she says) and set up a meeting at a local hangout where a couple of his friends work. He wanted to make sure I would be well looked after. We were both kind of shy, and it was awkward at first, but we sat and talked til 2am . . . it was great . . . we got together two times while he was in town and talked on the phone. Having had cybersex made it awkward for us, and we really wanted to be intimate, but we refrained.'

It sounds harmless enough (odd, but harmless), but things went wrong. What happened to sour the extra-curricular relationship? That age-old problem between the sexes. The guy's wife found out.

Andrew, a middle-aged man from the American midwest, is another who has kept his dalliances from his wife. He is planning to meet his online lover about the time this book comes out, the result of months of planning and talking about it. The father of teenagers says he was 'just looking for excitement' when he found cybersex. His wife, he says is 'a cold person. She doesn't show much emotion. I was looking for some passion.' He claims he can't leave the marriage — he does love his wife, he protests, he just isn't satisfied — and that the outlet the Net provides has, in fact, helped keep him in it. (How's that for a rationalisation!?!)

'Because I feel I've missed something in my life, passion, I've convinced myself that it would be worth the chance to cheat on my wife,' he says. 'I have fallen in love with two women. With my online friend, we started out at the cybersex thing. She was involved with another guy and she was going to meet him. She needed someone to talk to about her concerns and I was a willing ear. We became close friends and now lovers.'

Andrew says he tells the women he meets online everything about his life, the complete truth — 'I feel if we are going to meet then she had better know everything.' If the plan goes ahead, he and his lover will meet in a hotel halfway between their homes, a drive for each of many hundreds of miles.

'I can't wait,' he says. 'If I could, I'd do it tomorrow. I have worries and concerns, sure. But I'm not so much scared — more like nervous. I think I can take care of the wife thing. I'm worried about her finding out, but I think I can fix that. I want this to change my life. I want some excitement.

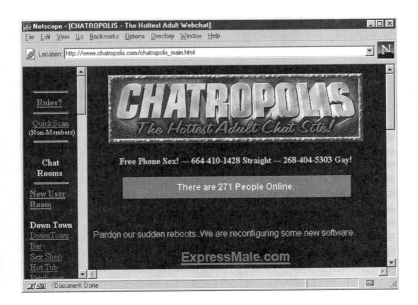

'I know I can't leave my wife. My lover is single and I would like her to find happiness in real life too. I know I can't give her that. I want to make her happy as long as I can, but I want her to get married and have a family. That would make me even happier. My dream for her is that she falls in love with a real man and dumps me on my ass. For me, it's just love and passion for as long as I can have it.'

Phew! On the whole, it's clear that relationships are hard enough in real life, without bringing machines into the bargain. But we don't learn much as animals, individually or collectively. And not only are we doomed to repeat our mistakes as a species, we're also in the process of creating a whole new arena to make new mistakes in. So if you're looking for a job that will get you through to retirement, set yourself up as a cybertherapist. There's about to be a lot of work coming your way.

Gender Swapping

On the Internet, the old joke goes, no-one knows you're a dog. We are all anonymous online, disembodied voices wrapped in whatever personalities we choose. There are no rules to follow in the creation of our virtual personae, no boundaries or restrictions. We can be anything or anyone we want. We can ask to be treated on whatever term we devise. Today, my terms are simple. I am Jenny. I am 26. And lordy, I am woman.

This morning, I woke up male. I'm kind of used to that, so it didn't faze me. And that somewhere between breakfast and now, as I stepped from the real world into the virtual one, my sex changed. I just reached into my brain file, clicked on the folder marked 'Underwear Contents' and reconfigured myself. Easy as that. Now I'm a card-carrying oestrogen supply. Because today, I want to know how the other half lives. And how it feels to have virtual breasts.

Let me introduce myself. I work in television publicity ('I hate actors'), I have dark brown hair, cut to a length that rests on my shoulders, and green eyes ('Some people think they're contacts'). I'm 5'7", and weight 125lbs (do the metric yourself). I live in a house I'm paying off on Sydney's northern beaches, alone except for my two Weimeraners, Jana and Ray.

I think I look a little like Elaine from *Seinfeld*, but really, I don't. I was a gym junkie a few years ago, but now think a long walk and a good diet is a better option. I had my navel pierced on a drunken weekend in 1995 but took it out because all my clothes rubbed against it. I drive a sporty little red Mazda but want to move up to a Peugeot cabriolet. I voted Liberal in the last election—I can't remember why—and now regret it . . . sorry, I'll get on with it, shall I?

I'm the kind of girl I would accidentally date and then wonder, just before the main course arrived, how I got myself into this mess. Anyway, my first port of call as Jenny (26) is 'the exquisite **L'Hotel Chat**, a five-star hotel located on the coast of Monaco. All guests have complete access to any of our following facilities: the conference room (The Dialogue), the ballroom (The Couplet) and the library (The Articulate). Enjoy fine dining at our hotel restaurant — The Chatter. Relax in our hot tub — The Gossip, or meet some new people in our singles bar — The Babble (Join us for cocktails during happy hour!). End your evening in our deluxe Penthouse Suite. When you are tired of our public facilities, book one of our Private Suites.'

Ignoring the fact that 'Articulate' doesn't really work as this kind of noun, I head into the 'library' room on this chat site, thinking it might be a more decorous place to start, a kind of wading pool — surely the inhabitants will be more couth than the usual parade of testosterone abusers that I have been warned about by everyone I have told of my plan. I decide to just sit quietly in the background, humming to myself and watching the parade. There are about 20 people with me in the room, some silent (or privately conversing), the rest babbling furiously about the usual concerns of cyberchat (Who are you? What are you? Where are you from? Would you care to relieve my tension?).

I'm quiet for a couple of reasons. First, I want to time how long it takes for a rogue male to make its move. The mythology of chat is well known (and true). If you're a woman online, you are constantly harassed by the moth males, drawn to your light and determined to batter themselves against it. Sometimes it's a little gentle fluttering here and there. Other times, you have to call the exterminators. Whatever, for many women, the hardest part of finding a cybersex offer is actually just turning up.

Surprisingly, it takes six minutes (none of my other forays will go for more than a minute without me being hit on). Some guy using the name «_¤Äñâ®©h¥ Äñgê£™¤_» (if you look

closely, it says Anarchy Angel, and maybe it's his real name—
maybe his parents loathed him on sight) finally pipes up, 'Hello,
Jenny. Do you want to chat?'

No, I respond, I'm feeling a little quiet today and I just
want to sit here for a while. He goes away. The other reason
for my need for a little peace is that I'm still trying on my new
personality, feeling my way around it. It's like a piece of baggy
clothing—I'm not quite sure where it fits and where it doesn't
and what it looks like to anyone else. So for the moment, just
sitting here is enough. I'm acclimatising—I have this strange
feeling that if I enter conversation, I'll give myself away. A
little later on, I see that «_¤Äñâ®©h¥ Äñgê£™¤_» has revealed
to someone else that he is 13. Though I haven't actually
resolved what I'll do if somebody does attempt to seduce me,
I'm relieved I didn't bite.

A few minutes later, someone calling him or herself Instant
Karma offers an 'Alo!'. I type back 'Hello', well okay, I type
back 'Bonjour', because I'm thinking that no self-respecting,
hormone-fuelled guy would use a pretentious French saluta-
tion. I figure it'll help my cover. I hate myself instantly for
being so obvious in trying not to be obvious. This is more
evidence of how paranoid I am about being caught.

His response? 'Aha! Bonjour! Ca Va, Madame? Where you
from? Quebec? Or France?'

Bastard. I am forced to concede that I don't actually speak
French and am from Sydney, Australia.

'I am from Rotterdam Holland!' he writes. 'Ever been here,
or have plans to?'

'I haven't been there, sorry. Is it a nice place?'

While I await his reply, someone called 'Anonymous' posts
a private message to me: 'Care to chat w.28, male from Ca,
L.A (Frank)?'

'Frank,' I reply ingenuously (I have made a decision to go

with this as a plan of attack—play the unfamiliar innocent), 'I don't know. What did you want to chat about?' He says we can talk about whatever I'd like, though really, I would have preferred he offered a suggestion. Imagine someone walking up to you at a party and saying 'Hi. I'll talk about whatever you want.' You'd be back at home on your couch, alone, in seconds. I restrain myself and just play dumb again, telling him I'm new at this and not sure.

Instant Karma reappears to tell me that Holland is not as big as 'down under' (and folks, using that phrase kills his chances right there). He says it is very crowded and very regulated. 'You will like it here, because if you travel a lot you can see very much here. In three hours, you can travel from the north to the south! Paris is four hours driving, and London one hour by plane or five hours by car!'

Oh-oh, travel nerd alert! I realise I'm bored with this guy and want him to go away. My God, I'm turning into a bitch already. The power of being in demand is going to my head, making me cool, aloof, distant . . . no, I was all those things before.

Frank/Anonymous messages again, enclosing his CV: '28, 5'6", 125 lbs, blk hair, brn eyes, in school part-time, major C.P.A., minor in accounting, work full-time at financial institutes (bank, FCU) as collateral analyst.'

Great, I'm being cruised by a guy who is shorter than me, lighter than me, and an accountant. Here is a man who is obviously not using the Net to indulge his fantasy version of himself, unless he's kinkier than I suspect. For this, I guess I should be grateful. But I'm not. Let's face it, a sexy picture is not emerging. If I were him, I'd be a dog. I like dogs. A dog would stand a better chance.

Before I can reply (I figure it's only fair to follow through with the formalities and give him my basic stats ('28, 5'7" blah

blah blah' in return), he whispers 'Would you rather chat on the phone?' I reel off the self-description and tell him that, as I live in Australia, I suspect he wouldn't want the phone bills.

'You are 28,' he says, 'and it's about time that I meet someone my own age.'

Damn! I've typed my age in wrong. I hurriedly type back, telling him I made a mistake, a slip of the finger, that I'm 26. He hasn't even noticed.

'I love your eyes,' he says. Hmmmm. I stare at the screen for a while before deciding that there's no possible response to that.

He asks what I do for fun. Still playing it straight, I tell him I go out a lot because of my job. I like to see as much music as I can. And I like good food. And reading. He says he loves sports, football particularly, reading at the beach and taking long walks (I love the way his words sound like those descriptions of hobbies and interests that you find on the back of Playboy centrefolds).

He then asks what I look for in a guy and I reluctantly tell him brains and someone who'll make me laugh. I can feel the whole thing petering out. I'm typing slowly, not flirting hard enough. I'm starting to wonder if there's somewhere else I should be, if this isn't exactly like every other party I've been to in my life, going nowhere fast.

'I am not that smart,' he posts, playing for sympathy, 'so I am out of the question.'

'Okay then,' I reply icily, spotting my chance, 'have a nice life.' But it's not enough of a hint.

'I want to get to know you,' Anonymous/Frank says.

'Why?'

'No answer. What I get instead is a proposition. 'Care to have candle dinner by the beach with me and chat?' Much as I think a little wax is an integral part of a healthy diet, I decline.

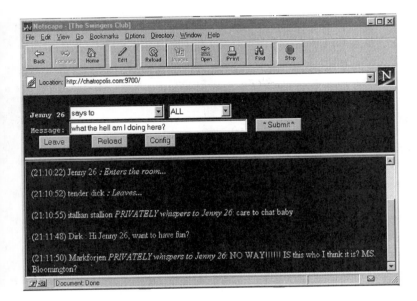

'Have you been to the USA?' he persists. 'And if you ever do, don't forget to look me up.'

'Yes,' I make the mistake of telling him. 'I visit the USA every year. I'll be there in summer.'

'Do you want to have dinner with me when you get here? When will you get here so I can make reservation right now?'

'You don't even know me!!! Why on Earth would we have dinner?!?!? This is getting a little too weird for me. See you later.' . . .

I hit the exit button and slump back in the chair. I'm sure he was harmless, but I find the note of desperation in his typing sad and upsetting. I'm thinking 'Hello stalker'.

Later in the day I try another chat venue, **Chatropolis**, a place which boasts more than 300,000 users a month, congregating in more than a dozen virtual spaces. Instead of choosing a room from the menu, I hit the 'Quick Login' button to let the site choose which of its rooms it wants to hurl me into.

I find myself in the Blue Oyster Bar, a lesbian hangout, surrounded by names like Amanda bi/f and Kinky Lez. Hmmm, I'm not quite sure this is where I'd been thinking of going with this experiment, but in for a penny . . .

It's a peculiar feeling to find yourself chatting to/up a member of the opposite sex who is under the impression that you are one of her own. I had been planning to look at male behaviour, but this is just as interesting. And more dangerous. Will they pick me? Will I be tarred and feathered? I get nervous again.

I shouldn't have. It was a pretty safe bet that boys would be so lust-crazed you could pretend to be anything ('Hi, I'm a donut!') and keep their attention online. But surprisingly, the same can be said of the girls too. Unless, of course, they were all just boys pretending to be girls . . .

It takes no longer for me to be hit on here than anywhere else. Lynn tries to grab my attention, but Veronica sends me a quite message: 'I started with her and all she could say was "OOOOOhhhhh baby you know what I like?" You've been warned.'

I think about the subtext of the message. Oh right, so he/she's male! I thank Veronica for the inside line on what is going on in here. 'I strongly suspect a bunch of high school boys laughing,' she says.

'Yeah, you're probably right,' I say back. 'Mind you, I've been a boy a few times in other rooms!!!!'

'Pretty grim being a boy, isn't it?' she responds. 'I tried it once, to find out if it was easy for guys to find a girl to fuck. It wasn't.'

Wow, I'm generating sisterhood! We're bonding! This is working! Then my browser crashes.

Later, I try again, logging in at random to Chatropolis's Hot Tub Club. It takes less than 20 seconds before the first 'wanna chat?' enquiries roll in. Feeling like a cocky old hand, I decide to play hard to get. In the course of half an hour, 24 male names run their pickup lines by me. None of them are even slightly convincing. I am, as usual, embarrassed by my gender—men are a tragic joke.

Someone called Minotaur leans over and whispers hello. 'Hello ancient dead mythological beast,' I reply. Oddly, conversation fails to develop.

After a while, bolstered by my experiences in the Blue Oyster Room, I try to chat up a woman called Lizzie. She tells me that she usually likes the bondage rooms, but can't find any takers today. She's a dominant, but will also be a submissive if the occasion demands. She says she's bisexual, on and offline. She's a 24-year-old redhead, a 'voluptuous 38dd who radiates sensuality'.

'In real life, I like tall, black-haired, pale-skinned, smart women. I like to be spanked and I have a serious vampire fantasy. Vampires are beautiful and they are very romantic. They represent the absolute loving of another individual in pain and pleasure, death and life. They're very sensual and erotic. They only take blood if both parties are interested and have to be together for a very long time, mated.'

Hmmm, is that the kettle I hear boiling?

I switch to another room, where I am cruised by six people in less than a minute, three female and three male. A woman named Jody whispers sweet nothings in my ear. I tell her I'm new at this.

'I always have a good time here,' she says. 'It's like my own little fantasy world. Just be yourself—that's the great thing about this place. You don't have to pretend. Just be real. I'm 33, married and bisexual. I've never been with another woman yet, except here in my fantasies. Have you?'

I'm considering my answer to this when Jody suddenly

moves up a gear, describing what she would be doing to me if we were alone in a room together. And we are right here in her fantasies. It begins with a slow dance but goes much further very quickly. Her hands are on my back, moving underneath the fabric of my shirt, tracing paths along my skin. She is telling me about her hot breath on my neck, her lips trailing along my collarbone, her body pressing against mine. I can, she says, feel the swelling warmth of her breasts against me. Her hands continue to move, down towards parts of me that don't even exist.

And you know what? I just can't go along with it. It's not that I don't find the idea of lesbian sex mildly arousing—as long as I'm one of the lesbians. It's just that I can't lie about something so intimate. It doesn't seem fair to the other person—not that they'd care. Really, it all gets too confusing. And too difficult. I decide to just go back to my old life of being a man pretending to be woman pretending to be a man. Things were a lot simpler then.

Web addresses

L'Hotel Chat
http://chat.magmacom.com/lhotel/hotel.html

Chatropolis
http://wwww.chatropolis.com

Live . . . Nude . . . Teleconferencing

WORDS are like children. Many of them seem really well-behaved on their own, stern, proper, noble even, but when you put them with their friends, they can become completely giggly and silly. It is easy to take three perfectly decent, well-meaning words, do nothing more than place them side by side, and make something very, very stupid. And no further proof of this is needed than an example recently thrown up by the Web: 'live . . . nude . . . teleconferencing'.

Yes, out there in Net land, there are people who are ready, willing and able to pay for the privilege of connecting their computer to another and watching a young man or (more often) woman take his or her clothes off. Welcome to the Internet peep show.

Why? Because the technology allows it. 'Follow the money' was the advice that Deep Throat offered to Woodward and Bernstein as they tracked the story that would become known as Watergate. Anyone wishing to find out what is really happening on the Web would be well advised to 'Follow the porn'. After all, pornographers have always been quick on the technological uptake.

'All successful technologies have passed through the pornography phase,' notes Paul Saffo of the Institute for the Future in California. 'The startled Japanese found out only blue movies could sell VCRs. And movies also went through this stage at the turn of the century.'

One of the pioneering cinematic efforts was a risqué flick called *The Kiss*. Erotic photos date from the earliest days of the camera. And as soon as telecommunications companies introduced 0055 numbers, we all know what use they were put to.

So it comes as no surprise that porn pedlars are at the cutting edge of Web development. Porn sites are the Web's best model of economic success—the bigger ones have development money to burn. And their competitive industry is driven by the excitement of the new—as the 3D Web becomes more of a reality, you can bet it will be the porn sites making the first use of it.

For now, the live video connection is about as far out as it gets. Cyber strip shows are taking place in virtual red light clubs all over—many are open 24 hours. The modus operandi is consistent. You get a few minutes of free chatting and then you pay through the nose, usually around US$6 per minute. Some places even have the CUSeeMe option—so the stripper can watch you at the same time (they don't pay).

Of course, I had to give this a go. I assuaged what little conscience I have left by reassuring myself I was doing it on your behalf (yeah, right), just an observer out there taking notes and trusting in prudence. It would be another day at the office. And speaking of the office, wouldn't it be worth it just to see the faces of the bean counters when I wrote 'live nude teleconferencing' on my tax return. So here's my experience . . .

Venturing into the club, I hand over my credit card information, wait for it to be checked, and then find myself offered a choice of 'models' (no photos), with short descriptions of the assets of each.

I click on my choice and wait as the model is ushered into the studio. A frame comes up with a black video screen on the left and a chat box on the right. 'Model enters', it says in the box.

I am asked for the last four digits of my credit card number as confirmation. The first time I send the information, nothing happens. The screen reloads itself every few seconds, but always comes up black. The second time, bingo, I get a picture, and there is my new best friend, happy as hell to see me judging by her grin. The 'model', who we will call Claudia (or Naomi

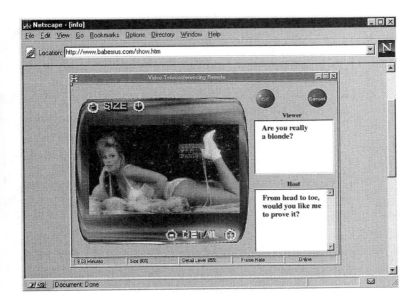

or Linda or Elle, depending on how it looks in the sentence), is a woman in her 20s with long, strawberry blonde hair and black, lacy lingerie.

I had been betting that, given the cost of connection, Linda would be wearing overalls and a parka, or something with 29 buttons, anything that would eat up time (and my money) as it came off. I also figured she would type . . . like . . . this, . . . that . . . is . . . to . . . say, . . . a-m-a-z-i-n-g-l-y . . . slowly . . .

'Hi, can you see me?' she types in breezily, and I answer in the affirmative.

'What's your name?' is her next question, but just as I'm about to type 'John Howard, Prime Minister of Australia' (I was dreaming that her response would be 'Oh, not you again Johnny, you naughty monkey!'), my browser crashes.

I try again, figuring third time lucky. The screen works. I can see a large bed behind Elle with a blue bedspread and a wooden bedhead. I'm meant to be thinking I have just stumbled into her boudoir, but it just looks like a studio—no windows, no bedside tables, no clothes strewn haphazardly, nothing visible but the model, the bed and the computer chair in the foreground.

Claudia is sitting on the chair, smiling as she types—this girl has skills. Her main one appears to be that she can smile while doing anything. It's obviously part of the job description, but after a very short while it looks less like good humour and more like rictus, like the Joker in *Batman*.

'Where are you?' Linda asks. 'Sydney, Australia' I type back, but before I can send my answer, she has leapt out of the chair and is twirling around the room. I realise after a while that this bizarre, inexplicable behaviour is meant to be some form of exotic dancing, but given that the browser is only refreshing itself at a rate of about one frame every three seconds, it's disjointed enough to just look odd—not exactly video as promised.

'I'M IN CHICAGO, ILLINOIS' Naomi types in capitals and I don't know if that's her loud voice or if she's left the Caps Lock button down accidentally. Then she is out of the chair, smiling and dancing again. Maybe the chair is not that comfortable—should she try something more ergonomic?

'Is it weird performing for a camera?' I ask.

'No,' Elle types quickly, 'do you think it would be weird?'

'Not necessarily. I was just wondering how it is for you.'

I sense I'm not really going to get an answer, and I don't.

'What do you do for a living?' she asks. I notice that every time Claudia sits down to type, the tip of her tongue pokes gingerly out between her lips.

'I write.'

'And do you like your work?'

'I love it,' I type. 'And you?'

'I love my work. I get to meet a lot of interesting people

[even though we must all look the same to her, just lenses that pass in the night] and hear their fantasies.'

'And what do most people want from you?' I ask, again not really expecting an answer.

'Your free time is up now,' comes the reply. 'What are your fantasies?'

I don't have the heart to tell her that most of them involve sleep and two consecutive days off work, so I offer something that seems harmless enough.

'Well, I guess I should start by asking you to take some things off.'

This gets a good response. I feel I have stopped confusing her and put her back on track. She smiles, pirouettes and delivers what might have been a coquettish wiggle of the hips, but I only saw frozen frame bits of it, so it's hard to tell.

The negligee comes off. I'm not sure if it went over her head or was dropped, I couldn't quite tell from the frame sequence. She stands in bra, panties and stockings. Suddenly, she's at the other end of the room, on the bed on all fours, pushing her hair back and showing me her teeth again.

I feel like I ought to be doing something. Linda's obviously just killing time.

'Umm, take your stockings off please.'

She obliges, dragging them slowly (four frames per leg) across her thigh before discarding them. And it is clear that she is playing for time again. The Web might be the only sexual arena in which time really is of the essence—a premature ejaculation problem would be to your financial benefit here.

Elle blows me a kiss. She sits on the chair and spins around. It's eerily like watching a four-year-old playing (psychologists, feel free to read whatever you want into that).

'Thank you,' I say. My mother taught me that if you don't have anything meaningful to say, at least be polite.

'You're welcome,' comes back.

I wait to get a sense of what's next, but again, there are no clues from her behaviour. This, it seems to me, could go on for longer than the Cold War. Oh dammit!

'Now take the rest off please.'

Almost to my surprise, Naomi obliges, then does one of those will-I-won't-I dances, covering her privates with her hands and forearms. If I am meant to be excited, I have somehow resisted it.

Elle's heading back over to the keyboard to read what I have just typed in ('And what do most people ask you to do now?') when my browser crashes again.

Obviously, it just couldn't contain itself any longer. The excitement was too much. I think about trying for a fourth time, but what would be the point? I got the drift.

The whole thing has taken about twelve minutes. I have just spent $60. I could have seen the same thing in the flesh at my local strip club for half the price. I could have bought it in a newsagent for a quarter of the price.

But I have done it on the Net, at the cutting edge of technological culture, for a whopping great fee, with little success. And yes, there is still one of us born every minute.

Web address

Porn sites move around a fair bit. Go to a search engine like **Yahoo** or **AltaVista** (those addresses, again, are **http://www.yahoo.com** and **http://www.altavista.digital.com**) and type in 'live nude teleconferencing'.

Flashers

The following is a public service announcement. Girls, next time you take the **Splash Mountain** ride at Disneyland, think twice about doing the big drop topless. Be careful too, when letting your boyfriend sit behind you. A lot of blokes seem to think it's pretty damn funny to lean around and pull up your t-shirt and bra, exposing your breasts to the elements on the wild and wet way down.

How do I know? Well, in case you hadn't noticed, there's a camera positioned opposite the Mountain slope, which records for posterity the joy and exhilaration of those on the ride. It also records the nudity. And a dozen of those revealing photos have been lovingly mounted on the Web for the amusement and arousal of the rest of us. Check 'em out—those nipples could be yours.

The Splash Mountain pictures are only a small part of **Look at Me**, a Web site devoted to flashing and flashers. Not dirty-old-men-in-long-socks-grubby-raincoat-style flashing, but young, lithe (mostly) women downing togs and taking on the world in the same condition that they entered it. There are 20 collections of photos available at the site, each with up to a dozen examples of the activity. Venues for these public displays include the beach, city streets, roadside verges, boats, cars and parks. It's all good, clean, full frontal fun, ordinary folks getting their kit off and breaking minor laws. Nothing you probably don't do yourself on a Saturday afternoon.

The flashers are colonising cyberspace. Just the other day I was actually flashed on the Net. There I was, minding my own business in a chat room, when a woman dropped by, introduced herself as Pauline and, before I could even type back a quick 'Hi', said 'This is me' and promptly posted a

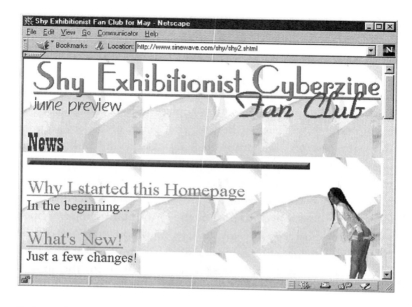

Polaroid of herself in the buff. Now there's a way to meet people. It sure beats handing out business cards.

Exhibitionism is a subsection of the enormous boom in amateur pornography online. The nature of the Web allows anyone to put up their own home page, anyone to publish their own words and anyone to make pictures of themselves, *sans underwear*, available on the online world. It's an exhibitionist's paradise. The vast bulk of amateur porn stars make their contributions in the comfort of their own homes but some, a more playful minority, like to do it in the open air and, preferably, with surprised flashes nearby.

The **Shy Exhibitionist**, otherwise known as Kris, is an American woman who has started a cyberzine of her own, dedicated to her exhibitionist exploits. Each week she heads out to a new location, with a new outfit and a photographer, to capture herself showing the world a little more than the world asked for that day.

Before the Internet came along, she used to wear the kinds of outfits that would give men 'accidental' peeks at her under-wear-free bod when she bent down at the supermarket. Cheeky, enjoyable, but not really serious, nothing more than an occasional thrill for herself and perhaps the object of her attentions. Then she tried posting a few pictures of herself, nothing 'too revealing' to the **alt.sex.exhibitionist** news group.

'The responses were all great! They gave me the courage and confidence to become even bolder. I started posting the stories and pictures of my escapades. I was also discovering something about myself. I really enjoy exposing myself. Much more than just a sneak peek at the grocery store.'

Kris continued to post pictures, getting more daring each time, but when the anonymous remailing service anon.penet.fi shut down, she was deprived of the anonymity that had made it an easy decision for her. Then, she found her pictures for sale at a Web site. So, in the end, she decided that the best thing to do would be to abandon her anonymity and build her own site, continuing her expeditions on a more professional and predictable basis. Now she publishes monthly updates, with photo spreads and explanations of how they happened.

Shelley, a strawberry-blonde from Texas, has taken things further. In her late twenties and, by her own admission, 'noth-ing special' in the bod department, she began experimenting with clothes-free photography in 1994, while living on her University campus. Her boyfriend took the snaps and, a few days later, posted the results in the **alt.binaries.pictures.erotica** newsgroup. Although she was pissed off that he hadn't asked her permission, she was more excited by the hundreds of e-mail responses that came in after the posting.

Three years later, she also maintains a Web site about her activities and, like Kris, has become more adventurous over time. The site archives photographs in series, including those

from her Caribbean honeymoon and a trip to Iceland (brrrr, chilly). There is even a Valentine's day set. Shelly also sells her own nude-in-public calendars through the site—the 1997 calendar, Sights from Texas, features the gal nekkid in front of various Texas landmarks.

Carol Cox, otherwise known as **Wild Rose**, maintains an Amateur Flashers Page as part of her larger, more catholic site. This Canadian mother of three describes herself as, among other things, a sex addict, and maintains a site of pretty hardcore content. (You have been warned.) The exhibitionist page is its mildest section and boasts pictures that other amateurs have sent to her for display. Both men and women take part and she encourages anyone who'd like to be hung in her gallery, so to speak, to send her their best snaps.

Another Web streaker is **Taylor** (she's kidding herself if she expects us to believe those are real). Taylor wanted to be a model but only just scraped over the five foot mark. She lives in California, 'with my four dogs and four cats, whom I love very much. My measurements are 36D–22–34. I was born in San Diego, CA, November 1970. That makes me a Scorpio, so you'd better watch out!!!!! My favourite colour is green but my favourite jewel is the sapphire. I enjoy reading romance novels and I love the true story murder-mystery books.'

She also loves to pose in the raw, or in as little clothing as possible. Her site has plenty of nudity in the great outdoors, with her photo shoots taking place in parks, by lakes and even while she's rollerblading. But, as you look closer, you see that her exhibitionist credentials are not what they seem. Sure, there's a fair bit of the outdoors in the photography, but there ain't a lot of flashing. She's doing it for the camera, but not for an audience.

And beyond that, the big letdown about the site is that, unlike others already mentioned, it's a tease. There's a lot of promising, but little actual nudity on offer, unless you fork out for a private membership. Where's the spirit of fun and adventure in that? There are plenty of other places that are also determined to open your wallet, such as those run by **Risque Renee** and **Lorie**.

Some nude Webbers want money. Some just want to have fun (crazy kids). But what most seem to want is attention. Many of these women say it makes them feel sexy to read the lusty howls of approval that flood in via e-mail. Many say it makes them feel powerful, gives them more confidence.

From the other side of the screen, the interesting thing about the phenomenon is that the success of amateur porn and flashing sites on the Web might say something about changing tastes. What the user sees is the girl next door, an ordinary woman disrobing. In the age of the supermodel, that kind of fantasy appears to be increasingly attractive for some men, those who see little point in lusting after Tyra Banks or Claudia Schiffer—the kind of fantasy that is unattainable.

Unfortunately for male exhibitionists, women have yet to follow (birthday) suit. Male flashing sites on the Web are few, perhaps because for me, flashing doesn't achieve the same responses. **Topbit's Exhibitions and Dares** site includes an essay on the key question: 'Are male exhibitionists kidding themselves?' Answer: Pretty much.

This 'trainee male exhibitionist/darer' doesn't include pictures on his site, because his ISP has made it clear that it's a no-no. 'I've long enjoyed simple nudity and fantasies of more complex dares,' he explains. 'In 1997 I've resolved to act on all of those fantasies and wishes.' His site is made up of exhibitionist stories (fact and fiction appear to mingle freely) from contributors, as well as information on exhibitionism and articles about the hobby.

And a link to the **Naked Mile Home Page**, the official site for the annual University of Michigan tradition, in which hundreds of people, mostly final year students, discard their wardrobes and run in celebration of the final day of classes. Check out the video footage. Coming soon: University of Michigan students attend Spring break at Disneyland!

Web addresses

Splash Mountain
http://www.gate.net/~defiant/Splash_Mountain.html

Look At Me
http://www.gate.net/~defiant/Warning.html

Amateur Index
http://www.amateurindex.com

The Shy Exhibitionist
http://www.SineWave.com/shy/

Shelley
http://www2.cy-net/~digitrix/

Wild Rose
http://www.carolcox.com/pictures/flasher.html

Taylor
http://qstart.com/taylor

Risque Renee
http://www.risquerenee.inter.net

Lorie
www.gentlement.com

Topbit's Exhibitions and Dares
http://www.geocities.com/WestHollywood/6027/exhibitionism.html#topbit

Naked Mile
http://www.angelfire.com/mi/nmile/

Bizarre Fetishes

SO anyway, I forget what I was looking for exactly—searching the Net is often like that—but one afternoon not so long ago, I stumbled across a site called **Whip Art**. The title offered the imagination a number of curious possibilities, so I clicked my way in to see what was happening.

Whip Art, it turns out, is a lesser known (the National Gallery has yet to mount an exhibition) field of the arts, in which the masochistic human being is the canvas, the whip (the bullwhip or the cat o' nine tails) is the paintbrush, and the sadist is the artist dreaming of a government grant.

If art, as it has been said, comes from suffering, this must be genius. Our Whip Art site host is a 50-year-old electronics specialist by the name of ZeroTSM. He uses the site to talk us through his first bullwhip art experience (with colour photographs).

'Although it is more traditional to receive a whipping standing up,' he writes, 'the artist said that he had more control if the "canvas" was horizontal, so I laid down on a table. Since it was my first session, we decided to try some strokes across the butt with my pants on to see if I could handle the pain. That was "nothing", so then we tried a few "light ones" across my bare back. I was quite surprised at how little those hurt . . . I got off the table and everyone was admiring the art. One artist in particular noted that I had a very nice back for whip art, and (said he) would like to "paint" me once the existing art had faded.'

Hmmm, remind me not to ask these guys to do my portrait when I'm elected President. My brush (sorry) with the weird obsessiveness of Whip Art took me back to a place I first found a couple of years ago, the **Long Hair Site**. This site, run from Belgium by a 31-year-old electrical engineer (is there a pattern forming here?) called Frank Ploenissen, presents pictures of fully clothed women with waist-length hair. Such has been its success that he is now selling some of his archive on CD-ROM. There is also a **men's version** of the site.

'I believe that I have loved long hair on ladies since I was a child,' Ploenissen explains. 'That time it was just wonderful when the hair of my neighbour's female playmate flew around and accidentally touched my face. Today, long hair is an erotic desire for me . . . Be informed that I am not planning to make this site an erotic site by publishing naked girls. My intention is to give those of you who adore long female hair the possibility to enjoy its erotic beauty without the need of nakedness.'

People, as some loser called Jim Morrison once noted, are strange. And though I know that some find this kind of stuff offensive, it doesn't so much upset me as pique my curiosity. I reckon folks should be allowed to enjoy what they want with other consenting adults, no matter how stupid or inane, as long as it's in private and doesn't require the services of the ambulance or fire brigade. And as long as it doesn't involve me.

If the Net is home to this kind of obscure fetish, I wondered, what else is out there? How polymorphously perverse does it get? The **World Fetish Center Home Page** wasn't much use — it's just the usual latex/rubber/bondage/discipline shtick (sigh, any old fetishist can get into that stuff). Similarly, **Mrs Silk's Magazine for Cross Dressers** was pretty much as expected.

It was clear that I was going to have to move out of the fetish mainstream, away from the maze of piercing, probing and posing, if I was going to find anything really out of the ordinary. Like its hair-oriented cousin, **Nails, Talons and Claws** is a site dedicated to length (size is everything). Its specialty is pictures of women with ludicrously long fingernails, the kind you see in old Asian films and *Nightmare on Elm Street*. The site is bursting with photo and video offers (get your

X-rated long fingernail clips now) as well as extensive and involved arguments about the virtues of real versus artificial.

That was interesting, but I didn't really hit weird paydirt though until I came across **Messy Fun**, the Web site of a company started in 1991 to fill what it thought was a void in the market: the lack of wet and messy erotica. 'We specialise in beautiful girls — most with very long hair — frolicking in mud, food, and paint; and in wet clothing (wetlook). We celebrate the fact that a coating of goo is very erotic both to look at and to participate in.'

Fans can subscribe to the Messy newsletter, buy copies of videos and photo sessions, or just peruse pictures on the site, arranged in handy categories such as: 'Gorgeous Ladies in Mud!', 'Messy Misses in Glop! (Food, Paint)' and 'Glistening Gals! (Wetlook)'.

This I had to see. In Messy Misses, the captions more than tell the story: 'The quintessential cheerleader, Beautiful Blonde Daizy, relaxes full length in the luxurious chocolate bath.' Look around and you'll find shaving cream, pie and green paint fun. Switching to the wetlook section, I learned that water, of course, is never enough. There was model Kassandra, in thigh-length boots and leather outfit, reclining in '24 gallons of corn syrup'. Elsewhere, gelatine is a pretty common accessory. The mud lovers section offered the biggest treat though — photographs of a mud wedding, no doubt between a pair of consenting mudults.

On a much cleaner footing, **Heliophobe** is soft core Goth porn, a magazine and Web site devoted to the glorification of pale-skinned women. 'Each issue,' it says, 'contains how-to advice on avoiding sunlight, beauty tips on accentuating paleness, and notices honouring albinism.' Here were people who would find street mimes a turn on. Now, I thought to myself, I've seen everything.

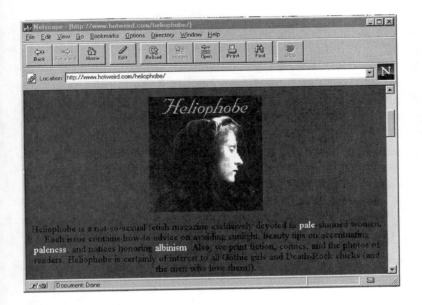

Heliophobe is a not-so-sexual fetish magazine exclusively devoted to **pale-skinned women**. Each issue contains how-to advice on avoiding sunlight, beauty tips on accentuating **paleness** and notices honoring **albinism** Also, we print fiction, comics, and the photos of readers. Heliophobe is certainly of interest to all Gothic girls and Death-Rock chicks (and the men who love them!).

Tom's Adult Tickling Site is for folks who like to get jolly while they're getting their jollies. Really, it's just a gallery of pictures of Tom's wife's feet, as well as links to a surprisingly large number of other tickling sites, and those dedicated to the tickling accoutrements, such as the human foot. **Celebrity Bare Feet** 'is dedicated to celebrity feet and celebrity tickling' and features shots of famous folk like Sandra Bullock, Courteney Cox and Elle McPherson *sans chaussures*. A more general appreciation of foot loving can be found at **Foot World**, with live foot chat and multiple photo galleries.

There are admiration societies for other parts of the body too, most notably including **The Stomach and Bellybutton Page**. There was an Underarm Home Page, but it closed down.

If you fancy your feet clothed, try **Terri's Shoe Page**, where she of the title updates regular photos of herself from the shin down, in various poses, with various pumps, sneakers and slingbacks. Terri is a below-the-knee exhibitionist ('American size 10, English size 8, European size 41') who just wants to show off. An even better version of this comes from **Frieda and Guido's Interactive Underwear** page. If you send them underwear ('Frieda's a 32C with a size 4 panty, and Guido cuts quite a figure with his 34" waist'), they will put it on, photograph themselves and post the results on their Web site.

More concerned with the other end of the body, **Smoke and Glamour** is one of a sizeable number of sites dedicated to the association of tobacco with sex. It keeps files of photos of women with cigars, celebrities taking a quick puff (Anne Archer, Glenn Close, Julia Louis-Dreyfuss, Helen Hunt and Gillian Anderson, among others) and even has an amateur section open to all us non-professional smokers (actually, I've never been a smoker, but gee whiz, if it's good enough for Gillian Anderson . . .).

Many of the sites devoted to these obscure peccadilloes are inspired by activity in the Usenet newsgroups. There are dozens of **alt.sex** and **alt.sex.fetish** discussion groups, ranging from **alt.sex.fetish.feet** (the obvious) to **alt.sex.fetish.giants** (return-to-the-womb fantasy of sex with incredibly large women) to **alt.sex.fetish.robots** (sex with plastic people, mannequins or robots) and **alt.sex.aliens** ('I wasn't just abducted . . .').

My favourite is **alt.sex.plushies**, a group for people who like to get it on with soft toys (or get it on while wearing fur suits). It has a few sister sites on the Web including **Plushies**, which boasts '25 Reasons Why It's Better To Sleep With Stuffed Animals Than Men'. While we're on the subject of children's toys, another corker is **Animals,** a site which celebrates the attractions of, oh, I'll let it tell you itself . . .

'Do you enjoy blowing up inflatables? I mean, REALLY ENJOY blowing up inflatables? Do vinyl pool toys and inflatable animals turn you on? Did you ever think you were the only one with this fetish and wish you could contact others like you? Well, your search is over!'

Following this trajectory further, we come to perhaps the weirdest of the Web lot (well, from my perspective anyway), the adult baby sites, places where people go to share their love of infantilism, where grown people pretend they are newborns or toddlers, finding some kind of pleasure in the sight of themselves, and others, in nappies and plastic pants. Though one of the sites, **Babylai's Babyland**, describes this as simple, harmless adult make-believe, the thought of bedwetting as fun just scrambles my brain . . .

At least the Web also provides something for these adult babies to do if they ever start to grow up. **Robby's Fetish Girls** showcases the work of a Swiss guy who dresses Barbies up in latex and PVC and sells them at 140 Swiss francs a doll. Just perfect for the adult primary schooler.

Web addresses

Whip Art
http://www.telcen.com/~zerotsm/whipart.html

Long Hair Site
http://www.tlhs.org

Men's Version
http://the-light.com/mens/longhair.html

World Fetish Center Home Page
http://www.idealine.com/fetish/welcome_netscape.htm

Mrs Silk's Magazine for Cross Dressers
http://www.CityScape.co.uk/users/av73/

Nails, Talons and Claws
http://www.ntcweb.com/nailz.htm

Messy Fun
http://198.151.175.26/messyfun.html

Heliophobe
http://www.hotweird.com/heliophobe/

Tom's Adult Tickling Site
http://www.televar.com/~thawkins/tickle.html

Celebrity Bare Feet
http://www.newreach.net/~marka/

Foot World
http://www.geocities.com/SunsetStrip/Palms/2973/

The Stomach and Bellybutton Page
http://ark.ship.edu/~md9033/

Terri's Shoe Page
http://www.thoughts.com/shoes/

Frieda and Guido's Interactive Underwear
http://www.moosenet.com/iu.html

Smoke and Glamour
http://www.wp.com/51824/smoking/

Plushies
http://www2.hawaii.edu/~mivillan/plushies.html

Inflatable Animals and Pool Toys
http://www.smart.net/~xydexx/animals.htm

Babylai's Babyland
http://home1.inet.tele.dk/babylai/index-uk.htm

Robby's Fetish Girls
http://ourworld.compuserve.com:80/homepages/Roger_Gerl/fgirls1i.htm

IT TAKES ALL KINDS

Collectors

THERE's a woman in the Blue Mountains, west of Sydney, who hoards those little plastic date tags that come with loaves of bread. If you think that's odd, there's a guy in Victoria who collects adjustable wrenches. And over in Western Australia, there's someone permanently on the lookout for razor blade wrappers.

People will collect anything. And we all do it. Anyone who can remember footy card swapping (or Barbie clothes trading) in the playground knows that Bill Gates and Rupert Murdoch are really just a pair of schoolboys trying to trade their way up to the full set. 'I want that network.' 'What'll you swap for it?'

The Web offers plenty of material for collectors. There are clubs of all kinds, archives, museums, trading forums and other resources. But what fascinates me is the growing number of DIY curators, obscure collectors displaying the results of their lifelong (or week-long) obsessions on the Net. Why? Why not?

Meet Celophaine, owner/operator of the Japanese site, **Bubble Wrap**, one of my favourite Web outings. 'Bubble Wrap is the most profound invention of the twentieth century,' he or she writes by way of introduction. Celophaine obviously isn't let out much.

Not that it matters. Anyone who devotes a site entirely to bubble wrap specimens from around the world has surely got something going for them. It's early days yet and there are only about a dozen to admire, but Celophaine clearly has big plans — she invites you to donate your workplace scraps.

Thankfully, you can do more than just admire the plastic specimens at the site. Sound files let you hear the popping noises of species with exotic names like 'American Big Wrap', 'Korean Standard' and 'Japanese Antistatic'.

There's also a section evocatively titled 'Fun With Bubble Wrap and Shredders', which advises that after you've pumped the wrap through the office machine, 'the other thing a shredder is good for is to take nori [sheets of seaweed for rolling sushi] and shred them into strips, which are good for sprinkling on miso soup and such.' See, you do learn something new every day.

Larry Hartman collects the colourful tags from **banana boxes**. So far, more than 120 banana labels are displayed on his site. Lynn Bry isn't as fussy, she collects any old **fruit stickers**.

Six years in the making, **Rubber Band Ball** is one man's attempt to create the largest rubber sphere in the universe. Not one of the bands has been bought, sitemaster Willie boasts— they were all either found or stolen. 'I am sure I could have accomplished something more significant and meaningful with the effort I have devoted to the ball, but I didn't. I just made this big honkin' ball o' bands!'

Likewise, **Aluminium Foil Ball** is a sphere composed entirely of bits and pieces of aluminium foil, mostly candy wrapper (the collector expresses a fondness for Peppermint Patties). 'The ball is more impressive in "person" than this page can hope to depict. When people are introduced to the ball, their first reactions are of surprise that it is so nearly perfectly round, smooth, and hard.

'This is no ordinary foil ball, created because some crumpled up foil was handy. This is a long term project. There isn't actually a goal size, so it is the intermediate results that are important. The round, smooth, hard attributes are achieved by applying new pieces of foil more or less uniformly about the surface, then rolling it around on a hard surface to flatten it. I also periodically whack it with a hammer, further compressing the surface and keeping it as round as possible.'

'It has been determined that the ball has gone beyond the danger assessment of "choking hazard", and now enjoys the

designation of "heavable projectile, such as might dent one's noggin"'. I'm hoping for "blunt instrument". It has been suggested that it might eventually become large enough to prevent me leaving the office, at which time it would cease to grow on account of my death from starvation.'

Meanwhile, winter in Europe appears to keep a lot of people indoors. And what better thing to do if you're trapped inside than develop a bizarre hobby?

'May I introduce myself, my name is Gemma Dickmann and I'm a collector of pencil sharpeners.' Gemma's **Pencil Sharpener Collection** contains more than 4500 different pencil sharpeners. 'Since hardly any new sharpeners are available in my country,' the Dutch woman writes, 'I would like to come in contact with fellow collectors to trade sharpeners with me.' Looking for Mr Pencil . . .

Then there's Madeleine Endre, of Sweden: 'It is I who creates the **Lipstick Page**,' she writes. 'The goal of this site is to create a lipstick library where you can find (or list) your old favourites and find new ones . . . You can, for example, read about what lipstick Winona Ryder prefers or which lipliner Linda Evangelista uses . . .'

Endre has more than 600 lipsticks (you might say the special ingredient is sheep fat) indexed, with sample reviews of more than a third of them and a growing number of pictures to help you tell the minute differences between them.

Bjørn Christian Tørrissen, a Norwegian, collects **Travel Sickness Bags**. And yes, he's wacky with a capital V.

'Sickness bags in general don't get the attention they deserve, except in those short, intense moments they are very much needed and appreciated. In a world where people collect all kind of things to preserve them for our children to see, I have chosen to concentrate on these gadgets.'

The main part of his collection is Scandinavian, but it is steadily growing. He also provides an 'introduction to sickness-bags-related terminology'. This tells you how to ask for a bag in different languages. If that idea sends your laffmeter into the red, you'll also appreciate *The Joy of Vomit*, a spewrious history of retching.

Just to be on the safe side when it comes to cleaning up afterwards, Bjørn really ought to link up with Mike Lewis, who edits online zine **Modern Moist Towelette Collecting**. 'Many individuals,' he writes, 'have asked me in past months, "Why moist towelette collecting? Why not stamp collecting or numismatics? To be different, perhaps?" Well, I must admit that at first that was part of the appeal, but I have since become aware of the strong movement of moist towelette enthusiasts, and accepted that I am not alone in my fascination/hobby. Each moist towelette is like a work of art.'

The weirdest collection I have seen online is also in the sanitary area. **Pads in the Hut** is a graphic display of one guy's collection of a friend's used panty liners. And I am telling you now, you don't want to go there. Really.

The online Web collections suggest that some people are born to the job and some have it thrust upon them. **75 Years of Band Aid** came about because a couple moved into a house in northern California and discoverer that the previous inhabitants had used Band Aid tins for storing nails, washers, bolts, and anything else small enough. Half a century of design variations are displayed on the site.

And **Jeff's T-Shirt Collection** is here because 'I seem to have gained a reputation as someone who has (and wears) lots of T-shirts, especially nerdy computer or SF related shirts. I've decided to open my collection to the public, so that everyone can enjoy them.' Jeff, do the words 'washing machine' mean anything to you?

Last but not least, another favourite of mine is the **Phallic Symbol Page**, a celebration of the root vegetable. Enough said. Now, has anyone out there got a set of 1974 football cards they'd be willing to trade?

Web addresses

Bubble Wrap
http://www.atom.co.jp/UNSOUND/Actual/Profiles/celopages/bubble/wrap.html

Banana Labels
http://www.geocities.com/TimesSquare/2355/banana.html

Fruit Stickers
http://pharmdec.wustl.edu/juju/Fruit/fruit.html

Rubber Band Ball
http://www.easttexas.com/pdlg/theball.htm

Aluminium Foil Ball
http://sunsite.unc.edu/lou/ball/

Pencil Sharpener Collection
http://www.universal.nl/users/dickmann/gemma.htm

Lipstick Page
http://www.users.wineasy.se/bjornt/lip.html

Travel Sickness Bags
http://www.pvv.unit.no/~bct/spypose/

Modern Moist Towelette Collecting
http://members.aol.com/MoistTwl/index.htm

Pads in the Hut
http://www.rox.com/quarry/XY/Hut/PadForm.html

75 Years of Band Aid
http://www.northcoast.com/savetz/bandaid/

Jeff's T-Shirt Collection
http://home.netscape.com/people/jsw/shirts/

Phallic Symbol Page
http://www.cs.und.nodak.edu/~gibbens/phallic.html

See also . . .

My Autograph Collection
http://www.midcoast.com/~scottj/autograp.htm

'I collect autographs primarily through the mail. From various sources, I have compiled a huge list of celebrity home addresses, and using this have been able to contact many of them to request an autograph. This listing describes the celebrity's name, what each one sent, how long they took to respond, inscription (if any), and my personal comments. It's a very interesting hobby — I never know who I will find in my mailbox each day!'

Hewlett Packard Calculators
http://ns.via.nl/users/mccidd/html/calc.htm

Maarten collects Hewlett Packard calculators. Prepare to be thrilled by his Dutch take on these adding and subtracting machines . . .

Things I Found on the Ground
http://www.web-cincinnati.com/bailiwick/things.phtml

A self-explanatory site run by a guy who obviously spends a lot of his time walking into telephone poles — his eyes are clearly focused on his feet. The artefacts he collects are usually of a creative nature, kids' drawings dropped at bus stops, a love letter left behind in his dentist's office, various essays found on campuses and in the streets. 'Each one is a little glimpse into some stranger's life and I have found them fascinating,' he says. 'I keep them in a file, right next to my taxes and insurance forms.'

KBS Beer Bottle Collection
http://rieska.oulu.fi/~psl/kbs/kbsbeer.htm

A huge collection of bottles, indexed by country of origin.

Mike's Meat Collection
http://www.bozosoft.com/mike/meat/index.html

Mike Epstein hoards tinned meats, but only weird ones, the kind you find yourself looking at on the supermarket shelf and thinking: 'My God! What kind of deviant would eat that?' Mike guarantees he hasn't eaten any of them.

Logo Buttons
http://www.geocities.com/SiliconValley/Pines/9210/

James Kupperian is a Web curator, a guy who is now exhibiting his not quite priceless collection of logo link buttons. What? 'Those little link buttons that are 31 pixels in height and 88 pixels in width, usually displaying a logo and the words Download and/or Now!.' Sounds like a dumb idea, but some of them are really rather sweet, and it's not impossible to conceive of yourself one day being nostalgic about some of them.

Dead Presidents
http://www.csn.net/~mhand/Presidents/

Manus Hand uses part of his spare time to photograph himself visiting the final resting place of almost every American president (three to go). The rest goes into putting up a Web site in tribute to his quest.

Rick's Chewing Gum
http://members.aol.com/RKaczur/index.html

'I've been collecting Chewing Gum Wrappers for 30 years. Do you have any you want to get rid of?' E-mail Rick and offload that box or two of wrappers that have been gathering dust in the garage.

Yossie's Handcuff Collection
http://www.blacksteel.com/~yossie/hcs.html

What will amaze you is not that it exists, but how big it is. And yes, there is a page of Cuff Links.

Licence Plates of the World
http://danshiki.oit.gatech.edu/~iadt3mk/index.html

I am frightened by the number of plates Michael Kustermann has. His massive global database has examples from more countries than I actually believe the planet has.

Sugar Packet Collectors Page
http://www.iquest.net/~phillip/

Another inexplicable hobby (they all are, from the outside, aren't they? I mean, who would want to drive toy trains around a track?). You know those little sachets of sugar you get in cafes and hotels? Well, some folk hoard 'em . . .

Online Diaries

THE Web is a double edged sword. So often, the beautiful idea is also the banal one. So often, the newfound power is a newfound waste. Everyone can be a publisher, and everyone has something to say, but is everyone worth listening to?

Therefore, depending on the way you're inclined to see these things, it's either very heartening or completely blood-draining to find out that the diary, that intimate, confessional forum for the anal expulsives among us, is having its own renaissance out there. If you're inclined to voyeurism/empathy, you'll find dozens of diaries slowly growing in all corners of the Web.

There are four basic types: the personal confession (many of these are connecting to each other via a **WebRing**—see chapter on Pregnancy); the Historical record (old diaries which would not be published in book form, but nonetheless make interesting curios); the quest report (a diary with a reason for existing); and the joke or hoax diary.

You can view them as harmless diversions, pointless vanity publishing or windows into whatever soul the Web may have, but the fact remains that, as with everything else, they seem to be multiplying. I spent a day wandering among their pages. The following is an alphabetical trawl through a few of the more interesting ones.

A Diary with Ferrets

One of the oldest diaries on the Net, this one goes back to 1992 and tells the story of a Swedish guy and his fur brigade.

Sample entry: *Today, we had Roxane spayed. She didn't like it at all, I think mostly because we had to wait a rather long time after the planned time before she was prepared for the operation.*

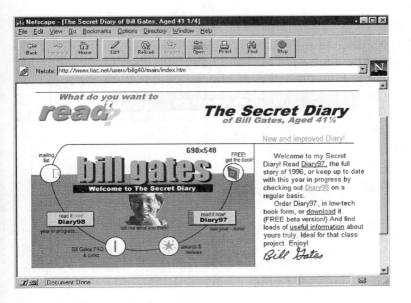

An Average Australian's Diary

Personal diary begun in March 1996 by Melbourne computer programmer Daniel Bowen.

Sample entry: *Today I arrived at work soaking wet. Well okay, not soaking, but certainly, undeniably wet. 'Was it raining?', I can hear the Sydneysiders snidely asking, "cos it always rains in Melbourne'. No, actually it's hardly rained a drop all week.*

Circle the Globe with Janet and John and Fargo

A quest diary, covering the international movements of Americans Janet and John Anderson and their frog puppet, Fargo,

245

on their 18-month holiday. It asks 'Have you ever followed a frog around the world?' Actually, yes I have.

Sample entry: *We are awestruck by our first glimpses of Australia. We have eaten dinner at a picnic table while we watched koalas run down one tree and up the next with babies clinging to their backs, had eye-to-eye contact with an emu that stuck its head in the driver's window and watched grey kangaroos bounce everywhere.*

Civil War Era Diary

A historical diary put online by Mark Bowden, who inherited it in a box of books from his grandfather. The diary appears to have been kept in 1861 and it is thought that the diarist was a young boy in his teens attending school at Greenshade in Decatur County, Georgia.

Sample entry: *Thursday, March 14th, 1861. Spent 35 cents for tobacco. J. F. Stanton went to Bainbridge and road [sic] J. E. Dodd's Mare. Moved a hog trough.*

Diary of a Madwoman in the Attic

Fictional diary by Sandra Kelley, 'a compilation of the trials and tribulations, joys and sorrows, thoughts and reflections of a wide variety of people (men and women) whose paths in life have crossed mine at one time or another.'

Sample entry: *Dear Diary, Two days in a row. This must be a record for me. Today I'm writing because my therapist thinks it would be a good idea.*

Guadalcanal Diary

Personal diary of the Battle of Guadalcanal by a 20-year-old corporal in the 11th Regiment, James R. 'Rube' Garrett.

Sample entry: *August 9, 1942. No air raids for a change. There was however a naval battle . . . Dutton was killed and we also killed a cow to the rear of the battery in the dark—we didn't know what it was.*

My Diary on Getting a Girlfriend

Personal/quest diary, beginning in 1996, chronicling the adventures of a college student on his hunt for a love object. 'Why am I writing this Web diary? Why not? I figured it might be fun to read how a guy makes a complete fool out of himself trying to find that perfect girl.'

Sample entry: *Jan 1, 1997. New Years Resolutions: Stop being a Loser. Stop being a Loser. Stop being a Loser. Get buff and studly-looking so that I can stop being a Loser. Kick super ass at school. Get out of the house more so that I'll stop being a Loser. Get a girlfriend that won't leave to be hundreds of miles away. And finally, stop being a Loser!!!*

oZ Diary

Personal diary and 'an exercise in self involvement' from Ophelia, a Hawaiian who lives in Waikiki. 'These are my words. Mere, unpolished and uncensored everyday words. Perhaps it's just a diary. Perhaps it's more.'

Sample entry: *Derek's been grumbling more and more about moving out. Anywhere else, you'd think 'it's about time', given his age. But in Hawaii, where rents are high and homes average around $300,000, kids pushing 40 still live with mom and dad. I think a fear of dishes* *(a chore that he's granted specific exemption from at home) is the only thing holding him back.*

The Diary Project

Inspired by the diaries of Zlata Filipovic, a young girl growing up in Sarajevo during the war in Bosnia, the site is a collection of diary entries from children around the world. You can take it from the top or browse by subject.

Sample entry: *Starting high school seems like a big step to me since I won't know anyone. I have this repetitive dream that keeps me awake every night: I walk into the cafeteria, and I don't know anyone, and it scares me because I'm used to having friends to be around.*

The Doggie Diaries

It just wouldn't be the Web without it, would it? Here is a diary kept by a Boxer named Auggie, who was born in June 1995.

Sample entry: *Molly, Foster and I had been chasing mice in the field when all of a sudden we came upon these huge dogs. One of the huge dogs came up and introduced himself. He said 'hello my name is Bob the horse'.*

The Secret Diary of Bill Gates

Is it a joke or isn't it?

Sample entry: *Just got back from Palm Springs. It's nice, but way too warm. I think I prefer plenty of rain. On the other hand, there's nothing like a couple of days of golf to get me relaxed and ready to face another year of competitor crushing.*

The Loser Living Upstairs

Perhaps the finest and most memorable piece of writing on the Web so far, this is a personal/quest diary of a year in which the guy in the downstairs flat spent his whole life wigging out about the guy in the upstairs flat. Just who was the loser?

Sample entry: *Wednesday May 3, 1995. Loser was up and around at five. There was pacing. There was a shower. There was more pacing and then Loser left at 6:05am. I left at ten and returned at 11:30am. No Loser. I left again at 11:45am. I returned at 1:30pm. Loser must have been sleeping, as he got up when I put on some rap tunes on my K-Mart all-in-one. I left again at 2:55pm and returned at 3:20 only to leave again . . .*

The Semi-Existence of Bryon

Personal diary of a customer support tech at IBM. Goes beyond the usual by providing a Cast Of Characters list with photographs and extra resources to help you understand his life.

Sample entry: *Chris let me borrow his new laser pointer to use as a cat toy. I have to think this is the ultimate cat toy! Ashley went insane chasing a red dot that she could never seem to catch. I would lead her into the kitchen and then run the dot behind the refrigerator and turn it off. She spent ten minutes staring behind the refrigerator waiting for the red dot to come out.*

Watching Parker Lee Grow

Don't just give your kids names, give them domain names as well. This personal number is a tribute diary from a loving father. Parker Lee's Web site began in July 1995, when he was five months old. 'Both the Internet and I have been growing like a wwweed.' There is a new photo every month.

Sample entry: *Photo of small child with balloon.*

Web addresses

WebRing
http://www.webring.org

A Diary with Ferrets
http://www.kd.qd.se/%7Egriffon/ferrets/diary/

An Average Australian's Diary
http://www.toxiccustard.com/diary/

Circle the Globe with Janet and John and Fargo
http://tawny.bu.edu/JandJ/

Civil War Era Diary
http://pages.prodigy.com/GA/daddyof3/diary.html

Diary of a Madwoman in the Attic
http://www.chiweb.com/entertainment/madwoman/

Guadalcanal Diary
http://204.49.53.2/~jrube/intro.html

My Diary on Getting a Girlfriend
http://web2.airmail.net/atapaz/diary/

oZ Diary
http://www.aloha.net/~ophelia/Diary/diary.html

The Diary Project
http://www.well.com/user/diary/

The Doggie Diaries
http://www.west.net/~ollybaba/diary.html

The Secret Diary of Bill Gates
http://www.tiac.net/users/billg40/

The Loser Living Upstairs
http://www.geocities.com/SouthBeach/Lights/5427/loser.html

The Semi-Existence of Bryon
http://www.master.net/bryon/

Watching Parker Lee Grow
http://www.parkerlee.com/

Those Wacky Royals

IS there something portentous about the fact that the design of Queen Elizabeth II's home page is dominated by a colour that is very much Empire Red? Is she planning to do to cyberspace what her forebears did to the globe a century and a half ago—paint as much of it red as possible?

Perhaps the slow winding down of the Commonwealth and the crumbling of Britain's sense of self-worth is leading her to strike out in search of new worlds to offer tea, cricket and middle-class repression to.

Whatever the long term intent might be, on 7 March 1997, the Queen cut the invisible ribbon on **The British Monarchy Official Web Site**, and took her first steps into the virtual world, becoming the very first cyber sovereign (if you don't count the self-appointed Prince Leonard, scion of **Hutt River Province** in Western Australia).

'The Royal Web site will, I hope, be an interesting and helpful source of information,' HRH told staff and students at a London high school, where the site was launched. 'I also hope that it will encourage you and others to make full use of the World Wide Web, so that we are able to learn more about each other and communicate more easily with each other, both here in Britain and elsewhere around the world.'

The site, which was so popular in its opening months that it crashed more often than, you know, one of those racing car drivers who crashes a lot, includes sections detailing the monarchy today, the palaces, the royal art collection, the Queen and the Commonwealth, the royal finances (nothing of Fergie's debt), details of the Queen's working day, an explanation of the accession process, biographies of members of the family (Di gets one but Fergie misses out) and a family tree dating from Queen Victoria onwards.

The most enlightening section is the Frequently Asked Questions list, in which we finally discover such things as:

- in 1995 the Queen sent 4,714 congratulatory telemessages to centenarians and 10,817 messages to Diamond Wedding celebrants;
- the Queen is *not* the wealthiest woman in the world;
- there are seven limousines, consisting of five Rolls-Royces and two Daimlers — they are painted in Royal maroon livery and the Rolls-Royces uniquely do not have registration number plates;
- the most exotic animal ever owned by the royal family was a giraffe, which lived during the reign of George IV; and
- the Queen not only keeps corgis (four of them, Phoenix, Pharso, Kelpe and Swift) but has branched out into the ownership of 'dorgis', dachsund/corgi crosses (hers are named Harris, Brandy, Cider and Berry).

All in all, it's a predictably sedate affair, long on brochure-style information and short on anything that might be construed as light-hearted or interactive. As a foothold on the Web, it's a tentative effort, marked by its conservatism — that reserve means that it isn't really a great advertisement for the monarchy. Then again, what would be? (Hey, surely I've got a right to one piece of gratuitous editorialising).

There are many other sites for royal watchers including **Royalty UK,** an offshoot of *The Daily Mail* which deals with the lifestyles, home and fashions of the royals, as well as their affairs and history. The only problem is that they want you to fork out about $20 a year for it.

The **Unofficial British Royal Family Home Pages** also offer the latest news, for free, updating daily by linking to sites around the Web. There's also an explanation of the laws of succession, and the opportunity to subscribe to a royals mailing list, as well as chat and postcard services. **Royal Palace News** is another news archive.

The most imaginative and entertaining is the **Royal Network** ('Your one-stop surfing headquarters for all the latest Royal Dirt!'), which marked the Queen's arrival in cyberspace with an editorial wishing her happy surfing and a list of handy bookmarks for sites devoted to corgis, horses and hunting.

The site's gossipmonger, The Peep, pulls no punches, providing all the palace scoops, but the site is notable for much more than its news value. It carries rather more candid biographies of the royal family and has great features like the Royal Swimsuit edition (mmmm, Camilla). The site offers Royal wallpaper samples for your computer, as well as 26 separate icons for free download.

To show that it has a heart, it's operating an ongoing appeal for donations to save Fergie from penury. At last count, it claimed to be up to $15,475. And it has a whole section dedicated to that 'Hunk in Training', Prince William, which offers the chance to declare your love for the Prince, or just write him a soppy poem (a half dozen are housed on site so far).

The best features of the site are the interactive ones, a dimension the official royal site really lacks. Fans can meet for live chat in the Royal Lounge or use the electronic postcard service to bestow a royal greeting via e-mail, choosing a (Photoshop-enhanced) portrait of the royal they wish to impersonate along the way, as well as background music—the choices run from *Rule Brittania* to the *Monty Python Theme*.

There is a tabloid headline generator, which allows you to nominate a couple of royals, type in a headline that links them—anything loud and ridiculous is good—and then let the site turn it into a printable tabloid front page for you.

The highlight is Club Di, which not only gives you the opportunity to write to Princess Bulimia, but lets you play

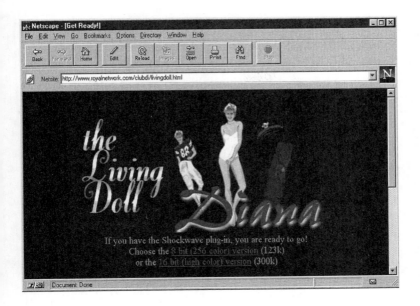

dress-ups with her as well. The Living Doll game, a
Shockwave-driven time waster, allows you to deck out (remember those old paper doll books) the **Princess** in a
number of costumes, from football player to nun to bondage
mistress.

If it's a longer term perspective you're looking for, Gail
Dedrick's **Guide to the Monarchs of England and Great
Britain** includes the Normans, the Angevins, the Houses of
Lancaster and York, the Tudors, the Stuarts, and the Houses
of Hanover, Saxe-Coburg-Gotha and Windsor.

Queen Liz and her wacky predecessors don't account for
all the royal Web action though. **Marivi's Royalty Buff Page**
is a Web directory, a list of associated links for everything from
Faberge eggs to news sources and genealogy sites. It also boasts
a comprehensive collection of links to sites dealing with other
royal families, from the **Greek Royal Page** ('Rumour: Prince

Nikolaos is dating model Elle McPherson') to **Thailand's Royal Family** to **Swedish Queens** to the **Hawaiian Monarchy**.

Royalty in History charts a path from Caligula, the Roman emperor who proclaimed himself a God and later inspired a very poor bio film, all the way through to the seventeenth-century crowned heads of Europe. The site's best feature is its alliterative monthly Mad Monarchs series ('Crazy Caesars of Rome', 'Sadistic Sultans of Turkey', 'Terrible Tsars of Russia', 'Kinky Kings of Spain' and 'Peculiar Princesses of The Netherlands').

The last category offers Anna of Saxony (1544–77) who was 'a difficult child, ugly, lame and hunchbacked, but widely regarded as the wealthiest catch of all the German princesses of her day'. As an adult, 'Anna was immoderate in everything. She had violent fits of temper, smashing everything to bits. At parties she boozed and flirted with the guests. Fits of gaiety alternated with drunken bouts of melancholy gloom.'

Anna publicly ridiculed the sexual prowess of her husband, William of Orange. She had children to other men and was confined in her later years as her mental state declined. 'She now talked nonsense, trembling and foaming at the mouth. A captain reported that Anna had attacked him with knives and was "raging and foolish as if she were possessed".'

Next to Anna, Fergie's indiscreet toe-sucking experiments seem like nothing to write home about . . .

Web addresses

The British Monarchy Official Web Site
http://www.royal.gov.uk

Prince Leonard of Hutt
http://www.wps.com.au/hutriver/hut1.htm

Royalty UK
http://www.royaltyuk.com

Unofficial British Royal Family Home Pages
http://www.etoile.demon.co.uk/Royal.html

Royal Palace News
http://www.itl.net/features/camelot/cgi/display

Royal Network
http://www.royalnetwork.com/

The Unofficial Princess Di Page
http://members.aol.com/douglasb52/index.htm

Guide to the Monarchs of England and Great Britain
http://www.ingress.com/~gail/

Marivi's Royalty Buff Page
http://www.serv.net/~marivim/royalty.html

Greek Royal Page
http://wwwedu.cs.utwente.nl/~kersten/royal/greece.html

Thailand's Royal Family
http://www.cs.ait.ac.th/~wutt/wutt.html

Swedish Queens
http://www.luth.se/luth/present/sweden/history/queens/

Hawaiian Monarchy
http://hawaii-shopping.com/~sammonet/monarchy.html

Royalty in History
http://www.xs4all.nl/~kvenjb/kings.htm

Cow Fans

ONE of the comforting things about the Web is that you can always find people who take your own slightly odd interests to such extremes that you end up feeling better about yourself. You feel somehow more normal.

By way of example, I've always been rather fond of cows (in the platonic sense of course). Perhaps the appeal stems from the sheer size and cartoonish rectangularity of these animals—they look so clumsily designed. Perhaps it's the fact that if you sit on the fence near a herd of Friesians, you can play cloud-watching games, spotting shapes in their black and white markings. Perhaps it's just because I love **cheese** . . .

Whatever the reason, no matter how much of a bovinophile I am, Big Dave will always make me look like a dilettante. 'I think cows are cool,' he says with more than a hint of understatement on his comprehensive, exhausting **Cow Page**. 'I don't know why; I just like them.'

Dave's site is an Internet hub for cow fans, a repository for all kinds of odds and ends. While not being huge on specific breed information, it carries trivia (a Holstein's spots, apparently, are as individual as a fingerprint or snowflake; the average cow gives nearly 200,000 glasses of milk in her lifetime) and links to many information-related sites.

There are sites that take things a little more seriously. If you're looking for cold hard data, try **Cow Net,** the Web front door for a cattle-oriented bulletin board, 'the Cattle Crossing on the Information Superhighway'. The World Health Organisation has a fact sheet about **Bovine Spongiform Encephalopathy** (Mad Cow Disease) available online. There's also a site that lists **Cows from Around the World**, starting with the Aberdeen Angus and winding through hundreds of breeds on the way to the Znamensk . . .

But enough usefulness. Back to Big Dave's site, which houses a library of cow pictures, sounds and ephemera. Marvel at the pictorial proof that cows beat mankind to the moon. Download logos, screensavers, icons and 3D cow pics. Listen to more than a dozen lowing beasties in the sound file area. Weep in the poetry wing (and you will, because most of it is *that* bad). Groan at the reworded, 'bovinified' pop songs. Or just check out the ASCII art.

There's an even bigger collection of cow art (and more soothing moo sounds) at **Cows Caught in the Web**, the Net's oldest cow fan site, a place which hasn't been updated for about a year, but still offers enough reason to drop in. Constructed by Neil Enns, in honour of his pet cow, Opt (it's a fake Neil—did you think we wouldn't notice?), it also boasts a handful of holiday snapshots of his pet and the rest of the cotton-stuffed herd.

If it's contact with a flesh and blood virtuality you're after, well, that's an udder question entirely (sorry). And it's a question to which **Kris** is the answer. This handsome eight-year-old Jersey may well be the only cow on the planet with its own home page. Certainly, it's the only one I've found with an e-mail address.

'Unfortunately,' Kris explains, 'I cannot type to log in, but you can send me e-mail anyway at *kris@cs.umd.edu*. Sometimes the other folks in my research group call me up on the phone and read it to me.'

Kris is the official mascot of the computer science department at the University of Maryland. His adoption certificate is available for perusal online. Clearly, these comp. sci. folk are not getting out from behind their desks enough. Still, the attempt to bring pastoral serenity in via a computer pet is rather sweet. The **Amazing CowCam** does something similar.

That's not the only link between cows and higher education. There's a site where you can play med student and **Dissect a Cow's Eyeball.** Another, the **Cow Simulator**, allows you to play God Farmer. Built along the familiar lines of other simulation games, it begins with a bit of virtual animal husbandry, after which your cow is born and ready for your tender loving care.

The object of the game is to milk the cow and sell the milk. But many things can go wrong between the blade of grass and the supermarket shelf. Are you ready for the test?

It isn't all scientific and serious though. The **Virtual Cow Experiment** doesn't experiment on cows at all—it experiments on software. It's a simple virtual tour around a co-operative cow named Laverne, completed in HTML rather than Java or VRML, just to prove it can be done. And it can, if you have a lot of patience. **Cow Morphing** demonstrates Glenn Lewis's 'puddling' animation program.

The **Cow Car** belongs to a guy called Tony. He painted the Mazda Miata to look like a Friesian (photos on site) for reasons he can't quite put his finger on. He has installed a horn that moos and the number plate reads HOW-NOW.

'The truth is that I asked for MILK-ME and the Registry people nixed it. I see HOW-NOW as reflecting a confident air that says, "I'm a cow car and I feel good about it. Who are YOU?" The subtext, however, remains "Milk me!"'

Game players are welcome to download **Apocalypse Cow**, a bovine slugfest. And if you'd like to see a cross-sectioned diagram of the **robot cow** at the 1933 World's Fair, there's a site to go to for that too. And speaking of fakes, **Dummy Cow** is an unintentionally funny animal husbandry site:

'Our mechanical dummy cows with built-in operator space are used regularly on nearly all bulls all over the world,' the company brags. 'Our new model is silent when moving and weighs 700kg to provide necessary stability. All movement and height adjustments are made by noiseless motors and hydraulic jacks, controlled by the operator seated inside or from outside controls. Safe inside the dummy cow, the operator properly positions the artificial vagina through an open slot designed in the dorso-posterior section of the dummy cow . . .'

The dummy looks absolutely nothing like any cow I've ever seen—which proves that bulls are very short sighted or, as they say in the paddock, 'you don't look at the mantelpiece while you're stoking the fire'.

Last and least, **Virtual Cow Tipping** is a deeply stupid site dedicated to the practice of pushing sleeping cows over on their sides. Supposedly, our bovine friends are too dumb to wake up when you start tilting them. The site asks you to click on the picture, which then inverts. **Cow tipping**, by the way, is something of an urban (rural?) myth. Cows are too heavy to tip over and they sleep lying down. If you must attempt to tip cows, about 15 per cent of the bill is the appropriate amount.

Web addresses

CheeseNet
http://www.wgx.com/cheesenet

Big Dave's Cow Page
http://www.gl.umbc.edu/~dschmil/cows/

Cow Net
http://www.cow.net/

Bovine Spongiform Encephalopathy
http://www.who.ch/programmes/emc/bsefacts.htm

Cows from Around the World
http://www.tc.umn.edu/nlhome/m121/puk/cowworld.html

Cows Caught in the Web
http://www.brandonu.ca/~ennsnr/Cows/Welcome.html

Kris
http://www.cs.umd.edu/projects/omega/Kris/index.html

Amazing CowCam
http://www.accsyst.com/cow.html

Cow's Eye Dissection
http://www.exploratorium.edu/learning_studio/cow_eye/

Cow Simulator
http://amsterdam.park.org/Netherlands/pavilions/typical_dutch/cows/simulator/

Virtual Cow Experiment
http://www.fractalcow.com/laverne/laverne.htm

Cow Morphing
http://www.gmlewis.com/morphing/cow.shtml

Cow Car
http://www.wildfire.com/~tony/cowcar.html

Apocalypse Cow
http://er4www.eng.ohio-state.edu/~cooperb/PinataFatala/apoccow.html

Robot Cow
http://brink.com/brink/author/1933/cow.html

Dummy Cow
http://www.ubi.com/imv/dummy_cow/

Virtual Cow Tipping
http://www-und.ida.liu.se/~c94magpe/engcow1.html

VRML Cow Tipping
http://www.digitalo.com/vrml/cowtip.html

The Museum of Dirt

SOMEWHERE in the **Henry Ford Museum**, in Detroit, there is a glass tube which supposedly contains Thomas Edison's last breath.

Think about it for a minute. Imagine yourself standing in front of that jar. Gee, it'd look exciting, wouldn't it? You've probably got a whole bunch of similar museum exhibits yourself, empty bottles in a cupboard under the sink.

But though I might gently mock the whole idea, there is something oddly compelling about it, something almost romantic embodied by that jar full of air. I'm sure that after a visit to that museum, no matter how many other things you saw, that's what would remain on the shelves of your memory.

Some things just seem to snag the imagination. And if a museum piece is supposed to transport you, to make you think, to connect you to the time, place or person it relates to, then a jar of air can be just as valid and effective as any other artefact.

Such a philosophy underrides the **Museum of Dirt**, one of my favourite Web sites. At first glance, the museum looks like another stupid Net idea. At second glance, well, it still looks like that. But if you take the time to consider it on its own terms, the richness of the idea reveals itself. The Museum of Dirt will snag you . . .

At the museum, the user can experience a spectrum of history, geography and pop culture, all expressed in the medium of dirt. Its showcase gallery includes more than 150 specimens, little bottles of dirt, each with its own story to tell.

There's dirt from famous places, from **Bondi Beach** to the **Great Wall of China** to the **Acropolis** to Cape Canaveral. There's dirt that is somehow linked to famous people: from the graves of **Gertrude Stein**, **Jimbo Morrison** and **Oscar Wilde**; from the backyard of film director **John Waters**; from the driveway of **Barry Manilow**; and from **The Simpsons** writers' bungalow.

And there's dirt from places of significant events: the **Berlin Wall**; the **Menendez** house; the site of **Yitzhak Rabin**'s assassination; the Alfred P. Murrah Federal building in **Oklahoma** City; **Abbey Road Studios**; the corner of **Sunset Boulevard** where **Hugh Grant** picked up Divine Brown . . .

Boston-based museum curator Glenn Johanson says the idea for the institution arose after he found himself captivated by a dirt collection at the home of a Texan friend.

He later sent his friend 'a pile of the Boston Common and a clump of Harvard Yard', before adopting the idea for his own museum.

'I've always had an interest in collecting things,' Johanson says, 'particularly from my travels. I like to bring something back of the places I've been, but not something sold for that purpose. Dirt is the best, because it's common to *every* place, and everyone can participate.'

The museum is both virtual and real. Each of Johanson's samples is 'proudly exhibited' on custom-made, brushed metal shelves in the offices of Planet Interactive, the multimedia design and production company he works for.

Though Johanson has collected dirt from around the globe, the bulk of the collection is actually donated, often by the person to whom the dirt relates. Johanson has regularly approached celebrities to donate dirt, sending zip-locked bags with official Dirt Specimen labels, asking for all the relevant data and a signature of the donor as verification of the sample's authenticity.

Cineaste John Waters was the first to respond favourably to his request, and his offering has been joined by those of many others, including Ted Turner ('Georgia dirt!'), **David Hasselhoff** (sand from the **Baywatch** set) and **Robert Redford**

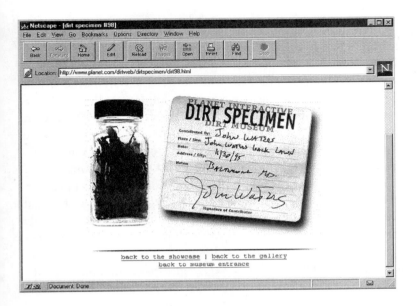

(dirt from his ranch). Johanson's rejection letters are also on view at the museum.

'Mike Eisner at **Disney** wouldn't participate because they didn't see a "tie-in" to Disney,' Johanson says. '**George Lucas** is "too busy making the next three **Star Wars** films". **Prince Charles'** assistant wrote, "His Royal Highness was grateful to you for writing and has asked me to send you his best wishes." But no dirt.'

When asked about the most covetable dirt, Johanson is at something of a loss to decide which way his dreams are pointing. He explains that he had been hoping Jennifer Saunders would respond to his request, but so far it's all quiet on that front. But then there's also the highly fanciable non-Earth dirt, dirt from the moon, Mars or an asteroid.

Similarly, he has no specific favourites in the museum, in terms of look and feel anyway. In terms of the meaning they convey, well, that's another thing.

'The conceptual ones are always a treat, because the contributors had to really think hard about their dirt.' For example, Tabloid Dirt is a collection of **National Enquirer** headlines and was submitted in a Listerine bottle (the only bottle which doesn't conform to the rest of the exhibits). Audio Dirt is a piece of police surveillance audio tape which captures a woman trying to hire a hit man to off her husband. No, really! **Dave Barry**, a syndicated humour columnist, sent lint from his dryer, saying that some of it might belong to **O.J. Simpson**.

'There's a dark side to the criminal ones which appeals to me. A chunk of granite from the Oklahoma City Federal Building is quite moving. People have also sent dirt from Nicole Brown-Simpson's front walkway, Jeffrey Dahmer's apartment site, the Menendez brothers' house, a piece of the bridge at **Chappaquiddick** and Yizthak Rabin's assassination site. It's America's sick and twisted obsession with the sick and twisted.

'And about 10 per cent of the museum is gay and lesbian, including dirt from **Stonewall** Bar in New York, Pedro Zamora Way in Miami, Cherry Grove on Fire Island, the grave of Gertrude Stein and Alice B. Toklas (they are buried together) in France and the Hordern Pavilion in Sydney, taken during the **Gay and Lesbian Mardi Gras**. These are cool.'

Web addresses

Henry Ford Museum
http://www.hfmgv.org/

Museum of Dirt
http://www.planet.com/dirtweb/dirt.html

Bondi Beach
http://www.voyeurmagic.com.au/

Great Wall of China
http://metrotel.co.uk/jvt/china9.htm

Acropolis
http://cal022011.student.utwente.nl/~marsares/

Gertrude Stein
http://www.magibox.net/~stein/

Jim Morrison
http://www.geocities.com/SunsetStrip/Palms/2914/index.html

Oscar Wilde
http://www.jonno.com/oscariana/1.html

John Waters
http://www.reed.edu/~mfagan/dreamland.html

Barry Manilow
http://members.aol.com/garyoye/barrynet/bmnet000.htm

The Simpsons
http://www.foxworld.com/simpindx.htm

Berlin Wall
http://www.users.dircon.co.uk/~chrisx/index.html

Menendez Brothers
http://www.courttv.com/casefiles/menendez/

Yitzhak Rabin
http://www.israel-mfa.gov.il/gov/rabin.html

Oklahoma Bombing
http://kwtv.com/news/bombing/murrahbomb.htm

Abbey Road
http://www.abbeyroad.co.uk

Sunset Boulevard
http://www.cen.uiuc.edu/~dd-moore/sunset-blvd.html

Hugh Grant
http://ucsub.colorado.edu/~kritzber/new/hugh/hugh.html

David Hasselhoff
http://www.ithaca.edu/shp/shp98/dwiller1/dh.html

Baywatch
http://baywatch.compuserve.com/

Robert Redford
http://www.tsr.srg-ssr.ch/emission/specialc/d004.htm

Disney
http://www.disney.com

George Lucas
http://www.tc.umn.edu/nlhome/m108/stef0056/lucas.html

Star Wars
http://www.starwars.com

Prince Charles
http://www.orioninc.com/Charles/

National Enquirer
http://www.nationalenquirer.com/

Dave Barry
http://www.herald.com/tropic/barry/

O.J. Simpson
http://www.cnn.com/US/OJ/index.html

Chappaquiddick
http://www.vineyard.net/mvol/map/edg-chap1.html

Stonewall
http://www.actwin.com/stonewall/theinn.html

Gay and Lesbian Mardi Gras
http://www.mardigras.com.au

RESOURCE FILES

Basic Toolkit

FIVE WAYS TO GET AROUND

Yahoo
http://www.yahoo.com

The Big Bang of the Web universe. Sometimes feels like everything expands from here. The best place to begin your journey if you have any idea what you're looking for. It's the simplest and most logical of the search engines and, for people new to the Web, the easiest place to dive in.

AltaVista
http://www.altavista.digital.com

There are plenty of other engines out there ready to behave like sniffer dogs, wandering around the Web, rooting out information for you. They're strange creatures, search engines—every one seems to have a different personality. Ultimately, you choose the one that suits you, that most matches your own logical processes. I use a combination of Yahoo and AltaVista, the former for simple searches, the latter for more involved meanderings, for searches where a little lateral thought is required. AltaVista is much broader than Yahoo, and returns many more options. It's much harder to wade through those responses, unless you have patience or curiosity, but it's usually worth it.

Web Soup
http://sctest.cse.ucsc.edu/roth/WebSoup/WebSoup2.html

This site just isn't as famous as it should be. In fact, I don't think I've ever heard anyone recommend it. But it's one of the places

I visit most, at least once a week. Carl Roth's Web creation is a thing of beauty, an absolute diamond. Here's how it works. There are places all over the Web that nominate cool, new sites every hour, day or week. Roth has built a site which saves you the trouble of going to each of those sites to read the latest nominations. Web Soup scans all of them for their links and then presents the Top Five suggestions from more than 100 sites, neatly arranged in tables on one Web page. 500 new and cool sites in one hit, with other people doing the sorting for you!

Deja News
http://www.dejanews.com/

A search engine for the thousands and thousands of newsgroups. Find out if others are talking about your subject of special interest, what they're saying and where they're saying it. Usenet grows by more then 500 megabytes a day. Let Deja News, which stores Usenet back to March 1995, do the walking for you.

Weird Places on the Net
http://www.euronet.nl/users/deiman/

Half the fun of the Internet is being taken off in odd and surprising directions, following your nose and ending up somewhere completely different than you intended, but just as cool. This place warns you that some of the sites it links to are so bizarre that you surf at your own risk, but really, most of the hundreds of things here will just elicit a smile or a shake of the head at their addle-pated idiosyncrasies. It's a small 'c' catholic archive of all kinds of fringe behaviours and ideas. And for that alone, is an essential bookmark.

FIVE INSTITUTIONS

EFF
http://www.eff.org

The Electronic Frontiers Foundation has been at the forefront of the fight for cyber rights for years. Based in America, it has spawned affiliates in other parts of the world. Its library carries extensive documentation on most of the key issues of Net civil liberties (free speech, encryption, privacy) as well as copyright and property questions. It takes a calm, rational approach to many of the problems that the Net throws up which, of course, does nothing to endear the organisation to those who would have us live in fear of the medium.

HotWired
http://www.hotwired.com

Wired mag's online sister started off a lot more pretentious and convinced of its own destiny than it is now. These days, it's just a damn good Web zine, with a solid history, a clear sense of itself, and a number of whipcrack columns. Oddly enough, *HotWired* seems less hyped about the digital age than the offline magazine, more willing to look at the cracks in the facade, to consider the possibilities of things not being wall-to-wall wonder.

Ultimate TV
http://www.ultimatetv.com

If you like television, there's really no need to start anywhere else. This enormous site not only generates its own television stories, but is the clearing house for links to pretty much every

TV site on the Web, thousands of them all neatly filed into the Ultimate TV database. Whatever you're looking for, it's here.

The Spot
http://www.thespot.com

Will it still be there by the time you're reading this? Who knows? The Spot has been having some tough financial times lately. But it deserves its place on the list as a true Web pioneer of interactive entertainment, even if the content of that entertainment has at times been lacking. The Spot, which won the 1995 Cool Site of the Year award, was the first blockbuster cybersoap, an online drama about the lives and loves of a handful of twentysomething mannequins. It was Aaron Spelling in a new medium. And it worked.

Firefly
http://www.firefly.com

This place started out as a strange little site which recommended rock records, based on information you provided about your own tastes. Now it has mutated into something much larger and more complex, a community of self-appointed buffs (aren't we all?) in film as well as music. It takes a while to work up to the stage where it's valuable (it has to get to know you, and it keeps asking questions about strange American bands you couldn't care about) but the rewards are there if you persevere. This is a place to spend some time, chatting with others who share your interests (you can find who is logged on while you are).

FIVE WAYS TO GET THE NEWS

CNN
http://www.cnn.com

See what happens when a major information company decides to put the time and effort into a new (news) medium. The site is arguably better than the cable station. It has a staff of more than 100 people. Its live and continuous news updates of important issues and events really demonstrate how useful the Net can be. An example: within six hours of a Paris subway bombing in 1996, the site had a lengthy report, video and audio from the scene, and maps of the Paris streets and subway, pinpointing the position of the explosion.

C/Net
http://www.cnet.com

Geek heaven. All the technology news you could possibly want, the latest in the browser wars, who's buying who, who's releasing what. C/Net is an ambitious news provider, with its own TV show and a sense of itself as a community rather than a service, as a place people come to hang out, to keep in touch with the news as well as each other. To that end, there are polls, contests and discussion areas, as well as games and shareware libraries, all kinds of things to be downloaded.

PointCast
http://www.pointcast.com

This is a stupendously successful, intelligent screensaver. You tell it what news you're interested in and while you're working, it wanders off at regular intervals to download the latest in those areas (and a bunch of ads). Then, whenever your screen is idle, it pops up the new headlines. Voila! Push media!

Timecast
http://www.timecast.com

Another site built around the concept of customisable news, this one deals in audio. It links to a number of sites which offer audio briefings in various areas of news, business, sports and entertainment. You choose which ones you would like delivered to you daily and the site puts them together as a neat package of audio for you to listen to while you're working.

Newslink
http://www.newslink.org

Then there's the old fashioned way of getting to everything. Newslink, run by the American Journalism Review, is dedicated to keeping tracks of the hundreds of news sources on the Net. Online newspapers from just about everywhere, magazines, radio and TV broadcasters and other information providers are all listed here. Choose your own media!

FIVE MOVIE SITES

The Internet Movie Database
http://www.imdb.com

An exhaustive volunteer effort in bringing together movie info. More than 200,000 people are covered, with credits for more than 100,000 films. And much, much more. Just go there.

CineMedia
http://ptd15.afionline.org/CineMedia/cmframe.html

Along with the IMDB, this is the largest film and media directory. Its cinema section features extensive round-ups of Web sites devoted to the movies, actors, studios, schools, organisations, directors, festivals and events, production details, histories, video and laser discs.

Mr Showbiz
http://www.mrshowbiz.com

Net landmark and one-stop shop for Hollywood goss. Film, TV and music all get good coverage. A pop culture obsessive's dream, with plenty of content you won't find elsewhere and writers of the calibre of Joe Queenan.

The Hollywood Reporter
http://www.hollywoodreporter.com

This site offers continually updated news briefs from the entertainment and media worlds. It has expanded coverage under various subject headings, and is great for the latest scoop, but if you want the full service of the magazine online, you have to pay for it (US$9.95 a month). Another great place for Hollywood goss is **E! Online (http://www.eonline.com)**.

The Oracle of Kevin Bacon
http://www.cs.virginia.edu/~bct7m/bacon.html

A legendary site dedicated to the idea that Kevin Bacon, in acting terms, is ground zero. Connect any major actor with Kev, within six short steps of acquaintance (a familiar idea to anyone who has seen *Six Degrees of Separation*).

FIVE MUSIC SITES

Yahoo Music List
http://www.yahoo.com/Entertainment/Music/

Last time I looked, there were more than 25,000 sites listed in its alphabetical 'Artists' section alone. You'll find directions to everything and everyone, from sheet music to karaoke bars, from chart histories to music videos to songwriting tips to trivia contests.

Internet Underground Music Archive
http://www.iuma.com/

A bona fide classic. This library of lesser-known acts has been growing like topsy since, oh, the dawn of Web time (1993).

Its archive covers new bands and keeps tabs on the old ones that have made it.

iMusic
http://www.imusic.com

The best all-in-one music site on the Web. Daily news, features (with occasional live performances), hundreds of bulletin boards to chat about your favourite bands, acres of chart info, contests, games and record reviews.

Hyperreal
http://www.hyperreal.com

Rave culture and dance music resources. This enormous, sprawling site is fastidiously maintained and exceptionally neat, given that it is probably run by people who spend their lives in a state of sleep deprivation.

Rocktropolis
http://www.rocktropolis.com

Part magazine, part theme park, part huge and bloated tribute to all that is excessive about rock. It's a monster site, stacked with designed goodies all the way to the roof, but not too slow on the download. It has gossip, concert archives, four radio stations, chat areas and a lot more.

FIVE GREAT TIME WASTERS

Useless Sites
http://www.go2net.com/internet/useless/

The guys who run this site have made it their life's work to track down and catalogue pointless and stupid Net destinations. For this, I am in their eternal debt.

Centre for the Easily Amused
http://www.amused.com/

'Our hard-working experts have been exploring the Internet since long before it was trendy in their search for the Ultimate Guide to Wasting Time.' Payload! A handy guide to oh, at least a thousand sites guaranteed to entertain you for a minimum/maximum of five seconds each.

The Interactive Ego Booster
http://web.syr.edu/~ablampac/ego/ego3.html

A site which behaves like a total fawning tart, worshipping obsequiously at the user's altar. It updates its sycophancy a few times every minute: 'No-one is quite like you'; 'You are the nicest person I know'; 'When they made you, they broke the mould . . .'

WebCam Central
http://www.cris.com/~jdholley/wcc/index.shtml

Want to drop in on someone else's world? This place has links to more than a thousand Net accessible cameras, pointed at all manner of pointless things.

Internet Anagram Server
http://www.wordsmith.org/anagram/index.html

Also known as 'I, Rearrangement Servant' and 'Inert Net Grave Near Mars'. Parliament, it tells us, is an anagram of 'partial men'. Clint Eastwood is an anagram of 'Old West action'. Type in a word and then let the computer rearrange its constituent elements for you.

FIVE ZINE SITES

John Labovitz's List of all Known E-zines
http://www.meer.net/~johnl/e-zine-list/

Pretty much every zine you'll find on the Web is linked alphabetically here. There are short explanations of the tone, content and frequency of each, with contact e-mail addresses.

Electronic Newsstand
http://www.enews.com

Magazine Central. Like Labovitz's list, this site links to online magazines, but this one catalogues the publications which have offline, often major, versions. This is the place to find the mainstream mag you're looking for. Search by name or subject area. Or just peruse their recommendations.

Suck
http://www.suck.com

Smart, cynical Web zine which sends up online culture, among other things. Begun by two guys out of a back room at *Wired*. Though it's long and lateral (it's more of an essay) it's worth digging about for the goodies. And just often enough to keep you coming back, it really sizzles.

Word
http://www.word.com/

Word is the closest thing the Web has to a coffee table magazine. It's as much an experiment in art as it is in publishing, an exploration of the medium. Ambiguous, amorphous section headings lead you off to feature articles that are a marriage of design and content.

Salon
http://www.salonmagazine.com

Probably my favourite site on the Web. A journal of literature, culture and ideas, it comes off like a groovier version of *The New Yorker*, and has big name writers to prove it. Some of its cultural criticism has been of a higher standard than the mainstream media has achieved lately.

FIVE THINGS TO PLAY WITH

The Electric Postcard
http://postcards.www.media.mit.edu/Postcards/

One of the sweetest and simplest sites yet invented. Judith Donath's server allows you to choose an image from the virtual Postcard Rack, compose and address a message to a friend and click the Mail button. That person will then be e-mailed with a note that includes a claim number and instructions on how to retrieve the card at the Electric Postcard Pick-up Window. Images include works by da Vinci, Vermeer, Gauguin, Van Gogh, Monet, Kandinsky, Magritte, Hopper and many others.

Web-a-Sketch
http://www.digitalstuff.com/web-a-sketch/

A site which invites you to twiddle with your keyboard and make onscreen drawings. Log in and see daily updates, featuring efforts along the lines of 'Naked Crazy Guy Taking Shower'. There are monthly awards and a hall of fame.

Ferret Frenzy
http://www.delphi.co.uk/delphi/interactive/ferrets/intro.html

The Web's first interactive ferret racing game. This playful British site gives you 50 quid and a choice of furry steed, all of whom sport names like Gnasher and Trouser King. You make your bet, head down to the track and watch your play money fritter away.

Piercing Mildred
http://www.mildred.com/

A game which lets you pierce an imaginary friend. Compete with play piercers the world over as you artistically arrange your bits and baubles on the cartoon Mildred.

Talk To My Cat
http://queer.slip.cs.cmu.edu/cgi-bin/talktocat

Chat to a moggy at Talk To My Cat, a Web document which uses speech synthesis to make your words audible to the animal near the owner's computer. Play with its mind. If it starts talking back, seek medical help.

Travel

USEFUL BACKGROUND

Travel Health Tips
http://www.cdc.gov/

The US Centre for Disease Control and Prevention site is an excellent resource for traveller's health advice. It boasts all kinds of reference materials, the latest information on disease outbreaks around the world, and geographically based health recommendations. Find out what you're going to die of if you leave the house. So good you might never travel again.

Universal Currency Converter
http://www.xe.net/currency/

A point and click way to keep track of exchange rates in the countries you're planning to visit (and why is it that, whenever you travel, your own dollar lurches downwards to make everything more expensive for you?). Updated daily, the site converts dozens of currencies from and to other ones.

Money Abroad FAQ
http://www.inria.fr/robotvis/personnel/laveau/money-faq/money-abroad.html

Contains general information about ways of dealing with money when in a foreign country. It tells you how to deal with cards and cash, and where you will run into problems. It's simple, direct, and honest. 'Practically, there are five exchange rates: 1. The black market rate; 2. The rate at which you can sell your foreign notes into your own currency; 3. The interbank rate (that's the rate you get in the newspaper—it is used by the banks to exchange currencies between them); 4. The traveller's cheque rate; and 5. The rate at which you buy foreign notes.'

Local Times Around the World
http://www.hilink.com.au/times/

This guide attempts to list all of the world's countries, and many of its islands, with the local time in each region. As I type, it's 3:58am in Rio de Janeiro. Just thought you'd like to know.

How Far Is It?
http://www.indo.com/distance/

Type in any two major cities and the site will tell you how far apart they are. Win bets with your friends. Did you know that Glasgow and Vladivostok, as the (very tired) crow flies, are 8288 kilometres apart?

Intellicast's World Weather
http://www.intellicast.com/weather/intl/

Ah, weather, friend and foe of the itchy-footed. Some people, like my partner, spend so much time poring over weather details that they sometimes forget to look at the sky. For meteorology junkies, Intellicast is a major rush, so be careful of the doses you allow them. This site carries weather details for all points. You choose continent by continent, honing in on the cities you're interested in. The site returns four-day forecasts, with satellite pictures. It also has temperature converters, in case you can't get your brain around Fahrenheit or centigrade.

The Universal Packing List
http://www.henricson.se/mats/upl/

Everyone, of course, is different. But someone had to have a go at making this list, which is actually a series of lists (things to do before you leave, clothing, money and documents, equipment, hygiene, health, electrical stuff, diving equipment, climbing equipment, comments by travellers). It does make a good fist of the job, by following the simplest of travel rules: 'We all carry too many things through life'. Step 1: get a smaller suitcase.

Mapquest
http://www.mapquest.com

This one has an interactive atlas, to let you find your way around the world. It has driving information and the opportunity to print your own personalised trip maps. There are all sorts of extra attractions if you're looking at US cities and towns, which are promised for the rest of the world as the site grows.

Subway Navigator
http://metro.jussieu.fr:10001/bin/cities/english

There are maps to help you with the subways in more than 60 cities, from Prague to Paris to Philadelphia, from Berlin to Boston to Buenos Aires. Not only does it use maps, it plans routes for you. Type in two places in a city and it will tell you which lines to catch to get from one to the other and where to swap trains on the way.

Foreign Languages for Travellers
http://www.travlang.com/

Select your own language from the list and the language you

want to learn (from 47 choices, last time I looked) and the site will return you a wedge of basic words and numbers, as well as useful phrases to do with shopping, dining, travel, directions, places, times and dates.

Adventurous Traveller Bookstore
http://www.gorp.com/atbook.htm

An online specialist in globetrotting books. Guide books, travelogues, CD-ROMS, calendars, videos. New releases lists and excerpts online. And a secure server to make your order safe.

International Clothing and Shoe Sizes
http://www.kisc.co.jp/KIEA/onepoint10.html

Japanese, American, British and European size conversion chart. For when that friend says 'Oh, and can you buy me . . .'

GUIDES

Lonely Planet
http://www.lonelyplanet.com

The best hard copy guide company offers the best online presence as well. Just choose your destination from their world map and click through into its library. I wondered if they had anything on Myanmar (formerly Burma). They had a map, pictures and information under all the following headings: Facts at a Glance, Environment, History, Economy, Culture, Events, Facts for the Traveller, Attractions, Off the Beaten Track, Getting There & Away, Getting Around, Recommended Reading, Lonely Planet Guides, Travellers' Reports on Myanmar and On-line Info. It also included an article about whether or not you should go to the country, given the

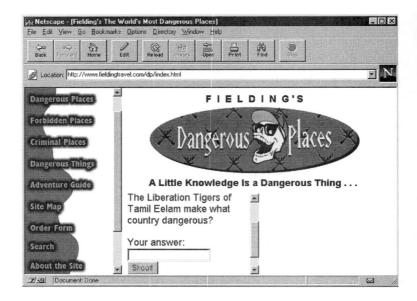

anti-democracy push of its government. Enough for you? Not all of Lonely Planet's book material is online, but more than enough for the user to make sensible decisions. And the level of detail is repeated for most of the world's countries. The enormous Lonely Planet site also contains up-to-date tips from people out there travelling now (they receive around 10,000 postcards a year), health advice and a secure server so you can part with your cash for their tomes.

Time Out
http://www.timeout.co.uk

Time Out's city guides are great (okay, okay, I admit, I worked on one). They cover Amsterdam, Barcelona, Berlin, Boston, Brussels, Budapest, Chicago, Edinburgh & Glasgow, London, Los Angeles, Madrid, Miami, New York, Paris, Philadelphia, Prague, Rome, San Francisco, Sydney, Tokyo and Washington.

The online city guides are a little slower in coming, but most of the cities are available, with the bulk of each book on the site.

Let's Go
http://www.letsgo.com

A very groovy-looking site from the Let's Go people, highlighting, I guess, the fact that these guides are aimed, first and foremost, at university students. The books are written by students and updated every year. The site has been down for reworking but should be back on deck by the time you're reading this.

Rough Guide
http://www.hotwired.com/rough

At the time of writing, its guides covered USA, Europe, Canada, Hong Kong, Australia, Mexico and India. Each section contains basic information on the destination, as well as advice on where to sleep, what to eat, what to see in the day, what to do at night and what's going on in the arts. The content, however, is simplistic and reads like it's been written by people just passing through and picking up brochures. But *HotWired* has always been good at integrating user feedback into its work, so perhaps with time the sites will come to life.

Rec.Travel Library
http://WWW.Solutions.Net/rec-travel/

This, as its title implies, is a giant archive for the postings of the **rec.travel** newsgroup. The Where To Go section breaks the world down into continents and then countries. Dig in and you'll discover all manner of links and information, from food guides to personal recollections to official tourism info. You'll find most countries represented here. The How To Get There wing offers advice on air travel, cruise ships, railroad timetables and accommodation. It gives you tips on how to pack for a trip and how to prepare for round-the-world travel.

Active and Adventure Travel
http://www.gorp.com/gorp/trips/main.htm

If you're looking for a bit more than sightseeing, whether it be whitewater rafting, biking, climbing or bushwalking holidays, this site will send you in the right direction. You can choose your holiday by the type of activity or the place and it returns information on adventure options. See also **Travel Source (http://www.travelsource.com/)**.

The World's Most Dangerous Places
http://www.fieldingtravel.com/dp/index.html

What's the point of going on holidays unless you're risking your life? I have a friend who always asks for the bulkhead seat on international flights. Not because it has more leg room. No. He just wants to be the first person sucked out if the doors are faulty. And any old wimp can go to London, Paris or New York. Why not spend your break in one of the world's trouble spots? The authors of this thousand page site (and the book that goes with it) have been on the ground in Bosnia, Chechnya, Chile, Cambodia, Guyana, Rwanda, Burundi, Turkey, India, Indonesia, Iraq, Kenya, Lebanon, Tanzania, Malaysia, Paraguay and Vietnam, looking for ways to get you as close to the action as possible. The site tells you what is dangerous, where that danger is, how to get there, how to get around once you are and how to get out intact. Good luck.

Roadside America
http://www.roadsideamerica.com/

The greatest ever travel book about the USA now has a handsome Web presence, promising offbeat attractions, hypertourism and 'vacation thrills!'. Its editors traipse back and forth across the States looking for the stupid, strange and unfathomable. For example, Australia may have the Big Merino and (my personal fave) the Big Potato, but Margate, New Jersey, has Lucy, the Big Elephant. 'She was built in 1881 by James V. Lafferty, a real estate developer with a knack for promotion. Standing six stories tall, weighing 90 tons, covered with 12,000 square feet of sheet metal, Lucy was more than an object of awe — she was a functioning building, serving first as a hotel, then as a tavern. She also gave people a reason to come to Margate City while Lafferty gave his real estate pitch. Lucy proved very useful. Jim L. made a bundle and went on to build other, even larger elephants in Cape May and Coney Island. Sadly, only Lucy has survived.' A must for anyone contemplating a holiday Stateside.

No Shitting in the Toilet
http://www.magna.com.au/~nglobe/nsitt/contents.html

'The travel guide for when you've really lost it.' The title was famously inspired by a sign on a toilet door at John's Café in the town of Dali, in the Yunnan province in China. 'NSITT is a celebration of everything that is perverse about travel. It's about getting stranded and ripped off. It's about sitting in a tiny room counting cockroaches and feeling sorry for yourself. It's about being totally clueless, hopeless and pathetic. It's about everything going wrong . . . and loving every minute of it!' It's a big and beautiful site with traveller's stories, a 'tribute to the

295

tacky, the sad and the rather strange world of postcard art', discussions of various travel nightmares and much more.

NB: **Yahoo (http://www.yahoo.com), Lycos (http://www.lycos.com), CitySearch (http://www.citysearch.com), Excite (http://www.excite.com)** and others have all been building City Guides in the last 12 months. These generally have maps, people finders, listings of hotels and restaurants and other services. The cities they cover are too numerous to list here.

GENERAL RESOURCES

Travel Network
http://www.travnet.com/

The future of the Net as a commercial arena is clear on sites such as this one and **Travelocity (http://www.travelocity.com)**. Online travel services are a model that big business believes will work. Increasingly, it is becoming possible to make all your travel arrangements from your computer. This site offers airfares and schedules for more than 500 airlines, a cruise ship database covering the activities of more than 40 lines, a database of more than 10,000 hotels, domestic (USA) and international car rental information and an extensive library of tours, packages deals and special offers.

Airlines of the Web
http://w1.itn.net/airlines/

Marc-David Seidel, assistant professor of management at the University of Texas, did his dissertation on the airline industry and found himself fascinated by its rapid changes. This led to the building of this Web site, which keeps track of all the home pages for airlines, passenger carriers and cargo ventures. Keep track of their stock quotes, frequent flyer programs, schedules and online reservation systems.

Tourism Offices Worldwide Directory
http://www.mbnet.mb.ca/lucas/travel/tourism-offices.html

Just type in a country name and it spits back the addresses of the official tourism information offices.

Air Traveller's Handbook
http://www.cis.ohio-state.edu/hypertext/faq/usenet/travel/air/handbook/top.html

Should you be travelling in the US, this regularly updated FAQ will tell you how to get cheap airline tickets.

Eventseeker
http://w3.eventseeker.com/

This is a calendar directory of worldwide events. You can search by country, date and area of interest. It catalogues festivals, carnivals, holidays, important astronomical dates and places, and business-related events.

Internet Café Guide
http://www.netcafeguide.com

A list of places where, if you're not travelling wired, you can drop by and e-mail home, catch up with your local paper or just keep in touch with your favourite Web sites. If you are travelling wired, you might be interested in **Modem Hoookup Info (http://www.cris.com/%7EKropla/phones.htm)**.

MAGAZINES

eTraveller!
http://www.empg.com/etraveller/index.html

'eTraveller! is an online magazine featuring the hard work and creativity of other magazines; a collection of travel articles, magazines, guides, books and videos scattered throughout the Internet.' Ah, nothing like making your living just by linking to the work of other people!

Epicurious Travel
http://travel.epicurious.com/

The excellent Conde Nast Traveller site was folded into this one, an offshoot of the *Epicurious* food mag. '*Epicurious Travel* is devoted to helping you find the best places to go, the smartest ways to go there, and the best things to do when you get there. It's also a place where you can swap tips and tales with other travellers.' It's a huge and impressive site, taking advantage of input from Conde Nast Traveller and Fodor's travel guides, as well as its own research and the considerable contributions of readers. It breaks down into four sections: Places (destinations), Planning (hints, tips, updates on special deals), Play (chat spaces, contests, book reviews, links) and Conde Nast Traveller (the magazine's site within the site).

Salon — Wanderlust
http://www.salonwanderlust.com/

A newish travel venture from *Salon*, the Web's best zine. 'Wanderlust is dedicated to putting the romance — the "unconquerable longing" — back into travel and the passion back into travel writing.' With writers of the calibre of Isabel Allende,

Jan Morris, Peter Mayle and Tim Cahill, they've been on to a good thing since the beginning.

Cyber Adventures
http://www.cyber-adventures.com

A Net-only magazine filled with stories from ordinary travellers. 'Join explorers and vacationers as they travel in "real time" to the many corners of the globe. Travellers record their observations on laptop computers and some take photographs with digital cameras. Transmissions are made to our site using modems with local telephone connections, in cyber cafes or with mobile satellite phones in remote locations. Use this site when planning a vacation or sit back and take some time to enjoy exploring the world from home. Cyber Adventures also features the Coolest Travel Site of the Week, Strange (But True) Travel Stories and Weekend Getaways.'

Web Travel Review
http://www-swiss.ai.mit.edu/webtravel/index.html

A site which specialises in heavily illustrated, detailed, personal first-hand accounts of journeys. It contains more than 2000 photos and 600 pages of text and features *Travels with Samantha*, an award-winning piece of Web writing about a three month trip from Boston to Alaska by a man and his anthropomorphised computer.

Business Traveller Online
http://www.btonline.com/

US, UK and German editions are all available from the site.

TRAVEL STORIES

Everest '97
http://www.everest.mountainzone.com/

'A live Cybercast of what it's really like to climb the world's biggest mountain. Historic multimedia cybercast includes: live sat-phone audio updates from Todd Burleson's Alpine Ascents International team as they climb Everest, video, animation, photo gallery, history, culture, high altitude physiology, in-depth coverage of each camp on the way to the summit, and all that makes an Everest expedition.'

Around the World in a 46-Foot Motor Boat
http://www.circumnavigator.com/

'One boat. One globe. One Internet. Infinite possibilities.' This site describes a three-year journey around the world in a 14-metre motor boat. The boat will depart from the west coast of the US sometime in 1997, with a plan to reach home on New Year's Eve, 1999. Nice work if you can get it. 'Taking digital pictures all the way and putting them up on the Web, we'll keep our followers informed right here on the World Wide Web of how it's going. We'll mount a remote control camera so Net surfers will be able to scan the horizon for ships or whales or porpoises or landfall! We'll put up audio from above and below the waterline. Of course, the Captain's log will be posted each day.'

Wheels on the Rim
http://www.efaxinc.com/WheelsOnTheRim/

'Riding mountain bikes and carrying all they need, Jennifer Fox (29) and Patchen Homitz (33) embarked on a two-year trip to circle the Pacific Ocean that will take them over 20,000 miles. These experienced cyclists will visit the countries and people bordering the Pacific Ocean to promote the use of bicycles as transportation and recreation. Heading south from the Seattle area on 23 June 1996, they will visit 23 countries, cycling clockwise around the Pacific Rim.' The journey is updated with letters, photos and postcards, and a monthly journal. Last time I looked it seemed to have been quiet for a few months. Maybe something happened to them . . .

MayaQuest '97
http://www.mecc.com/maya97/news/news.html

In 1995, the MayaQuest team explored 30 archaeological sites, biked 1,100 miles and took 22,332 photographs. They also told the Web about what they were doing. They say one million people have dropped by to see their site. In 1997, they did it again. In April and May, the MayaQuest team members cycled through the rainforests of Mexico, Belize and Guatemala in search of undocumented Mayan cities. They were linked by computer to the Web and classrooms around the world, allowing students to interact with online archaeologists and experts, and even choose the directions the team should travel in.

Skate around the World
http://www.cora.org/world.phtml

Fabrice Gropaiz of France is attempting to skate around the world on inline skates. He departed from San Francisco on 30 March 1996 with plans to cover 33 countries and 19,000 miles (27,000 km) in about 18 months, stopping occasionally to answer e-mail and post the evidence of his experiences on this Web site. It really does take all kinds.

RoadTrip America
http://www.RoadTripAmerica.com/

'These are the adventures of Mark, Megan and Marvin the Road Dog. When they lost their home and business in a California wildfire in 1993, they hit the road in the Phoenix One, the one-of-a-kind, four-wheel-drive motor home that rose from the ashes. Join them as they explore North America in search of the fascinating & entertaining.'

Live from Antarctica 2
http://quest.arc.nasa.gov/antarctica2/index.html

Despite the name this is an archived site, but it still has much of interest. Twice, from November 1994 to February 1995, and from January to March 1997, a team of scientists on the coldest content kept journals and interacted with teachers and students back home. 'Experience life boat drill on the roughest waters on Earth! Go study penguins amid the most spectacular scenery on Earth! Interact with researchers at Earth's most remote research laboratory for marine biology and global climate change!'

Yahoo's Guide to Travelogues
http://www.yahoo.com/Recreation/Travel/Travelogues/

A collection of links to sites about the personal journeys of travellers, stories from around the world, sites devoted to all kinds of travel and all sorts of obscure and not so obscure destinations. From a journal of a two-week tour with The Grateful Dead to the tales of a 20-year-old Japanese student who travelled around the world for two years with only $300.

AND BEFORE I FORGET . . .

How to be Obnoxious in French
http://yoyo.cc.monash.edu.au/~mongoose/french/

You never know when you'll find yourself in Paris, pretending to be Cary Grant or Audrey Hepburn in *Charade*. So it's best to start preparing for your trip now. How to be Obnoxious in French offers some excellent tips on how to abuse a phrasebook before getting down to a serious list of insulting French phrases, with phonetic help, such as 'T'as une tête à faire sauter les plaques d'égouts!' (ta zoon tait a fair saw-teh leh plahk de-goo), which apparently means 'You've got a face that would blow off manhole covers'.

Roadkill Bingo
http://www.netads.com/netads/games/tccc/games.html

Your family holiday need never be boring again with the introduction of Roadkill Bingo. Download the bingo card and cross off every dead thing you see. You'll need to adapt it from its American version (it's reasonably unlikely that you'll hit an armadillo between here and the next town), but after a couple of simple changes, you'll never look back. The site points out that you can also use the cards for Roadkill Lotto. Now you'll look forward to school holidays.

Food

GENERAL

Kitchen Link—What's Cooking on the Net
http://www.kitchenlink.com/

These foodies really know how to network. This site bills itself as a master index to more than 6,665 food and cooking-related sites. I hate to do this to you, but I think I have to, just so you'll get an idea of the breadth . . . These are the categories of its links: consumer information, cookbooks, cooking for beginners, cooking for kids, cooking tips, culinary careers, diets, dietitians, e-zines, famous cooks, FAQs, food allergies, food companies, food safety, food service, forums, glossaries, health, hunger relief, magazines, mailing lists, news articles, newsgroups, newsletters, newspapers, nutrition info, professional chefs, recipe archives, restaurant menus, restaurant reviews, schools, institutes, search engines, site lists, software for cooks, TV and radio shows, Usenet FAQs and Usenet newsgroups.

FoodWeb
http://www.foodweb.com/

This is also a great place to start your wanderings, a clearing-house for more than 4,000 links. I won't list its attributes, but they're also considerable. And it's well-designed and easier to use than Kitchen Link.

The Internet Food Channel
http://www.foodchannel.com/

All the food news on the Web, culled from various newspapers

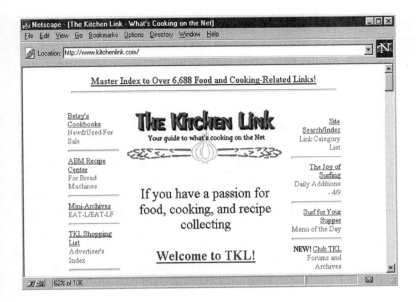

and zines. Plus recipes. There's a daily food fact, places to chat ('shut up and eat') and more.

Epicurious
http://www.epicurious.com

A funky little food mag on the Web, courtesy of CondeNet. It draws from offline magazines *Gourmet* and *Bon Appetit* and has a sense of humour in its approach to serious dining. It's Playing With Your Food section features all kinds of fun, from a hole gauge for circular foodstuffs to a guide to handling problem foods in public.

EGG (Electronic Gourmet Guide)
http://www.foodwine.com/

Another good foodie mag, with columns and lots of special

features. It's basically monthly but includes more frequent updates in specific areas. Its archives are good. There's an online store. And lots of little curious corners of the site to get yourself lost in.

Gourmet World
http://www.gourmetworld.com/

'Like to cook? Or maybe just enjoy the results? Gourmet World serves up a banquet of information about food and its preparation from all over the world and presents it to you with just a click of the mouse. Gourmet World is home to the first Internet cooking program by internationally-known expert Graham Kerr. Tune in to "A Tale of Three Chickens" for a delightful excursion into Graham Kerr's wit and wisdom in preparing healthful food.' It's a good site, but the downloads are killers.

Interactive Food Finder
http://www.olen.com/food/

Dedicated to bringing the user fast food facts. You just pick the franchise of your choice and the site will tell you the amounts of calories, fat, cholesterol and sodium in each of its products. It makes for cheery pre-lunch reading.

RECIPES

Internet Chef
http://www.ichef.com/

'An electronic archive dedicated to the worship of food.' An online mag featuring monthly articles, a recipe of the week, food news and columns, tips and hints, a recipe archive, places to chat about food and swap or request recipes, and directions to other Web resources.

Recipes Archive
http://www.neosoft.com/recipes/

The text-only files on this site are a collection of recipes from the newsgroup **rec.food.recipes**. Thousands and thousands and thousands of them. No-one, mercifully, has had to count them. There are 54 separate sections, from appetisers to vegetarian.

Searchable Online Archive of Recipes (SOAR)
http://soar.Berkeley.EDU/recipes/

Exactly as its title promises, this whip-fast archive had at last count passed the 35,000 recipe mark. The ethnic section alone deals with African, Argentinian, Armenian, Australian, Basque, Belgian, Brazilian, British, Cajun, Canadian, Carribbean, Chinese, Colombian, Czech, Danish, Dutch, Egyptian, Ethiopian, Filipino, Finnish, French, German, Greek, Hungarian, Indian & Pakistani, Indonesian, Irish, Italian, Japanese, Jewish, Korean, Lebanese, Mexican, Middle Eastern, Native American, Norwegian, Persian, Peruvian, Polish, Portuguese, Russian, Scandinavian, Scottish, Spanish, Swedish, Swiss, Tahitian, Thai, Tibetan, Turkish, Venezuelan, Vietnamese and Welsh. Phew!

Veggies Unite!
http://www.vegweb.com/

A fantastic site, well made and easy to navigate. A veritable garden of facts, with loads of recipes and reasons to follow the veggie lifestyle. There are newsletters, event notifications, places you can chat, and even a composting guide. The site's mission is 'to enhance public awareness of the many benefits of a vegetarian diet and lifestyle. VU began in the summer of 1994 with only a few recipes and a search engine. When its popularity grew, the Honours Division of Indiana University generously hosted it for several months. Now 2,000+ recipes and 20,000+ members strong.'

Aphrodisiac Dishes
http://www.santesson.com/recept/aphrlist.htm

'Can food really be an aphrodisiac? Yes, indeed! Just read what **Encyclopedia Britannica (http://www.eb.com)** has to say on this subject: ". . . the psychophysiological reaction that a well-prepared meal can have upon the human organism. The combination of various sensuous reactions—the visual satisfaction of the sight of appetising food, the olfactory stimulation of their pleasing smells and the tactile gratification afforded the oral mechanism by rich, savoury dishes tend to bring on a state of general euphoria conducive to sexual expression."' Entrees, soups, fish and shellfish, sauces and condiments and desserts are all catered for in separate sections.

RESTAURANTS

Dining Out on the Web
http://www.ird.net/diningout.html

This is an umbrella site for various city restaurant guides. It provides links to guides for places in all the states of the USA and 18 other countries as well. The quality of the content differs greatly from one to the next, but it'll give you an idea of what the food is like wherever you may plan to be going.

Dine Net
http://www.menusonline.com/

Another restaurant service, this one features the menus of hundreds of restaurants, so you can make your choices from home. At this point, it's America only.

World Wide Sushi Restaurant Reference
http://www.cis.unisa.edu.au/~cisjpm/Sushi

The main attraction here is the listing of sushi restaurants (well above the thousand mark), grouped by country, state and city, with commentary from various Net citizens. Summaries of these lists without the comments are also available. There's a fairly large glossary of Japanese sushi terms, and most Japanese words in the site are linked to their definitions in the glossary. The comments are linked to a contributor's page. There's also a number of recipes, a page of sushi bar etiquette and beginners' tips, a list of sushi societies and some other miscellaneous information.

Kosher Restaurant Database
http://shamash.nysernet.org/kosher/krestquery.html

Enter a city or a country or even a name and the site will search itself and bring back (quickly) a list of possible matches. Text only, very fast.

Eat Germany
http://www.eat-germany.net/

Before it eats you.

A FEW FOODSTUFFS

The Potato Page
http://imcom.com/~james/potato/

The Potato—'it's brown and has lumps'. Now there's a marketing slogan! This site looks at the spud's religious significance ('In the year 3000310, THE nuclear holocaust will have struck, leaving only cockroaches and potatoes. In the next 17 years, the cockroaches and potatoes will grow in population and size. In the year 3000327, the great potato will descend upon the earth, enslaving its people . . .'), at different cultural viewpoints on tubers (how to say 'I am a potato' in seven languages) and at the Web of spud links. You'll find more serious spudology at the **World Geography of the Potato (http://julian.dac.uga. edu/intro.html)**.

Official French Fry Page
http://www.select-ware.com/fries/

While we're on the subject, this is the place to find out too much about the ongoing love affair between potatoes and hot fat. Check out 21 things you didn't know about French Fries ('13. French Fries are the number two "drunk food"—what people eat when they've had too much to drink. 14. Pizza is number one') or 22 things to do with French Fries besides eat them ('1. You can use them to fill small cracks and keep out drafts').

Codfish World
http://www.bacalhau.com.br/

Ah, fish and chips. This Brazilian site seeks to introduce you to 'a noble and nutritious fish', the cod. 'We would like to dedicate this home page to Norway, the Viking's country, whose rich and sympathetic people have been exporting the codfish to Brazil for 153 years.' Learn about the fish and the industry which surrounds it, its history (dating back to famous cod of the fifteenth century), the kinds of cod that exist and the nutritional value of them. There are also recipes and cooking tips.

Rhubarb Compendium
http://www.clark.net/pub/dan/rhubarb/rhubarb.html

Everything you wanted to know about rhubarb, its history (I was never aware that there were vegetable historians until I became a Web surfer), growth, harvest, storage and uses. Sing the Rhubarb Tart song. Or just look at the pretty pictures.

The Bagel Page
http://jaka.ece.uiuc.edu/~scott/bagels/

'The first bagel rolled into the world in 1683 when a local baker wanted to pay tribute to Jan Sobieski, the King of Poland. King Jan had just saved the people of Austria from an onslaught of Turkish invaders. The King was a great horseman, and the baker decided to shape the yeast dough into an uneven circle resembling a stirrup. The Austrian word for stirrup is *beugel*. In Poland, bagels are officially sanctioned as an appropriate gift for any woman in childbirth.' Bagel info, recipes and scholarship.

The Garlic Page
http://www.garlicpage.com/

A site devoted to the joys and wonders of the 'stinking rose'. Check out the Fun Facts and Fiction section. Garlic as a recreational drug?

CheeseNet
http://www.wgx.com/cheesenet/

A huge and impressive site, stuffed with information. 'CheeseNet began in March 1995, and has been growing ever since. Our aim is to disseminate information on cheese and its many uses, in the interest of increasing Netizens' cheese knowledge.'

Its World Cheese Index is a database of more than 60 cheeses, which offers pictures and detailed information. There are poems, short stories and plays in the Cheese Literature and the list of Cheese Links is loooong.

B's Cucumber Pages
http://www.lpl.arizona.edu/~bcohen/cucumbers/info.html

I'll let Barbara tell you herself: 'One day, late in spring 1995, I had a hankering for a good cucumber. Naturally, this hankering led me to the Web, to cruise for information on how to grow my own and what I could do with them once I had grown them. Imagine my shock and dismay when extended searches and many devoted hours turned up close to nothing about the family, history, or culinary uses of this time-honoured vegetable!! So instead, I used my old-fashioned library skills and a bit of HTML knowledge to find and compile more information about cucumbers than anyone ever needed to know—including me.'

The Banana Museum
http://www.geocities.com/NapaValley/1799/

'The most delicious thing in the world is a banana'—Benjamin Disraeli, 1831. Banana Museum curator Ann Lovell has assembled more than 3,500 banana artefacts, on display at her shrine and this site. It's not technically about the fruit itself, but it is a fructal obsession, so I thought I'd mention it.

Durian Online
http://www.ecst.csuchico.edu/~durian/

'Name: *Bombaceae Durio zibethinus L/Murr*. Better known as: *Durian* (Malaysia/Worldwide), *Duren* (Indonesia), *Thurian* (Thailand).

From: *South East Asia*. Occupation: *King of the Fruits*. Part-time job: *Handy as a weapon.'* A Web page devoted in its entirety to the durian, with photos, recipes, books, facts and figures and news reports.

Broccoli Town, USA
http://www.broccoli.com/

You have to love a vegetable with its own domain address, even if the site is a corporate one, from Mann's packing company. Take a virtual tour of the farm to learn how broccoli grows. Drop into the kitchen for cooking tips. Send your children off to the Broccoli Institute to get some learnin'.

Toast Resources on the Net
http://www.dsp.com/tritone/toastlinks.html

Believe it or not, there are a lot of virtual shrines to the fine art of toasting, so if you want to look, you might as well go to the master list. Don't forget to drop by the haiku section for gems like the following:

A slice of calmness
In mankind's world of bloodshed
Spread some marmalade

MISCELLANEOUS

McSpotlight
http://www.McSpotlight.org/

A wonderful site which offers a little public resistance to the franchise, concentrating on the famous McLibel case, a public relations nightmare for McDonald's, which sued Helen Steel and Dave Morris for allegedly producing a critical factsheet entitled 'What's Wrong with McDonald's'. 'Contained within this section are the court transcripts for the entire 313 days of the trial, various legal documents, and a comprehensive guide to the witnesses.' The site also offers tours, not only of itself, but also of the official McDonald's Web venture.

The Anti-Blue M&M Page
http://www.mines.edu/students/l/lbecker/mm/

A conspiracy theory site based on the 'mysterious disappearance' of the tan M&Ms and their replacement by the much more suspicious blue ones. 'Coincidence? We think not. The blue M&M's® are Murderers. They killed the tan M&M's® in order to infiltrate the M&M® Mars distribution center of candy. This brutal and unnecessary killing has not gone unnoticed . . .'

Internet Pizza Server
http://www2.ecst.csuchico.edu/~pizza/

Order your pizza over the Web or by e-mail. The site will make it to your requirements and send it to you. Choose from a long, long list of toppings. The meats section alone includes: bacon bits, beef, beetles, Canadian bacon, eyeballs, goblins, kittens, pepperoni, pork, salami, sausage, fingers and something called Curly.

Food in the Bible
http://www.value.net/~esoteric/bro/foodsite.html

Proving that holiness and yumminess are related. In many categories. Here's what the Bible has to say about chickens: Matt.23:37 'O Jerusalem, Jerusalem, thou that killest the prophets, and stonest them which are sent unto thee, how often would I have gathered thy children together, even as a hen gathereth her chickens under her wings, and ye would not!'

The Barney Cookbook
http://www.wco.com/~keebler/cookbook.html

One of the refreshing things about the Web is the amount of fear and loathing directed towards Barney, the giant purple dinosaur and kiddie program host. Anyone over the age of six who has sat through a half-hour of his singalong playtime will have an entirely different vision of Hell to that usually conjured by Bible fans. The Cookbook is a contributor-based series of recipes involving large purple dinosaurs, meat grinders and lots of pain. Some may find it cathartic.

Food Gone Bad
http://www.eit.com/~bolhuijo/gallery.html

A tribute to mould and its capacity to colonise perishables. In glorious colour. Not for the queasy. Growing at such a rate that it has opened a Coffee Gone Bad wing for aficionados.

People Eating Tasty Animals (PETA)
http://www.mtd.com/tasty/

A Web site devoted to the other side of the arguments put by the People for the Ethical Treatment of Animals (PETA). It's 'a resource for those who enjoy eating meat, wearing fur and leather, hunting, and the fruits of scientific research (and more!)'. Outrage your vegetarian friends.

The Uselessness of Food
http://www.go2net.com/internet/useless/useless/food.html

From our very, very good friends at the Useless Pages site, this is a carefully curated collection of idiotic food links. Here you'll find directions to amazingly, brain-frying sites such as the Cabbage Appreciation Society, the Bacon Worship Page, Bananarchy and X-Rays of Cakes.

Zucchini Haters Anonymous
http://www.netonecom.net/~seguin/zha.htm

There's nothing to the site but a list of its teenage members and a declaration of loathing for the poor, little, under-rated vegetable. Pick on someone your own colour, guys.

Insect Recipes
http://www.ent.iastate.edu/Misc/InsectsAsFood.html

Mmmmmmmm, crunchy.

Butchering the Human Carcass for Human Consumption
http://www.envirolink.org/orgs/coe/e-sermons/butcher.html

A step by step guide, with handy (sorry) hints on procurement. 'The human being (also referred to throughout culinary history as "long pig" and "hairless goat" in the case of younger specimens) is not generally thought of as a staple food source. Observing the anatomy and skeleton, one can see that the animal is neither built nor bred for its meat, and as such will not provide nearly as much flesh as a pig or cow (for example, an average 1000 pound steer breaks down to provide 432 pounds of saleable beef). The large central pelvis and broad shoulder blades also interfere with achieving perfect cuts.'

ART

TEN MUSEUMS AND GALLERIES

Le Louvre
http://mistral.culture.fr/louvre/louvrea.htm

The Web site for what many would argue is the epicentre of the art gallery world (hey, Ms Lisa lives there) is another which is a lot more substantial than first glance might lead you to believe. There's a lot of practical information on getting there and opening hours and all the usual stuff, but there is also a refreshingly solid amount of wordage dedicated to the collections, with just enough examples of actual artworks to convince you that you have to make the journey, next time you're passing through Paris.

Smithsonian Institute
http://www.si.edu/

If you've ever spent a day or two wandering around the Smithsonian's many buildings, you'll know how big it is. Thankfully, so is its Web presence. It houses 16 museums, 12 research centres, 16 administrative offices and four affiliated institutions. And that's not counting all the special events, activities, resources and tours. This is a Web site with a lot on its plate. You could spend days wandering about its environs. Some of the museums are a little sketchy, but others have leapt at the chance to expand into the virtual world. The National Museum of American Art, for example, houses about 750 works in its two buildings. Its Web section boasts 1300. Take the 150 year celebratory tour (no, it doesn't take that long) to get an idea of the goodies awaiting. Oh, and should your eyes be failing you a little, you can have the Smithsonian Web read to you if you download a little of the appropriate software.

Metropolitan Museum of Art
http://www.metmuseum.org/

You'll think you've stumbled onto a holding page, a site that is just the back end of some online New York tourist brochure. But the Met reveals its layers as you head in, taking you on a complex tour of its collections and special exhibitions, and casting an eye towards its future, with a discussion of its plans for the new millennium. There are disappointingly few illustrations from its vast collections, but enough to whet your appetite. The Watsonline database gives biographical details for around 70 per cent of the museum's holdings.

Centre Georges Pompidou
http://www.cnac-gp.fr/

A great modern art gallery, but the site is in French, except for a single page which tells you the opening hours and how to get there. You, of course, read French perfectly, so you'll love the site, whereas I can't even read my own handwriting.

Guggenheim Museum
http://www.guggenheim.org/

You'll find information on the four main museums and collections that make up the Guggenheim legacy. Each part of the site has details of the museums, as well as past and present exhibitions. But it's all a bit like a brochure.

Los Angeles Museum of Contemporary Art
http://www.MOCA-LA.org/

Information on exhibitions (current and upcoming), its permanent collection, special events, educational resources and store. As with the Guggenheim, it's basically still a promotional arm of the museum, rather than a curatorial one.

Museum of Contemporary Art — Sydney
http://www.mca.com.au/

A simple, classy site for this institution, which is 'home to over 5,000 artworks acquired since the 1960s through the JW Power Bequest. With extensive Aboriginal collections also held in trust, the MCA is committed to celebrating the living indigenous culture of Australia in all its artforms. In addition, the Museum has an active program of changing international exhibitions and has worked with many of the world's leading contemporary art museums.' There are online versions of current and past exhibitions, as well as educational information, merchandising and links.

Don't miss the virtual tour of Jeff Koons' Puppy.

Uffizi Gallery
http://www.uffizi.firenze.it/

Another gallery site which seems weak at first but as you click in, you'll find a gradual project unfolding. Go to the gallery map and you'll discover most of the rooms in the museum have their own pages, with lists of the artworks on show, and photos and explanations of many of them. In time, this will clearly become a fine Web tour.

Victoria and Albert Museum
http://www.vam.ac.uk/

'The world's finest museum of the decorative arts, founded in 1852 to support and encourage excellence in art and design. Today the beautiful Victorian and Edwardian buildings house 145 galleries containing some of the world's greatest collections of sculpture, furniture, fashion and textiles, paintings, silver, glass, ceramics, jewellery, books, prints and photographs.' You can't, unfortunately, make similar boasts for the Web site, which is a bit dowdy really, and very text heavy. The information is good, consistent and solid, but the thrill of the art is absent.

Museum of Bad Art
http://glyphs.com/moba/

You'll either get it or you won't. Some people hate this site. Others love it. It's 'a community-based, private institution dedicated to the collection, preservation, exhibition and celebration of bad art in all its forms and in all its glory. The pieces in the MOBA collection range from the work of talented artists that have gone awry, to works of exuberant, although crude, execution by artists barely in control of the brush. What they all have in common is a special quality that sets them apart in one way or another from the merely incompetent.' There could be a heck of a lot more works in the online collection, but the few that are available through the site manage to crack me up every time.

RESOURCES

World Wide Arts Resources
http://wwar.world-arts-resources.com/

'The biggest gateway to the arts on the Internet—from happening, groovin' art events to traditional planar exhibitions and museums to way out 3D cyber galleries—you'll find it here!' This site is a specialist search engine for the arts. You can search by name or browse directories of subject-specific sites, indexes for more than a dozen areas of the arts and their related resources.

The Art Site on the World Wide Web
http://cwis.usc.edu/dept/annenberg/artfinal.html

Margaret L. McLaughlin, of the Annenberg School for Communication, University of Southern California, contributes this thoughtful, hyperlinked essay about art on the Web. It's good background for anyone wanting to look at the Net as artform as well as library. McLaughlin looks at the evolution of electronic art on the Web and what the experiences of its pioneers have shown us.

Art Links
http://www.fine-art.com/link.html

A simple, comprehensive index service for art sites, broken up into nine major areas: artists, galleries and exhibits, organisations and business, museums, mailing lists, indices and search engines, Usenet resources, applications, and a miscellaneous section for the overflow. Simple to use and extraordinarily broad.

Art on the Net
http://www.art.net/

'This is a virtual space where artists join together in sharing their art with others on the Internet. This site offers artists a place where they can have studios and gallery rooms that can be accessed via the WWW. This is a place where artists can come to learn how to get themselves and their art up on the Internet. It is also a meeting place where people can come to find out about art happenings on the Net. Currently we have 100 artists at our site, from around the world, so we are international. There are poets, musicians, painters, sculptors, digital artists, performance artists, animators and much more.'

FineArt Forum Resource Directory
http://www.msstate.edu/Fineart_Online/art-resources/

Another 'resource and jumping-off place for people interested in art, and in the possible relationships between art and technology'. This one not only links to gallery and artist sites, but to discussion areas, schools and services for artists.

ArtLex
http://www.aristotle.com/sskystorage/Art/ArtLex.html

'A dictionary/glossary for artists, art students, and art educators in art production, art criticism, art history, aesthetics, and art education.' This lexicon began in late 1996 and has been growing every week, adding new words and terms to its archive.

Multimedia and Clip Art
http://www.itec.sfsu.edu/multimedia/multimedia.html

A library of images, graphics, icons, clip art and sounds for the electronic artist in all of us. Links to other sites and resources.

Pictures
http://www.yahoo.com/Computers_and_Internet/Multimedia/Pictures/

This is the other place to go if you're on the hunt for imagery.

Yahoo links to hundreds of thousands of pictures, under subject headings from 3D to flags, fractals to weather. If you can't find it here, you're not looking.

Silicon Graphics Image Gallery
http://www.sgi.com/Fun/free/gallery.html

If you're going to look at computer-generated images, you might as well go to the company that designed half of the technology that made them. Silicon Graphics has all sorts of interesting galleries of images. The most interesting are the artworks made by the artists-in-residence, employed by the company to show them what their own machines are capable of. Check out Stewart McSherry's work.

PHOTOGRAPHY

International Center of Photography
http://www.icp.org/

The centre was established in 1974 to collect, preserve, and exhibit notable twentieth-century works, with a special emphasis on documentary photography; to teach photography at all levels; and to provide a forum for the exchange of critical ideas and information. There are two galleries in Manhattan and a third on the Web.

LIFE Magazine Home Page
http://pathfinder.com/Life/lifehome.html

The site carries many recent photos and special features (a rock and roll gallery last time I was there, but for shutterbugs, the Virtual Gallery is the place to go. It links to *LIFE*'s own collection of photographic exhibitions and to other major shows around the Web.

Photojournalism
http://www.yahoo.com/Arts/Visual_Arts/Photography/Photojournalism/Photojournalists/Personal_Exhibits/

Check out Yahoo's list of photojournalists. Each of the people on the list (well over 100 of them) hosts a site of their own work. All points of the globe are represented. Check out George Azar's photographs of Sufi mystics, lost desert cities and grand bazaar, Brian Cheuk's news and sport shots from Hong Kong, Piet den Blanken's views of Cuba, Dan Habib's essays on teen sexuality and Alain Le Bacquer's collection of hip hop images from the streets of Paris.

Dennis Kunkel's Microscopy
http://www.pbrc.hawaii.edu/~kunkel/

I love microscope photography, all those close-ups of the eyes and mandibular arrangements of strange insects, shot in lurid fluorescence. The look like '50s B-movie monsters. Kunkel's site is a beauty, with exhibitions not only of bugs and little things that fly into your open mouth while you're sleeping, but microscopic plant life as well. And it has a sense of humour — its Most Wanted Bugs section features mug shots of the various household pests.

Wade's Photobooth Gallery
http://www.cris.com/~Wadet/

Some of the best shots I have ever taken have been in a photobooth. This says something about me or the machinery, but I'm not sure what. The idea for a Photobooth Gallery was conceived in London in the spring of 1996,' Wade says. 'It was there, passing a photobooth everyday in the Tottenham Court Road tube station, that I realised how genius [sic] these humble boxes are. I vowed to document their art, along with the mugs of all the hipsters I know.'

Distortions
http://www.ibsnet.com/ndl/distortions/

An art gallery with a difference or two. Here, the electronic artists take the visages of well known people and alter them for your enjoyment. Want to see a rearranged supermodel? Or perhaps the cast of *Friends* after a nasty electronic collision? Reminiscent of Ralph Steadman's polaroid manipulations.

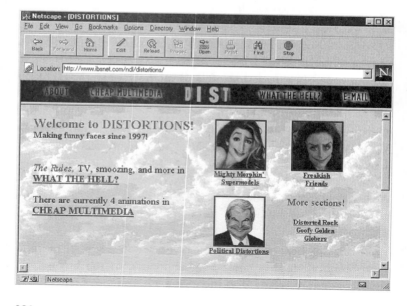

ONLINE EXHIBITION SPACES

artnetweb
http://www.artnetweb.com/

'artnetweb is the creation of artists Remo Campopiano and Robbin Murphy. The Web site is the third phase of a process to establish an art colony in cyberspace. All three parts are integral to artnetweb.' The first was the establishment of a reading room in New York's SoHo, where artists could experience the net. The second was a local BBS. The third is this Web site, 'our doorway to the world with a curated area for projects, writings and resources, a section for arts organisations and the arts commerce section for galleries, artists and companies to do business'. It's a lot more interesting than that simple description sounds, more like a funky art forum, with special features, chat and audio areas, and a regularly updated list of all that is happening on the Web, digital art-wise.

Virtual Exhibits on the World Wide Web
http://library.wustl.edu/~prietto/exhibits/

A guide to virtual exhibitionism (of the right kind), updated once a month by Carole Prietto.

The Web Museum
http://watt.emf.net/wm/

An attempt to do for the Web what the Metropolitan does for the city of New York, this site is an attempt to collect as many artworks as possible in one place, from different eras and schools. There are, for example, more than 100 works by Paul Cézanne alone. The Famous Paintings section has the works of more than 200 artists. Each of those artists is usually represented by multiple works, along with potted biographies.

ArtServe
http://rubens.anu.edu.au/

A huge archive of online images. Last time I looked, it had more than 27,000 images on its server, with plans for another 5,000 in the short term. The pictures are mainly of art and architecture from the Mediterranean basin. The site has become so large that its curators have had to start charging for downloads.

Foundation for Digital Culture
http://digicult.org/

An umbrella organisation for 16 online galleries, the Foundation for Digital Culture 'is a not-for-profit organisation whose purpose is to promote and support digital culture and art on-line'.

6168
http://www.6168.org/

Peter Horvath and Sharon Matarazzo run this stylish digital artspace, so it's no surprise that their own works dominate. The Web offers the artist the chance to be a gallery owner as well, without having to fork out for staff and enormous rental fees. The works are Net-specific art, interactive installations, like Mona Says, a reflection on the contents of the mind of Mona Lisa as she sat for her portrait.

911 Gallery
http://www.iquest.net/911/iq_911.html

A not-for-profit organisation whose goals include: 'promoting public awareness and appreciation of digital media in the fine arts, and encouraging the development of innovative, quality digital art'. It carries exhibitions from a number of digital artists, with a layout that suggests a real museum while its pieces suggest anything but. From digital abstractions to an interactive tarot to an animation corner . . .

Bibliotheque Bajazzo Amsterdam
http://www.xs4all.nl/~arthur/

A gallery of 'online experimental art' from the Netherlands, with a lot of sections whose titles don't make much sense. Like many online galleries, the navigational aspects of the site are thought of as part of the artwork. So, if it made perfect linear sense, it wouldn't be art, would it? Images appear and disappear, mutate and dissolve. Don't ask me what it's all about.

Entropy8
http://www.entropy8.com/

Sculptor Auriea Harvey lets loose her talents on a Web site which is as arresting as it is sophisticated in its use of texture, colour, image and animation. 'Since 1989,' she writes, 'Entropy8 has been dedicated to bringing you the finest in innovative imaging, multimedia creations, and conceptual design. In the realm of the Web I will continue to further the cause of beauty and ugliness in the world. E8D exists to spread artistic freedom and uncommon functionality to the Web and beyond.' Mercifully, she offers directions for the use of the intensely graphic site.

Digitopolis
http://www.digitopolis.com/

The home page, on my visit, was a distorted image of a body, with its arterial system on the outside and a starfish discreetly covering the genital area. I clicked on the head, which took me in for a closer look, before informing me that it had four clickable areas. Try the eye, I thought. It told me what the artist had seen, a site belonging to Spanish performance art guerillas **La Fura dels Baus (http://www.teknoland.es/fura)**. Hmmm. This intriguing site wants you to think of the body as navigational metaphor and the Web as art space and artwork simultaneously. And why not?

Elevator
http://RECOMPUTER.ELECTRICFROG.CO.UK/elevator/

'Scotland's first online forum for electronic art and multimedia. Here you will find a selection of new works specially designed for the site plus coverage of electronic and multimedia events and discussion.' There's a special section for Super 8 works, a number of floors of artist exhibits, news and links on the ground floor and a basement full of essays and ideas.

Putrid Afterthought
http://www.mayhem.net/mendoza.html

'Putrid Afterthought is what is seen at the end of a double-barrelled shotgunned cesspool of hyperreality. View at your own risk. May cause irreparable libidinal damage.' I like a site that carries a health warning. Artist Antonio Mendoza pieces together savage, usually ugly and confrontational collages. His intent is to disturb and he often succeeds.

The E-Wall
http://www.geocities.com/SoHo/3672/

A virtual wall on which you are invited to hang a piece of your own work. The artist, you, is allowed to submit up to three works (keep the file size under 40k), which are then displayed on the wall. Artists from many different countries are represented, with digital images, oil paintings and photographs of sculpture rubbing shoulders.

OH, AND A FEW OTHER THINGS ...

Waxweb
http://bug.village.virginia.edu/

Waxweb has been one of the Internet's prime art experiments since 1994. Is it a movie? A book? A virtual reality environment? Even its creator, artist David Blair, isn't sure. It's a loose, not exactly linear narrative with 90 minutes of video and 25,000 hyperlinks included. But it's not like reading a book or watching a movie. It's like entering an altered state of consciousness, a clickable dream.

Mondrimat
http://www.stephen.com/mondrimat/

Okay, just because Mondrian was the test pattern we had before television came along, doesn't mean he didn't do some cool stuff. Now you can emulate his feats, thanks to Mondrimat ('where the beautiful people come to flex their minds'), a site which allows the user to 'experiment with space, colour and visual rhythm in accordance with the theories of Piet Mondrian'. It's point and click fun and, much to my own embarrassment, I spent hours there.

Kids' Sites

A FEW HINTS FOR PARENTS

Child Safety on the Information Superhighway
http://www.missingkids.org/childsafety.html

'Although there have been some highly publicised cases of abuse involving computers, reported cases are relatively infrequent . . . The fact that crimes are being committed online, however, is not a reason to avoid using these services. To tell children to stop using these services would be like telling them to forgo attending college because students are sometimes victimised on campus. A better strategy would be for children to learn how to be "street smart" in order to better safeguard themselves in any potentially dangerous situation.' The Amer-

ican National Centre for Missing and Exploited Children offers guidelines for parents and a set of simple rules for online safety to be given to children.

Parental Control FAQ
http://www.vtw.org/pubs/ipcfaq

The folks at Voters Telecommunications Watch have put together this Frequently Asked Questions list to help parents understand Net realities. It's a text file which deals with parental guidance, government restrictions, author ratings systems, proof of age shielding systems, proprietary environments, phase detection systems and third party ratings systems.

The Kids on the Web: Safety
http://www.zen.org/~brendan/kids-safe.html

'There are a number of software packages available that try to help keep children safer on the Internet. While there is no ideal solution, as with life in general, the packages help take a first step to protecting children in Cyberspace.' Site author Brendan Kehoe provides links to a dozen companies dealing in Net protection software.

Platform for Internet Content Selection (PICS)
http://www.w3.org/pub/WWW/PICS/

A cross-industry working group to develop technologies that will give users of the Internet control over the kinds of material which they and their children access. 'PICS members believe that individuals, groups and businesses should have easy access to the widest possible range of content selection products, and a diversity of voluntary rating systems.' An even better explanation of PICS can be found at **Filtering Information on the**

Internet (**http://www.sciam.com/0397issue/0397resnick. html**), a special report from the March 1997 issue of *Scientific American*.

LAUNCHPADS

Yahooligans!
http://www.yahooligans.com/

'Yahooligans! is a searchable, browsable index of the Internet designed for Web surfers ages 7 to 12.' And it's the best bookmark you could have. Like its elder sibling, Yahooligans! is a simple, subject-based indexing system, which allows kids to follow their noses and discover lists of sites that are relevant to their interests. Its main sections include Around the World (info on other countries), School Bell (sites that will help with study), Art Soup (aesthetic pursuits), Science and Oddities (space and dinosaurs are a big draw), Computers, Games, and Online (techie stuff), Sports and Recreation (self evident), Entertainment (pop culture) and The Scoop (news, weather and comics).

Bess the Internet Retriever
http://www.bess.net

Bess does something similar to Yahoo, even going so far as borrowing certain design elements. 'Bess the Internet Retriever Service is named after a real live Chesapeake Bay Retriever. Bess, the dog, is one and a half years old, weighs about ninety pounds, loves kids, has mounds of energy and will retrieve just about anything you will throw for her.' Like Yahooligans, it filters the content of the Web and offers sites under category headings that parents can trust are safe.

Berit's Best Sites for Children
http://db.cochran.com/db_HTML:theopage.db

A really great links site, which not only puts the sites into more than 20 subject categories, but includes annotations and reviews, so you know what you're going to get before you click through.

CyberKids
http://www.cyberkids.com/

Launched in 1994 by a couple of software engineers (who were also parents of primary school children), CyberKids exists to publish the creative work of children. 'Our goal is to create and promote youth community worldwide, and give kids a voice and an interactive place to express their creativity. Young people all over the world make CyberKids a sharing, caring space. CyberKids is a place for kids' creativity to flourish while getting feedback from others; a space to read stories, to listen to kids' musical compositions, to view artwork, to meet keypals from all over.' See also: **Cyberteens (http://www.cyberteens. com).**

Kid's Space
http://www.kids-space.org/

Another site specialising in the online work of kids, this one is aimed more at the early teenage end of the market. It has a series of art galleries, story areas, a collaborative picture book project, a concert area where musical works can be heard, and a number of guided tours of the Internet, to teach children how to use it well and safely.

Bonus.com
http://www.bonus.com

This fascinating site has arrived at an ingeniously obvious way to reassure parents about the safety of their Web-surfing children. Using software called Web Scooter, Bonus.com launches itself in a separate browser window, with its own controls, so kids can't go clicking their way off the site. And though it carries ads, the balance is well in favour of content — there are more than 500 parts of the site — and the quality is high, with a high level of interaction. If not a mini-universe, the site is definitely a solar system. It's a guarantee of hours of interest. Its Godzilla section alone kept me rapt for ages.

WWW 4 Kidz
http://www.4kidz.com/

'We're here to help you have a fun, safe online learning experience. There's lots to do, so just click on one of W Whitaker Webb's buttons or scroll down for more information.' The site offers homework help, tips on using the Web, kid's reviews of books and movies, things to make with your hands and various weekly contests.

THE CORPORATE GIANTS

Lego
http://www.lego.com

Join the Lego surfer club. You have to build your own virtual Lego page to do it, but hell, there's nothing on TV today is there? If you join, you get free downloads of wallpapers, screensavers and video clips. Find out about the company, the whole range of products ('Mum, here's something you haven't had to buy me yet!') and the latest Lego news. Older folk can even apply for jobs with the company. Oh, and there are online contests too.

Disney
http://www.disney.com

I have dreams of throttling Pocahontas, but I have come to accept (after years of therapy) that many other people really like Disney cartoons (OK, Robin Williams was good in *Aladdin* and *Toy Story* was fantastic, but the rest? Sheesh!). Anyway, the site is home to the Disney Store online, information about the various Disneylands and Disney Worlds, the company's publishing and broadcasting ventures, and Disney Interactive, which makes the CD-ROMs. It's all a bit merchandise heavy for me, but kids get to look at the pictures of their favourite characters.

Warner Bros Kids
http://www.kids.warnerbros.com/

Part of the larger company site, this little corner has some cool things to do, including: Looney Tunes karaoke, an interactive Web postcard service and a Do It Yourself guide to animation techniques.

Sega
http:www.sega.com

An online shop for strategy guides. A Games directory. A Games room, where you can enter contests or have your high scores added to the champions lists. Extra levels of games not in the packaged versions. All the latest news. And discount deals.

Nintendo
http://www.nintendo.com/

Development updates from Japan. New hardware and software news. Special sections for many of the popular games. Company information. Game hints. And the chance for you to design your own game, as long as you're aged between 5 and 12.

Fox Kids Cyberstation
http://www.foxkids.com/

'Hi There! Welcome aboard the Fox Kids Cyberstation Control Tower. Through your viewscreen you are looking at the fleet of Fox Kids Ships you can visit in this website. There's a Show Ship, a Contest Ship, a Totally Fox Kids Ship, an Activities Ship . . . well, you can see 'em all for yourself! And on different ships, you guessed it . . . you can do different things: like hear Fox Kids characters talk, watch movies, play games, create coloring pages . . . even request your fave song from our Countdown radio show!' The home of cartoons from the Amazing Spider-Man to Attack of the Killer Tomatoes to the Tick and the X-Men. Look on the parent site and you'll find the official Simpsons home as well (there are more than 700 Simpsons sites out there if you really want to trawl).

Nickelodeon
http://www.nick.com/

In the process of rebuilding as this book went to press. Try it now.

The Marvel Universe
http://www.marvel.com/marvel.html

A huge and sprawling mecca for comics fans, with everything

you could want to know, all the latest release news, previews of upcoming issues, store locators, special artworks, live appearances of artists, trading card info, games, and company details.

DC Comics
http://www.dccomics.com/

Home of Alfred E. Neuman, Superman, Batman & Robin, Sandman and a whole bunch of other comic heroes. There's information on all the comics and upcoming releases, as well as submission guidelines for those who'd like to try their hand at comic writing.

Children's Television Workshop
http://www.ctw.org/

OK, so it may not be a corporate giant (though it did clean up on Tickle Me Elmo dolls). The online home of *Sesame Street* is split into sections for kids and parents. The kids get to hang out with Elmo in online storybooks, play games and print out special counting and colouring pages. The adults get some advice on child rearing, immunisation, family holidays and more. There are also short videos from the show available on site.

BOOKS

Children's Literature Web Guide
http://www.ucalgary.ca/~dkbrown/index.html

The best overall guide to what's going on in the world of kid's literature. It offers round-ups of books, recommendations, discussion areas, references for students and teachers, links to sites about authors and books, and all manner of online resources academic and commercial. It also publishes the writing of children.

The Internet Public Library
http://www.ipl.org

This site turns out to be much, much bigger than its discreet front end suggests. It offers a wealth of material for students and teachers, broken up into dozens of easily searchable subject categories with loads of special features, exhibits and interactive areas.

Alice's Adventures in Wonderland
http://www.megabrands.com/alice/doalice.html

A Net novel that hints at the directions the Web is moving in, behaving more like a CD-ROM than most static texts. The home page has theme music and a pleasing Cheshire Cat animation. The pictures throughout are gently animated, and the music changes with each chapter. Click on the white rabbit and it says 'Oh dear, I shall be late!' Very sweet.

Seussville
http://www.randomhouse.com/seussville/

The Cat in the Hat's online home has a library of Seuss information as well as trivia contents, Seuss events and a stack of online games including: Who Said That?, The Cat's Quizzer, Oh Say Can You Say?, Green Eggs and Ham Picture Scramble, The Cat's Hat Maze, Horton's Who Hunt, Connect the Dots and The Cat's Concentration Game. There's a great unofficial tribute site too, **CyberSeuss (http://www.afn.org/~afn15301/drseuss.html)**.

KidPub
http://www.kidpub.org/kidpub/

Not an underage watering hole, as you might expect. But a pub as in publishing house. Here you will find more than 10,000 stories 'written by kids from all over the planet!'

FUN & GAMES

Happy Puppy
http://www.happypuppy.com/kids/index.html

One of the most popular sites on the Internet, this is the place to start if you want to download and play free computer games. Happy Puppy is an extraordinary resource, with giveaways, new games all the time for PC, Mac and consoles, games reviews, demos, shareware, cheats and tips, and a special children's section. It also has directions to other games sites on the Web.

Tigger's Shareware Page
http://www.gamesdomain.com/tigger/sw-kids.html

Grace Sylvan writes: 'Here you'll find shareware and freeware for the Mac and PC, commercial demos, reviews of children's software, and other fun activities for kids. Along with educational titles, there's lots of fun freeware from Disney and other sites. Many of the programs are recommended by families or teachers, and are often tested by my own family.'

The Adrenaline Vault Game Site
http://avault.com/

For older kids, this site offers game reviews, previews, cheats and hints, a chat room, Java and Shockwave arcades full of games, latest game release info and its own newsletter.

Gamekids
http://www.gamekids.com

'Gamekids is a gathering place for kids of all ages to learn and exchange non-computer games and activities. Each month, selected games and rhymes (traditional and contemporary), activities, and recipes will be selected from around the world for you to download, print out, and play. YOU are invited to collaborate with us! Submit your favourite games, stories, poetry, artwork, sleepover and party ideas, photographs, and favourite recipes.'

Carlos' Web Colouring Book
http://www.ravenna.com/coloring/

Choose your picture to colour (apple, birthday wish, computer help, Easter egg, Leprechaun, Santa and Rudolph) and click on your choice of ten colours as well as the area of the picture you want to colour in. Don't go over the lines.

Optical Illusions
http://illusionworks.com/

A fantastic site which makes up for the slow downloads by offering illusions of all kinds, from antique puzzles to three dimensional stereograms (you know, those Magic Eye pics). This is science made interesting and fun.

CyberJacques
http://www.cyberjacques.com/

I don't know about you, but I'm a sucker for Old Salt vernacular, and this site is full of it. 'Aarr, me Hearties! Me name's Cyberjacques, and I'm the captain of the grizzliest, silliest site on the high seas of the Internet! So unless ye got barnacles on the brain, ye'll be wantin' to weigh anchor fer awhile and have fun! Aarr!' Beyond the lingo, it's full of simple games for young 'uns, from Connect the Dots to Hangman to Simon Says.

Hands on Children's Museum
http://www.wln.com/~deltapac/hocm.html

The site has a handful of fun mazes for kids under 10.

MISCELLANEOUS

Dinosauria
http://www.dinosauria.com/

Kids and dinosaurs. It's a relationship, a bond, a fascination that never seems to go away. Dinosauria is home to the DinoStore (for your merchandise needs, including fossil replicas), Jeff's Journal of Dinosaur Paleontology ('articles and discussions from enthusiasts and actual paleontologists on various dinosaur topics'), The DOL Dinosaur Omnipedia (a reference guide for dinosaur enthusiasts) and Jeff's Dinosaur Picture Gallery (paydirt for the kids).

Cockroaches As Pets
http://www.ex.ac.uk/~gjlramel/roach.html

'There are nearly 4000 species of cockroaches (*Dictyoptera*,

343

Blattodea) in the world, of which only 25 to 30 (or less than 1 per cent) have any pest status, the rest are innocent members of the earth's fauna, some of which are clean, gentle, peaceful and, as such, make great pets.' Yes, you read that right. Pets. This handy site offers tips on housing, feeding and breeding the little critters, as well as a link to more information on the marvellously-named Madagascan Giant Hissing Cockroach.

Jennifer Warf's Internet Barbie Collection
http://ezinfo.ucs.indiana.edu/~jwarf/barbie.html

Arrrggghhhh!!! The Pink! The Pink! Really a page for collectors, but kids will find plenty of Barbies to look at, especially in the special release wings, where rare and ever sillier Barbies congregate. Viva La Plastic Princess!

PetNet Selectapet
http://www.petnet.com.au/selectapet.html

In search of a furry friend but not sure exactly which pooch or moggie to get? Here's a site that helps you choose a suitable dog or cat based on your needs. It asks a lot of questions such as where you live, who you are, how much exercise you're going to give your pet and so forth, then makes a number of recommendations, with separate home pages for each breed on its list.

Virtual Mr Spud Head
http://www.westnet.com/~crywalt/pothead/pothead.html

Dress your favourite vegetable.

Leftovers

Laziness Central
http://www.laziness.com

I wouldn't want you to think that this site advocates doing nothing. It's more a stop-and-smell-the-fishtank kind of place. 'Life has become overcomplicated,' it says, 'filled with tasks to complete, obligations to be met, and so on. The freedom and happiness once instilled in us all has dissolved, leaving many imprisoned in the terrible day-to-day, nine-to-five lifestyle. It is time for a change!' Home of the Slackers Quarterly.

White Trash Online
http://www.vu.union.edu/~spitzera/trash/

The one-stop guide to redneck culture, with links to all sorts of places. The best part, however, is the Are You White Trash quiz, which allows you to determine your quotient by looking for any of dozens of tell-tale signs. You know you're white trash if: 'You ever cut your grass and found a car; you own a home that is mobile and 5 cars that aren't; you think the stock market has a fence around it; the Salvation Army declines your mattress; you've ever raked leaves in your kitchen; you were shooting pool when any of your kids were born; your wife can climb a tree faster than your cat; your mother has "ammo" on her Christmas list; the Home Shopping operator recognises your voice; your family tree does not fork; your house doesn't have curtains but your truck does; you wonder how service stations keep their restrooms so clean.'

Early Screen Tests
http://ssnet.com/~fatsteve/tests.html

Inspired by the fact that William 'The Greatest American hero' Katt almost got the Luke Skywalker gig in *Star Wars*, Early Screen Tests presents its version of tapings that might have been. Hear a scene from *Reservoir Dogs* with Arnold Schwarzenegger as Mr Pink, William Shatner as Nice Guy Eddie, Sean Connery as Mr Brown, Freddie Krueger as Mr Blonde and the *Today* show's Gene Shallit as Mr Blue.

The Unoffical Guide to Drinking Games on the Net
http://kalypso.cybercom.net/~japril/games/drgamesw.html

Far be it from me to recommend anything stronger than lemon cordial, but this is such a painstakingly researched and compiled site that we feel obliged to recommend it purely for its social history value. Here are games based on dice, cards, coins, endurance, skill and co-ordination and, more importantly (from our pop cultural perspective), on film and television, from *Batman* to *90210* to *Ren and Stimpy* to *Reservoir Dogs* to *The Simpsons*.

The National Miniature Donkey Association of America
http://www.teleport.com/%7Ematrixd/animal/info/nmda/

These people want you to know everything there is to know about the bonsai mule, a stubborn little critter which just refuses to grow more than a metre or so in height. Apparently, they originally hail from Sicily, which would explain things — Italian apartments are pretty small. 'Miniature Donkeys possess the affectionate nature of a Newfoundland, the resignation of a cow, the durability of a mule, the courage of a tiger, and the intellectual capability only slightly inferior to man's.'

Monkeys Typing Shakespeare
http://bronte.cs.utas.edu.au/monkey/

Another Net project dedicated to one of those eternal questions. A random typing page, it is attempting to see how long it will take the virtual monkey to type the 40 lower case characters of 'to be or not to be that is the question'. Apart from the full stop, it's not picky about the punctuation. So far, the best the little critter has done is 'ujgdejoxenotejotmbgtang ircpqbgluzstizg' — 12 of the characters are right.

Elvis Sightings
http://www.elvissightings.com/

Elvis, as we all know, has been much more fun since he died. Before that, his career was nowhere, in painful Vegas mode and spiralling. Nowadays, he is again part of a thriving cultural ecology. People from all over the world flock to see him. This Web venture keeps track of the various death hoax and sighting stories, offering you the chance to add your versions.

Punch Bill Gates
http://www.well.com/user/vanya/bill.html

Sometimes, a cute little animation is enough. Punch Bill Gates is a site that lets you do exactly that. And it's a surprisingly soothing activity. Then, just when I was thinking to myself what a useful public service the site is providing, I spotted its options area, which also allows you to deliver the left jab to the faces of John Tesh, Michael Jackson ('Just beat him') and William Shatner (in Kirk mode).

The Astounding B Monster
http://www.bmonster.com/

This site declares itself 'The Offbeat Film Authority'. A Web zine devoted to all things celluloid and tacky, and not always in that order, it specialises in horror, sci-fi and cult films. Fans of the obscure should hunt it down. It's a little thin, but what content there is works well. Check out the reader debate on which film features the best severed head.

Angry.org
http://angry.org/

Pissed off? Mad as hell and not going to take it any more? Well, perhaps unsurprisingly, there's a ready-made Net service out there to help you vent some steam. Angry.org, the self-appointed 'crankiest site on the Net', is the home of the short, bile-filled rant. Broken up into categories marked companies, groups, people and things, it is a collection of hundreds of pieces of, well, spleen. If anything at all makes your blood rise mad, feel free to contribute.

The Cosmic Ray Deflection Society of North America
http://www.geocities.com/SunsetStrip/1483/

I don't know about you, but I find that when I'm choosing my clothes every morning, standing there with a towel girding my loins, gently dripping excess shower water on the carpet, I often think 'You know Jon, a home-made aluminium foil hat would go well with those jeans.' The friendly folk at TCRDSONA take things even further in their attempts to ward off evil radiation from the skies. They cover their whole bodies (and their cars!!!) with anti-ray protection of their own devising, many of which are on display at their Web site. The cosmic ray deflection hat, by the way, should have as many useless trinkets attached to it as possible. The car should be pure sculpture.

Latin Mottoes and Phrases
http://www.cco.net/~jcurtis/latin.htm

Sometimes, particularly the way I speak it, English just isn't enough. Erin Curtis, in her second year of Latin studies, has compiled an online list of useful and useless phrases. There are those you're bound to find a use for: *Morituri te salutamus* (We who are about to die salute you) and *Mihi ignosce. Cum homine de cane debeo congredi* (Excuse me. I've got to see a man about a dog). And those it's worth actually contriving a reason to use: *Sentio aliquos togatos contra me conspirare* (I think some people in togas are plotting against me) and *Vah! Denuone Latine loquebar? Me ineptum. Interdum modo elabitur* (Oh! Was I speaking Latin again? Silly me. Sometimes it just sort of slips out).

The Pot-Bellied Men of America Home Page
http://potbelly.com/index.shtml

This one is waving its meaty arm in the air and shouting big is beautiful. A serious, actually quite moving site (read the Inspiration section), it argues that heroes come in all shapes and sizes and makes a personal attempt to recognise some of society's little guys, particularly the ones who aren't little. Mmmmmm, pin-up of the month.

The I Can Eat Glass Project
http://fas-www.harvard.edu/~emollick/glass.html

Here's one for you wandering surrealists, a quest to compile a list of ways to say the phrase 'I can eat glass, it doesn't hurt me' in as many languages as possible — 110 and counting. 'The Project is based on the idea that people in a foreign country have an irresistible urge to try to say something in the indigenous tongue. In most cases, however, the best a person can do is "Where is the bathroom?" a phrase that marks them as a tourist. But, if one says "I can eat glass, it doesn't hurt me", you will be viewed as an insane native, and treated with dignity and respect.' Good luck.

Sheri's Adopt a Pet Rock
http://www.geocities.com/TimesSquare/Arcade/3412/petrock.html

This page will send you hurtling back to '80s fad-dom. Choose one of four: the happy, snuggly, licky, pet rock; the one that kisses; the one that complains; or the one that bites. Actually, come to think of it, they all bite.

Cretins Inc, Adventures in Corporate Incompetence
http://www.nembley.com/

A Web site for anyone for whom the sound or look of the word 'bureaucracy' induces shudders. Originally conceived as a CD-ROM game, it's now a self-guided, role-playing tour. Welcome to BilgeCorp, a model of consumer underconfidence. You, its latest employee, must keep up with what is going on by visiting all the floors and taking in the full horror of the company that has just employed you. Oh, the pain.

25 Weird Sex Laws
http://www.palace.com/page9.html

A list of peculiar local ordinances, each pertaining to a carnal don't. A law in Fairbanks, Alaska, does not allow moose to have sex on city streets. A law in Oblong, Illinois, makes it a crime to make love while fishing or hunting on your wedding day. In Aimes, Iowa, a husband may not take more than three gulps of beer while lying in bed with his wife. A law in Alexandria, Minnesota, makes it illegal for a husband to make love to his wife if his breath smells like garlic, onions, or sardines. Plan your holidays accordingly folks.

Driveways of the Rich and Famous
http://www.driveways.com

There are six billion people on this planet and many of them seem to have too much time on their hands. This is the home site of a US public access cable TV program which surveys, well, precisely what the title suggests. Sometimes the hosts meet neighbours and mailmen and grill them on their brushes with fame. Sometimes the stars in question come out to chat, usually about the paving. If you have a yen to see the asphalt, concrete and stone that famous people, from Andre Agassi to Robin Williams, drive over, this is the place for you.

Magellan's Search Voyeur
http://voyeur.mckinley.com/voyeur.cgi#voyeur?1

What do other people get up to on the Web? Well, this is one of the best places to find out, a constantly updating page showing 20 recent searches that people have carried out using the engine. When I dropped in this week, some of the things that came up were: *Melrose Place*, yoghurt bacteria, pen pals, weird sex positions, American Arabic radio, scout record keeping, Chernobyl and enemas. The pages reloads every 20 seconds.

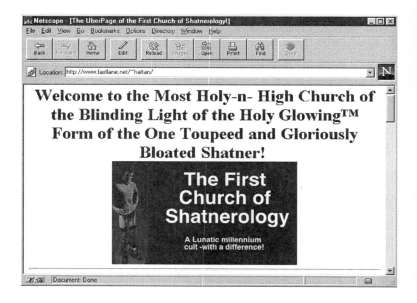

First Church of Shatnerology
http://www.fastlane.net/~hattan/

I saw a band once called William Shatner's Pants. It must be hard being old Bill, when nobody much takes you seriously. The Singalong with Bill Web site has been doing great business for ages. The latest cab off the rank is the Church, 'a lunatic millennium cult with a difference'. Devotees 'worship the holy essences of the most benevolent ShatnerBeing! We are transfixed by his magnificent TOUPEE [their capitals, not mine] and girth!' The site has everything from scriptures to sex haikus.

The Great Awesome Goat Click Page
http://www.hut.fi/~marje/goat.html

Of course, I read it wrong. I thought it said the Great Awesome

Goat Lick Page. Anyway, once I got there, I found another great exercise in Net Zen. Click away friends.

Denounce
http://www.denounce.com/

Pardon me while I come over all geeky for a second. If, like myself, you've been inundated with pointless press releases from technology companies, or even if you're just sick of the techno-hype, you'll love Denounce, a site which specialises in spurious tech news, announcements that we're unlikely to see: 'Apple Drops Retail Prices by 100%', 'Microsoft to Drop Its "Where Do You Want To Go Today?" Campaign', 'Unreleased Kenny G Recordings Wind Up On Internet'.

Minor Celebrity
http://pw1.netcom.com/~zymrgist/celebrities.html

There just aren't enough celebrities in this world. We won't have real global peace and harmony until three out of every four people have a good shot at making the cover of next week's *Who* magazine. So get famous and do it now. Who knows, you may even be a Minor Celebrity yourself. If you are, and you'd like to become just that teensy bit bigger, hike on over to the Minor Celeb site, a place where people come to record their brushes with fame. Example: 'I'm a Minor Celebrity because a few years ago, I went to the Edinburgh Film Festival. While I was standing at the entrance, actor Keanu Reeves and a small entourage came in to view his latest picture. I pretended I was with their party and was actually seated directly behind Keanu. Only for a short while, however. Someone must have gotten wise, because two of Mr Reeve's bodyguards came over to "escort me out". As I walked out, I noticed Keanu glaring at me. Being a gentleman, I turned to him and said, politely, "Sir, you couldn't act for toffee".'

The Love Calculator
http://www.xs4all.nl/~kink/love/love.html

A piece of online software which determines the romantic suitability of any set of two people, based on their names. You type yours into the handy space and the site returns a percentage chance of success. It's not that the calculator itself is any great shakes. What really attracts me to the site are the names of the sweet couple who built it — Matthijs Sypkens Smit and Thijs Kinkhorst. Maybe there is something to this name business.

The Ants Are My Friends
http://www.mcs.com/~bingo/lyrics/

The name will make more sense if you consider it in the following sentence: 'The ants are my friends, is blowing in the wind . . .' A 'Mondegreen', according to this site, is a lyric which is heard incorrectly. The most famous of these is the Jim Hendrix line 'Excuse me while I kiss the sky', which many people think is evidence of his homosexuality — 'Excuse me while I kiss this guy'. This site is building a library of mishearings. See if you can match the song with the Mondegreen: I want a piece of bacon (The Ramones); Baking carrot biscuits (Bachman-Turner Overdrive); Just slip out the back, Jack; make a new plant stand, don't need to be corduroy, just listen to me (Paul Simon).

Digital Nostalgia
http://www.negia.net/~msakey/

A library of downloadable game classics, 'a high-tech memory lane' for those whose childhood began with Pong, that riveting tennis video game. Many are slight variations on the original. All are for PC.

Movie Bloopers
http://www.geocities.com/Hollywood/1353/K.html

In *Scream*, when Tatum goes to get the beers in the garage and gets killed, she tries to get back into the house but the door is locked. Yet when the killer tries the door, it has become mysteriously unlocked. In *Braveheart*, in the first battle, one of the extras can be seen messing around with a sword as if he thought the cameras weren't rolling. In *First Wives Club*, at the end of the movie when the three friends are singing, Goldie Hawn's shoes change from white lace-ups to thick-heeled white shoes. Amuse your friends with your trainspotting genius.

The Bathrooms of Madison County
http://www.nutscape.com/~fluxus/

Did you find *The Bridges of Madison County* as bile-inspiring as I did? One guy obviously did, and this would explain why he has built this Web site, the story of his holiday in the area, with extra special attention paid to restroom detail.

The Book of Cliches
http://utopia.knoware.nl/users/sybev/cliche/

A handy guide to hackneyed phrases, so that you will never have to go without one again. It's handily arranged into chapters based on possible social or personal situations you might find yourself in, so that you'll never be without a banal reaction to life.

Blenderphone
http://www.cycoactive.com//blender/

Tom Myers had nothing better to do, so he got into a bit of machine husbandry and crossbred his blender with the phone. 'The "ringer" is the blender motor, which pulses like a telephone bell, except angrier. To answer, pick up the pitcher out of the base and put it to your ear. Usually, the caller can hear the motor spinning down just after you pick it up. To hang up, replace the pitcher in the base, just like all the other boring telephones.' And it still works as a blender (but you will, as the site points out, spill your margarita if you answer the phone). Now you can buy one too, for a measly US$200.

Marduk's Guide to Garbage Digging
http://www.psrc.usm.edu/macrog/marduk/garbage.html

One guy's advice on dumpster diving, his hints on why and where to dig. 'Garbage picking is good for the earth! Every goodie I swipe from a dumpster is something that won't take up space in a landfill. Also, everything I get from garbage is something I won't have to buy new. This means the energy of making a new product will be saved, as will the materials. This means I'm using less of the earth's precious resources.'

Killer Fonts
http://www.killerfonts.com/

Strictly speaking, this is one for designers, but it's odd enough to be brought to your attention. It's a collection of fonts available for PC and Mac, all based on the handwriting of murderers. 'Tired of the same old Times love notes? Promise someone you're really helter-skelter for them in the script of Charles Manson himself.'

356

Virtual Vomit
http://www.xvt.com/users/kevink/sick/sick.html

Both fake *and* virtual.

The Amazing Pecking Chicken!
http://www.vanderbilt.edu/~dotedu/staff/cluck/

Amazing!

Bill Gates Personal Wealth Clock
http://www.webho.com/WealthClockRealTime

A site which calculates Chairman Bill's current worth based on daily Microsoft stock prices. Last time I looked it was $26.6 billion. Yes, but is he happy?

Executive Decision Maker
http://clevermedia.com/arcade/execdm.html

Like one of those adult office toys, this site allows you to play a little game that puts the future of your company, your employees or your career (your choice) entirely at the whim of a bouncing ball. And as anyone who has ever worked will know, that makes about as much sense as any other management method.

Shakespearian Insults
http://www.nova.edu/Inter-Links/cgi-bin/bard.pl

Insults sound better in Shakespearian English. Everyone knows that. 'Thou saucy crook-pated dewberry.' 'Thou errant fen-sucked ratsbane.' This site generates random insulting phrases from a set of quasi-Shakespearian nouns and adjectives.

15 Minutes Of Shame
http://www2.ucsc.edu/~thebrain/shame/

'Welcome to 15 Minutes of Shame! This page is dedicated to those that have achieved dubious fame only by means of the television camera. The individuals featured on this page are just average people that happened to do something sensational enough to merit a sound bits, a videoclip, or the occasional political cartoon.' Sigh. Fame really isn't what it used to be. We're going to have to invent a new goal to replace it.

Ka-Boom! A Dictionary of Comicbook Words on Historical Principles
http://www.intergate.bc.ca/business/kjohn/

I love comicbook words, those strange collisions of consonants meant to convey the sounds of explosions or fists thudding into abdomens or minor superheroes being electrocuted. Kevin Taylor likes them even more—enough to have compiled an entire dictionary, from 'AAAA!', a cry of pain from *Dare Devil: The Man Without Fear* (Vol.1, Issue 3, 1993) to 'ZZZZZZZTZZTZZZ', the sound of mechanical parts coming undone, from *Dead Pool: The Circle Chase* (Issue 4, 1993).

Heartless Bitches International
http://www.heartless-bitches.com/

Girls, are you fed up with useless, whiny men and the weak women who chase them? HBI is the club for you, a place where women who aren't afraid to be harsh with life's losers get together. 'Heartless Bitches International is NOT about man-hating. We don't discriminate against stupidity, arrogance, irresponsibility, bloated egos or immaturity on the basis of gender.'

Sell Your Soul Online
http://www.nwdc.com/~demona/soul.htm

This site offers you the chance to part with that spiritual appendage. Tell the online Satan your name, your e-mail address and what you want in return. I got rid of my soul ages ago, so to test it out, I sold him yours. And, frankly, I didn't get much for it.

Toilet Training
http://gpu.srv.ualberta.ca/~msykes/thome.html

I've noticed, in the course of my short and pathetic life, that many women are fascinated by what goes on in men's toilets. What do we do, they ask? Do we look at one another? Do we talk? Michael Sykes, who describes himself as a urinalologist, is the author of *Toilet Training: An Online Guide To Urinal Etiquette*. It's all here, girls.

Grossology, the Science of Gross Things
http://www.northcoast.com/~bsv/grossology.html

'Sometimes it's stinky. Sometimes it's crusty. Sometimes it's slimy. But, hey, it's your body.' How to make fake blood, snot, vomit, wounds and other stuff. Great if you're about seven years old.

Ronan's Karaoke Page
http://www.visi.com/~dowling/karaoke

Start spreadin' the news, this site lets you howl along to more than 90 great pop-tastic classics, from Queen's *Crazy Little Thing Called Love* to the Doors' *People Are Strange*. All songs are rendered in that cheesy el cheapo computer keyboard sound.

Tickle Elvis
http://www.auschron.com/mrpants/elvis.html

Go on, see if you can wake him up.

Acknowledgements

Parts of this book have appeared, in various guises, in the *Sydney Morning Herald*, primarily in the Driftnet column. Many of those same parts also surfaced in *The Age*.

I am indebted to the Web inhabitants who answer my e-mail, offering directions and explanations. Thanks also to Sophie Cunningham, for making sure it happened; Emma Cotter, for overseeing the editing and production; James de Vries, for his grasp of things lurid; my colleagues at the *Herald*, for their continued encouragement; and Helen Greenwood, the cyber widow, for being pleasantly zen about the idea of me locking myself in a room for weeks on end.

This book was written, at time obsessively, to the accompaniment of: The Fountains Of Wayne's self-titled debut album, The Aphex Twin's *Richard D. James*, Telek's self-titled effort, The Guo Brothers' *Yuan* and The Justin Vali Trio's *The Truth*. Thanks to all these musicians for making it more enjoyable.

POSTCARDS FROM THE NET

An Australian's guide to the wired world

JON CASIMIR

Postcards from the Net is a travel book like no other. Fast and funny, it's a thirty-countries-in-thirty-days trawl through the weird, wired and wonderful parallel universe of the World Wide Web.

Too many books about the Internet tell you how the road is built rather than where it goes. They tell you how much land there is in cyberspace, but not what the weather's like. They tell you how many computers are linked up to each other, but not whether the natives are friendly. They tell you how you can get to a place, but not why you'd want to go there.

Postcards from the Net is not the usual how-to guide. It's a where-to, why-to and what-to that will take you to places the others don't go. It will introduce you to the minds that feed Net culture, from the input of mainstream media corporations to Japanese Haiku obsessives. You'll meet celebrities, footy fans, cyberfeminists, X-files nuts and people who just want to put up home pages for their pets.

Jon Casimir writes on popular culture and technology for the Sydney Morning Herald. He is a regular Mr Rent-an-opinion on ABC Radio.

ISBN 1 86448 233 8